D0185976

Son of a Silverback

HIGHLAND LIBRARIES

WITHDRAWN

www.penguinrandomhouse.co.uk

Son of a Silverback

RUSSELL KANE

BANTAM PRESS

WITHDRAWN

TRANSWORLD PUBLISHERS
61–63 Uxbridge Road, London W5 5SA
www.penguin.co.uk

Transworld is part of the Penguin Random House group of companies
whose addresses can be found at global.penguinrandomhouse.com

Penguin
Random House
UK

First published in Great Britain in 2019 by Bantam Press
an imprint of Transworld Publishers

Copyright © Russell Kane 2019

Russell Kane has asserted his right under the Copyright,
Designs and Patents Act 1988 to be identified as the author of this work.

This book is a work of non-fiction based on the life, experiences and
recollections of the author. In some cases, names of people, places, dates, sequences
and the detail of events have been changed to protect the privacy of others.

Every effort has been made to obtain the necessary permissions with
reference to copyright material, both illustrative and quoted. We apologize
for any omissions in this respect and will be pleased to make the
appropriate acknowledgements in any future edition.

A CIP catalogue record for this book is available from the British Library.

ISBN 9781787632141

Typeset in 13/16 pt Garamond MT Std by Jouve (UK), Milton Keynes
Printed and bound in Great Britain by Clays Ltd, Elcograf S.p.A.

Penguin Random House is committed to a sustainable
future for our business, our readers and our planet. This book
is made from Forest Stewardship Council® certified paper.

MIX
Paper from
responsible sources
FSC® C018179

1 3 5 7 9 10 8 6 4 2

Thanks to the poet Maggie Butt and novelist
Sue Gee for taking a punt.

Thanks to Mum for waving me on.

Thanks to Lindsey for keeping me upright.

And thanks to Dad for all the material that follows.
You miserable bastard. Love.

Contents

Contents

CONTENTS

Foreword

By primatologist R. D. Grineau

The western lowland gorilla is the biggest of all the great apes. This meaty, knuckle-walking, bipedal primate gives the nimble chimp a run for its money as the most famous ape. If you could choose to observe only one in the wild, be honest, would you choose Cheeta or King Kong? Of course, to actually see one you must travel to central Africa. Yes, contrary to popular belief and recent sightings, these creatures don't nest in Romford, Newcastle or Cardiff.

The 200kg males, in particular, are astounding creatures, moving in slow motion through the fetid swamps and forests like a steroided man from *The Only Way is Essex* going to the bar for a lit sambuca. Gorillas dress to impress too. Coarse jet-black fur, and once they reach adulthood the distinctive silverback. What is more unusual, however, is the lack of other males in the group. Most species in the primate order have multiple man-monkeys and apes in their groups. Chimps and bonobos have a chaotic mix of man-slag challenger Garys, Terrys and Kevins all fighting each other to be leader and for shagging rights with high-ranking Tinas, Donnas and Kellys, most of whom are opportunistic floozies when their chosen fella isn't keeping tabs. Not so with gorillas. No 'slappers'. Don't get me wrong, you do occasionally find the odd gorilla troop with more than one adult male, but it's rare.

You might observe a few adolescent blackback males flanking the double-hard leader for protection – but once their post-adolescent fur starts silvering, they're expected to sod off from their natal group and 'earn their own fucking living'.

The dominant male gorilla is not a bad being. He's not evil, he's not even that violent – he's just a big scary silverback who likes to be in charge, and whatever he says, goes. 'I'm paying, I'm saying.' He decides where they live, what they eat, what they do, when they sleep, play and talk. When it comes to making up a troop, girls and adult females are usually welcome, but if you're a boy you've got about twelve years before you need to get out of his way – and no amount of fur-grooming or arse-kissing will help you. You'll never be the silverback.

'You're on your own. Good luck, boy,' said the dad.

Prologue[*]

My dad Dave – the steroid-using doorman, lifeguard, sheet-metal worker, builder and bodybuilder from Barking in Essex – clutched his chest and dropped down dead in September 2003. For me, *that* was the moment I went from child to man. It shook up everything. It was the day I began my big-boy life.

Maybe I'd never really left my Moses basket. Certainly my old man's sudden death was my Red Sea moment. Scary, waves crashing, but somehow I just walked through. It was the crazy miserable old bastard's final act in the making of me. That's why it belongs before my beginning (the beginning's in a minute – keep reading).

He wasn't 'old', my old man. It turned out the most powerful muscle in his fifteen-stone, still-ripped, weightlifting body was his neck – his ability to thrust it into the ground meant he ignored the warning pains in his chest, the breathlessness, his body's hints to see a cardiologist.

Those of you reading who are also members of the Sudden-death Dead Parent Club will remember that plummeting feeling of finding out. It's a bonding experience when you meet someone else who has gone through it; so much so that when in 2006 I began chatting to a girl online

---

* Or as my mate Warren said as he unblocked the toilet when we were in Butlin's: 'Now that's Pro Log.'

about it, we thought it only proper to immediately start grief-shagging and then get married (and divorced within six months). It turned out trauma sex was an awful foundation for long-term love, but it goes to show the power of parental loss in bringing strangers together.

The unexpected international phone call. The inside-out adrenaline drop, like stepping into a lift shaft and realizing too late there is no lift in there. Just a dark, brutal descent. *Boom*. Right in the guts. No one would wish any sort of slow terminal illness on a loved one. In fact, most people themselves hope for a sudden, unaware journey from this world into the next – the next world for us atheists being nothingness, except for being eaten by slugs and peed on by tramps. But isn't it so much harder for those left behind to process – the quick dispatch into oblivion?

In my case, the fit, muscly Dave went on holiday with Julie to Cyprus (the Turkish half, mind you: 'The bargains you get when a country's unstable, boy. Steaks the size of an arse cheek'), then one night after dinner, dropped down dead.

Everything that happened after that phone call I've spoken about before. Lots. On stage, in interviews – and really, everything from that moment is my career. It's all in stand-up sets on YouTube, Netflix, iTunes (oh, and telly – do you remember telly?), and to write about what's already there would be, to me, utterly uninteresting. Even the phrase 'comedian's memoir' feels like a chewing-on-a-whole-pack-of-sleeping-pills level of yawn. What I've never really written down is all the stuff that came before. I'm not about to tell some mouth-gaping rags-to-riches story, oozing with facile gratefulness. I was never in 'rags' and I'm not really rich. I started life in a solid working-class household. So piss off, pity party. I never went hungry, we even had a few decent holidays to Spain and I had my own car when I was seventeen. Yes, OK, I'm a relatively successful stand-up now, but if the next tour bombs, I will have to get an office job or work in a shop just like I used to. No yachts, no first-class flights. It's premium economy and a buy-to-let. That's my pension plan. So no rags, and as yet (nor ever, is my guess) no Kanye level of wealth. I suppose there is still time for me to go full *R*-Diddy, but then I'll be old and shit so it won't matter any way. Most importantly, how boring would it be – to simply tell *my* story, I mean. And how interesting to tell my sad, funny, aggressive yet not physically violent, mentalfucker Dad's story. So if you have to put that in rags-to terms, it's my dad's story, and in his mind, he did indeed start in rags, but finished with a shitload less than he wanted. Rags to Primark trousers, let's call it. I wish he'd lived a bit longer – but then I wouldn't have had the courage to rip the living piss out of him onstage, or to carry it on in book form. And who knows what would have been the Me, Now.*

A note on the text. (I've always wanted to write 'a note on the text' – this is the level of nerd we are talking.) I have no real plan or message. I'm a massive fan of the novelist Murakami – just tell a story and watch the characters be weird. Except this shit is true. Everything here is what happened to me and how it led to me being a jester for a living with a nice house, a gorgeous wife, and a daughter so satanically charged with energy that she cries if holy water touches

---

* Actually, I do know. I would have continued to work in a solid job in marketing. But it sounds more mystical and impressive to end on a self-analytical speculation.

her skin and sizzles. The stories that seem the most unbeliev-
able are the most true, both in content and how they shaped
me, but I've changed the names and obscured the identities
of most people in this book. Except my mum and dad. They
can handle it. Well, he's dead – literally no choice. My early
life had a Dickensian cast of manual labourers, imprisoned
violent relatives, weed-smoking, swearing, fighting grandmas,
and a bodybuilder/model dad who was nothing like me but
was the main reason I became me.

If you read this book and hate it, you have only proved my
father right. Life is shit. Every fourteen-year-old would
surely love to hear the words I heard one Saturday night as
my old man drunkenly drained the biryani sauce from his
silver takeaway carton:

'Life's hard, boy. It's shit and it's hard. We die in pain, and
you have to work like a proper cunt in between . . . Right,
I'm going a-bed.'

And as he walked upstairs he farted. Loudly.

I should just pick up on that loud fart my father issued as
he ascended the Wilton-covered stairs of my childhood
home. Having spoken to people, I now realize that a 'temper
fart' is not normal fatherly behaviour. It was one of my father's
most emphatic quirks. It's a fine example of how he approached
life. Visceral, angry, funny, blunt and offensive to the senses.
Whenever there was a debate or an argument he used his
own anal gas as a full stop. He could be in full flow with
Mum, clashing over some household matter, and then he
and his arse would deem the exchange finished.

'We need to talk, Dave.'

'No, Julie – we're done . . .' then a thunderous walk-
off, sometimes with a Godzilla-tail after-waft using his

hand as a fan. This was my dad. Furious to the point of flatulence.

I'm ready to begin, but before we emotionally disrobe and jump into the turbulent stories of father and son, let me share my current setting. It feels relevant.

I'm wearing: a porridge-stained mauve vest, an echo from a former Ibiza life; lower down, I'm in yesterday's underwear with a yoghurt smudge near the fly opening (which doesn't look like yoghurt to anyone with a mucky mind). A green toddler-snot-scarred hairband prevents the wild twigs of my hair from stabbing my eyes. Footwear: one flip-flop. Where are you, darling Flip-flop Left? Although four coffees deep (*espressi* in the plural, although using that plural rightly attracts fists), I haven't yet eaten. Instead I've saved time by drinking butter and coconut oil with my coffees, because I'm a victim of a stupid faddish diet that will be laughed at in a hundred years when we're all dead from hypercholesterolemia. It's 10.14 a.m. I've written a silly foreword under a fake name about gorillas, but that will never make the cut.

Yeah, OK, I'm in a lovely chill-out room. A gorgeous room. The fantasy room of my intoxicated student brain a few years ago: book-lined, with leathery Evelyn Waugh editions here and there, an Edwardian smoking table, an actual marble bust of Beethoven (*Beethoven?* I like hard house and San Antonio Bay, Ibiza, for fuck's sake), an old desk and a real Persian rug. So, that's all good. There is even a Freudian chaise longue next to me. But it's what's upon that gorgeous piece of eBay-bought antique furniture that is the source of my mood and my clothing. It's a small human female. My daughter. Minna Agnes Kane. She is like me, and therefore profoundly irritating and with so much energy it's like Stephen Hawking, RIP, developed her using powerful machines in a physics lab. She is singing 'Happy Birthday' (it is not her birthday). She is eating a hard-boiled egg like an apple, spraying moist crumbs into my 1902 furniture, which she then jumps on, fossilizing the yoke into the brushed blue fabric. She is naked from the waist down and the 'white' vest on her top half has a brown upward smear at the back – a shitty Nike tick that symbolizes the speed and filth of being two.

She is my child, and I am her dad. And right now that's everything. *Oh God, no*, I don't mean in the wanky 'I love my babies, they are my world' way. Panic not. None of that crap from me. No, sod that. I mean that the relationship – that defining, chaotic mixing of two lives, Dad and Tot – is everything, energy-wise. At least, that's been my experience. It has been my main relationship, in my childhood, in my adulthood. Now it's her turn to be on the receiving end, and my turn not to have a clue if I'm getting it right. It's my turn, for example, at pretending happiness while holding in my temper because my car keys have been taken by Dynamo the Magician and magicked God knows where. Is that a fleck of silver on my back fur? Yes. Just a speck. I'm turning into the silverback, the alpha. I'm the Daddy now and, just like my old man before me, I have none of the answers.

A Story via My Dad

Dads: we become like them, or we become their opposite. If they are absent, we pour energy into that void and it takes on any old random shape, like *Terminator 2*. Mind you, their over-presence can also be somewhat challenging – see *all* the following chapters. Maybe I do overplay the 'Dad thing', but I saw life through a big Dad-sized lens (probably meat-coloured, given the man's brawn and his addiction to roasted proteins). I know, I know, the self-centred *me* generation – but it's my honest experience of the world.

See, most things I've done, nearly every place I have gone, almost every keystroke I've made, have been shaped by my idea of and my experience of fatherhood. Often, as I read some voguish rant about masculinity on a vegan blog some-where (I'm not vegan, please keep reading), I think: Is it really masculinity you're talking about? Do people sometimes mean fatherhood, that clumsy fist on the potters wheel of child psychology? Is it that, in fact, which has lost its way? It affects girls and boys equally after all.

Humans are (un?)lucky enough to be like seahorses and birds. Dads are super-involved; or worse, supposed to be and super aren't; or, worse still, super too much. We are never really told how to do it, nor how to receive it. Is there a correct way? Maybe there isn't. Maybe it's just like motherhood – here's your infant, good luck, beyatch. (Imagine if a midwife said that.) There is a complicating factor with being the man parent, however. Turns out you always feel a bit of a fraud in the Daddy role; like a crap assistant manager dawdling on the periphery, hoping to feel something more profound, or find something substantial to do – a nappy audit maybe. 'We're out of Size Sevens – I'll run to the shop.'

Ladies: imagine being so emotionally involved in something you have Nothing To Do With. It's not your body, it's not your rights, it's not your club, you have no invite, no wristband. You're just a lucky member of the public who fooled the Bouncer of Life and is now standing in the VIP area, hoping to get into the inner circle. Which you will, but not until your baby's about two, or twelve. I know some girls are reading this thinking, 'Bullshit, my Danny was involved from the first scan – we did this together.' Really? Ask him. Ask him if he felt like a silly fake who could be fired at any minute. Most men do. And if they did feel super-connected and involved from the first cell division, they have the opinions of other men to deal with: 'Silly wanker who's lost his bollocks', that sort of charming thing. Masculinity, perhaps justly, perhaps karmically, is in a mess.

Adding to this emotional muddle is the fact that *what dads used to be* has become rather unfashionable, while what we're trying to be is often made to feel limp and insubstantial – something silly and effeminate to be taken the piss out of. If you're not careful, you get trapped between the two stools of Meathead Gary and Broken Barry – and before you know, you're a weird dad too.

Of course, I have to confess here, I am an oddity, an exception. I'm OK with being thought effeminate. I make a living out of being conspicuously so. I get a lot of work out of it. As sexist as the idea is, certain traits are still, even now, 'boyish', and I happen to be world-class awful at those. I can't park, barbecue, do DIY or enjoy fast cars properly. I've never had a fight, and all sport makes me cry soil – even darts. I never remember when my country is playing football, and I'm usually deep into wondering if the streets are empty because of a zombie apocalypse before I remember that England are up against Belgium or something. But then, this just complicates the question further: what is the frigging point of Parent Me? The job of me *as Dad*? That's why I'm sat here typing, trying to explore my own dad. There must be other blokes like me. Skinny Peperamis with hair on who cry at *The Notebook* but still slam doors in a pig temper because they're running late. Men who accidentally ogle a breast, then cut meals because they want 'abs'. Men (and women here too I guess) who try to see their stories in terms of male role models, but find the definitions tossed about from *Daily Mail* opinion piece to lefty university campus and back again. If we're not careful we're going to end up with dads who are a bizarre blend of Gazza from *Geordie Shore* and David Furnish.

By the way, before we get going, I don't want any of my sensitive readers flinging this book in the recycling bin with the hummus pots and the sorted foil and cardboard. When I say male, for father, I don't even mean *a man*. Having grown up in a council street, I know from witnessing it that a mum is sometimes a dad. A dad can be a woman, two men, two women – it's the person who raised you and took on that role – whatever the hell it is – and certainly not the biological provider of genetic material. And of course, of all these styles of dadding, the most complex of the lot – and this was very common where I grew up – is Absent Dad, a nothing. The No-dad Dad seems sadly to be the most influential Dad of the lot.

So this is why I'm going to tell you a story via my dad. A psychologist might say I'm messed up. (I *am* messed up). Or as the kids (under-forties) might say, Hashtag Overshare. And in the age of self-publishing every molecule of yourself on social media, splurging your inner psychological being in an actual book with pages seems almost quaint.

Sometimes, as I sit at this 1950s teacher's desk on the old rug in the book-lined room, dipping my sugar-free protein madeleine into green tea (Proust is looking down on me, in two senses), I honestly struggle to think of a single thing to do with me which does not connect back to Dave Sidney Kane (and now forward on to Minna Kane). My dad. My old man. The fifteen-stone, low-body-fat, steroid-using, weight-lifting, Essex-boy lagger and doorman, whose seed somehow sowed the book-loving, skipping twat that is me.

I feel I should put in an aside about swearing, a sort of 'fuck' disclaimer. I am hoping whoever edits this stuff lets through as much foul language as fucking possible. To leave it out of a book like this would be to deny my heritage. If I spoke Greek at home, this book would be soaked in Greek linguistic references; were I Pakistani, smatterings of Urdu wherever you looked. Well, I grew up council, then right-to-buy in a council street. Swearing was both a primary mode of expression and a tool for fighting that stopped you getting cut . . . with a real tool. A wordy trepanning that lets out steam in a controlled, safer way. And not always even in anger.

Sometimes, it was simply the ambience. The word *fuck* is the 40-watt lamp of my childhood. Always there, always on, lambent within each sentence without you really noticing. Sometimes the swearing served no function. My dad would swear while he was thinking – like that little spinning circle you get on a computer as it buffers. My dad muttered the F-word while his thoughts gathered.

'Where were we the other night, Julie? What's that restaurant called . . . fucking . . . fucking . . . fuck, fuck, fuck . . . the pizza place down the road . . . Fucking rip-off. Pizzas were like fucking biscuits. I had a cheese sandwich when I got in.'

My mum's mum (more about her later) was perhaps the most proficient at obscenity. She was the first person I heard conjugate the C-word as the present participle.

'Get my cunting slippers.'

Cunt-ing! *Ing!* You could put *-ing* on the end! I was only eleven when I learned this, and at school I was king for a day.

'Warren, it's time for cunting History.'

Warren Evans's face fell into an expression of worship.

Lindsey, my Mancunian Mrs, is fascinated by Dave. She often says to me:

'Would I have got on with your dad?'

It's a tantalizing thought experiment. The silverback king of negativity coming face-to-face with the relentless, indefatigable northern wife.

'We can't eat at that restaurant, Lindsey. It'll be a rip-off and the food will be shit.'

'Pipe down, Dave, you miserable sod – we're going.'

And then my imaginary scene fizzles out. I simply cannot imagine his response.

What would Dave in his seventies be like? Just as angry? Vigorous? Still smashing the gym three times a week? Screaming about no-deal Brexit? Or would he have, as my mum keeps saying, become 'like butter once he had a grand-daughter . . . it was girls he needed'.

Again, I struggle to envisage it.

It seems awful to say, but rather than a Dave-sized, gorilla-shaped hole in my life, I feel stronger thanks to his absence. He's turned into my foundation, the cornerstone. (Is that a Tinie Tempah lyric?) Dave, as Dad, did his best to provide, but he also gave me something much more useful: he showed me what not to do – rather, how not to *be*. I find myself sometimes catastrophizing, declaring that all will fail and go wrong . . . then I stop. That behaviour made Dave miserable, so why choose it for me? Who cares if a drink is spilt? Who fucking cares? A half-glass of water was enough to set Dave off.

'Waheey! Floods of it. Fuck sake. Meal ruined. Trousers soaked. Let's leave.'

I wouldn't want my manic, weird, attention-junkie tiny daughter to absorb a vibe like that.

The only bittersweet thing about the Dave-less present is that I would love my old man to have seen me onstage, just once – or to have bought him a nice car. But then I probably would have fucked it up and bought the wrong one.

'That's the worst Mercedes ever made, boy. Thanks for trying, though.'

2.

Prince of Essex

When my mum, Julie Jacobs, fell pregnant by my dad in 1975, it was not planned. When I was twenty-two, my dad, Stella Artois-sodden, blurted out his version of my conception in one sentence:

'I saw her in Epping, boy, your muvva – in the Treetops nightclub. Next thing I know, I blow my biscuits and she was up the duff. I was fucked. That's how you came about. Never have kids. That's my warning to you.'

It's a unique mixture of sensations. Being warned by your own father not to create what you yourself are, his child. I know, I know. Amazing, isn't he? I'd love to pretend I'm exaggerating, but my dad's way of speaking was halfway between a Guy Ritchie character and a Harold Pinter play. Like a posh person wrote a working-class character and got it wrong by going too far.

That's how I began. I was the ball of cells that started dividing in a 21-year-old girl's body and into the life of a 35-year-old Neanderthal man.

Dad was still living at home with his mum in Barking, Essex. Thirty-five years old, about seventeen stone at this point, 7 per cent body fat, Dave Kane had never moved out. King Baby still inhabiting his box room overlooking a small square of yellowing garden strewn with rusting small weights, his first self-built bench and pull-up frame, all the metal ghosts of the puny boy he used to be – oh, he had a real gym membership now. In fact, he was one of the biggest men at the Barking gym. He had his clothes specially altered, as though he were afflicted with a pituitary malfunction that made his bulging muscles rip through whatever he wore. ('Like the fucking Hulk I was, boy.') The fact he had achieved his bulk and brawn with thousands of Deca-Durabolin steroid injections in both legs and arse did not matter. Not back then. Any crampon to the summit of man meatiness was allowed. No one knew, least of all my poor old-young dad, that main-lining enough of that shit could calcify one of your three aorta flaps (that's the heart valve that looks, ironically for my German-motor-loving Dad, like a Mercedes sign), so you die of a massive heart attack waaaaay before your time (take note, all you waxed *TOWIE* and *Geordie Shore* Christmas-ham bodies). But here, back when he was thirty-five, he was flying high. And wide. And with very yellow piss. The muscly boy-man who loved the ladies.

Dad's sister Brenda had long ago fled to the USA to seek a new life, but she was to violently cameo in my childhood several times over the years as a full American, more American than the ones who were actually born there. An alcoholic, flowing blonde-haired, sneaker-wearing mental bastard, who cropped up and always delivered a solid gold anecdote. I can't wait to tell you about the beer can she threw at my head when I was fifteen while screaming at me that I was 'a motherfucker'. For now, though, it's Dad, the Goliath-David – still in Sandringham Road, Barking, Essex – indulged as though an only child, Brenda long Yankeed by then; a full fried breakfast waiting every weekday morning at 6 a.m., before he set off to smash at sheet metal and dominate fibre-glass and insulation with the suppressed rage of a failed Butlin's Redcoat, model and actor; surprising details that, I know, do not fit with the rest of the man. Dave, son of Eva – it was she who made sure his tailored seventeen-inch collar shirts were ironed before he hit the Essex nightclubs at the weekend. The son, of course, of Eva *and* Sidney.

'Who the fuck was Sidney?'

I have found out as much as I could, and having known my grandma Eva – and having grown up feasting on my mum's descriptions of the things she said and did – I have come to the terrible conclusion that Sidney, though odious in his method, probably did what was best for his sanity. He'd got trapped in a relationship with a miserable person he didn't fancy so he ran off with a woman called Rose and started again. And they were happy, at least according to my secret aunts, uncles and cousins I eventually tracked down using nascent Internet resources when I was at university. My granddad Sidney had popped his clogs from stomach cancer in the late 1980s but not before he'd made my old man a half-brother and a half-sister.

Whenever I seek out remote corners of my family, I keep hoping against hope to find another hyperactive weirdo like me. One who grew up in a council area with no books, no culture, surrounded by hard manual labourers and people who actively told you education was a load of old bollocks and a waste of time, who somehow Penguin Classic'ed through every projection of who he could become. Is there one? Fuck knows. People mistakenly think I fit the stereotype of the working-class person who made it to university because their parents *meant well*. Not me. I didn't have poor-but-bookish parents. I didn't have a teacher dad or a degree-educated mum. I didn't go to a grammar school and get a miracle skimming off to Oxbridge. None of those things happened. I was just odd, thankfully. Oddness saved my arse. And when I hunted out my new cousins I was hoping to find another like me. But none. Just smiley builders, beauticians and very young mums.

Sidney ran off with a younger, happier woman when my dad was tiny – allegedly clearing all baby David's toys from the house for selling, thus funding his playboy flight from domesticity. I always thought this claim reeked of bitterness and overdramatic fabrication, but my dad believed it his whole life, his eyes frequently moistening after a few Stellas when he retold the story.

'I had nothing. He took everything I had and flogged it so he could run off with that slag. My poor dear old girl!'

Was she dear, though, Dad? Or was she a miserable, spiteful lost soul and a contagious emotional influenza?

I managed to acquire a picture of my granddad. I look a bit like him. We have the same rakish side-smile, as though about to take a taxi into town and cause mischief with a bevy of companions. When I produced this black and white snap one evening, my old man would not even look at it; he actually left the room when I told him about his half-siblings. He went to have a drama-sob in the living room, looking out from the bay window and cursing his 'arsehole father' through gritted teeth. Eva had poisoned him good and proper. Of course, there is always the chance that Sidney really was as my dad so eloquently described him to me when I was seventeen:

'My old man – didn't have anything. The cunt was just a stain. A fucking stain.'

My dad loved the C-word. He wasn't as deft with it as my nan (my mum's mum) but his use of it was more liberal. Everyone was a cunt. Everyone we passed. Every other driver, waiters, people in the street, me, my brother, my mum. All cunts. Objects were cunts. The Dijon mustard, when it ran out: total cunt. Sometimes my dad would say it so many times during a meal that my mum would get annoyed. One Sunday, after my dad had been cut up by a 'black driver' on the way home from the pub, he had a sort of cunt-fit, using it for every other word.

'Dave – can you stop using that word, please?' my mum had implored.

'Whoops,' he said, looking at me with wonky Stella eyes. 'I've made a cunt of myself.'

But to my dad, Sidney (his dad) was the biggest C-word of them all, even though he could have been a well-balanced, ordinary chap who quite reasonably sodded off. Eva was, after all, a dark and poisonous soul. My memories of her are of a downcast woman, always in mildewy corners, full of phlegm, with a bronchial sneer raised to the world; the type of lady who'd laugh if a cat's tail got severed by a garden gate (that actually happened). And if you're wondering how I dare type this about my dear deceased paternal nan – well, the answer is hidden in the question. *Everyone on that side of the family is dead. Everyone.* It is strange that on my dad's side clog-popping is so expertly done while on my mum's side many appear immortal. (At the time of writing, my granddad and his Mrs, my nan's older sister and her husband and *loads* more across that generation are still going strong.) I think it would be uncontroversial to throw in here that miserable people die earlier. It's statistically true (there'd be a footnote here if

I could be arsed).* My *paternal* nan and granddad are dead. My dad's sister, his half-brothers and -sisters, all his aunts, most of his cousins – all dead, and many of them early too. Cancers, freak accidents, suicides – all Deady McDeadface. Many quite Jewish too – like they were *doing* Jewish characters.

The only actual Jew was my dad's granddad. Benjamin Wolff: the miserable bastard dad to end them all. The father of screwface Eva. Great-granddad Wolff had the most complex Jewish trait of all. He was an anti-Semite. Wolff, a blond-haired, blue-eyed Jew (there are lots of them, by the way), had fled Europe and had no time for anything connected to the race and religion that nearly got him and his family into the hottest water Europe's twentieth-century immersion heater ever produced. Benjamin Wolff arrived in England from cuddly old Germany and never entered a synagogue again. Dad said that Benjamin Wolff would cross over to the other side of the road to avoid passing right in front of a synagogue. He felt that betrayed by his tribe. He started four hairdressing shops in Essex and Jews weren't very welcome. No Yiddish was spoken, no Hanukkah candles were lit. No one married a Jew (it was discouraged). Pork was joyously eaten every day – as though by biting into the meat he was tearing the gristle from his tough life. The only thing Wolffy kept, as did my Nanna Eva, his daughter, was a sort of parodic Jewish demeanour – hard for me to expand upon without sounding un-PC. Let's call my nan Eva and my great-granddad 'gesticulatory Jews'. All the voices and hands – recipes passed down – but about as pro-goyim as you can get.

* I cannot recommend enough *The Village Effect*, by Susan Pinker.

Could great-granddad Wolff be the source, the river mouth of my dad's poison lake of negativity? Is Benjamin Wolff patient zero of Miserable Git Disease? He certainly was one massive, miserable twat of a man: the prototype, perhaps, for the more refined depressive (and loving, in his own temper-farting way) Dave Kane. He was 'tighter than a gnat's arsehole' according to my dad, and used to spend hours just hanging out with his hairdressing accounts books, tracing the profit margins with his fingers. My dad told me he only ever saw Wolffy smile once. It was when Dad stepped on a nail in front of him.

'. . . just the corner of his mouth, boy . . . it twitched . . . he smiled. The only time I ever saw it.' My dad would often point to the circular scar on the top of his foot, reliving not the injury but the shock of seeing his granddad's only smile.

My dad inherited the Judaeo-sceptic gene but by the time the DNA got to him, he was only 25 per cent Ashkenazi anyway. I had my DNA tested in 2015 and, sure enough, it came back 12.5 per cent Jewish. Just a few per cent more and I'd have had something substantial to do stand-up about. Alas, it's white, male and heterosexual for me. Thank God for a touch of working-class emotional abuse and Essex regionality or I would have nothing interesting to pick apart. I also have really bad flat feet. I should do more about that. Poor and with bad feet. Shit! I've got a serious case. Must remind my agent tomorrow.

I have no idea to what extent the doomed legacy of pessimistic German-Jewishness affected the Wolffs. Perhaps they were just a family of grade-A miserable bastards, and laying culture and race over that would be to let them off the hook. Like putting my pug Colin in a tutu – it's still the same wheezing creature, even in a dress. Sorry, Colin.

They were a maudlin, self-indulgently despondent lot. And Eva, 'Nanna' Eva as me and my brother styled her, was a prime example of the Wolffy line.

From the moment my dad had language he was poisoned with the holy commandments of Wolff, and he tried, inadvertently, Lord love him, to pass them on to, into, me.

1. Life is shit and hard.

2. Nothing you attempt to do will ever be successful.

3. There are Haves and Have-nots. We are Have-nots – always will be.

4. Never rely on anyone. They *will* let you down.

5. I'm paying. I'm saying.

And the Golden Rule:

Take care of number one, and fuck everyone else.

I've spent my whole life coming to terms with the golden rule. There is some soundness buried within individualism, of course, muffled, but it's dodgy. Take care of number one can be the scaffolding of self-reliance and financial rectitude, the steel joist that held me up during some of the more astounding up-by-the-boot-strap transformations I pulled off when I was nineteen. But it has always – and still does – played on my noggin. How can a dad be number one when he has a child? Surely the kid is number one. Maybe it's just something my old man said to look tough, or to temper me for life's knocks. But his behaviour suggested he believed it.

The curry out or the £50-worth of lottery tickets always trumped the school trip or the financial help with a poncey uni education. Understand – it wasn't done in a nasty, neglecting way. It was the pure and liquid execution of a Wolffy Golden Rule. Take care of yourself first. No one else will. Maybe it was a lethal mantra, particularly when blended with Sidney sodding off and leaving little David to it.

'There are Haves and Have-nots. We are Have-nots – always will be.'

Must have been tough being exposed to that when he was little. He grew up into a man who believed it from the bicuspid aortic valve of his doomed heart, scowling at a world full of 'piss-takers', thieves and immigrants who want one up on you; his dreams were always just over there – in that posher postcode, where we'll never live, no matter how hard we try – and when we did try, well, it would probably turn to shit. Writing it here, it seems so bleak – you're either smiling at the outrageous miserable bastardness of it or frowning in pity – but when I was kid, it was just normal. In fact, it was funny. Me and my brother used to impersonate my dad. We'd stage mini-tragedies such as a glass of water being knocked over, then I would play Dad doing biblical scale wailing about tides and floods and how it is the End of Man, and James would play beleaguered Mum, plaintively crying back, 'Daaaavve, Daaaavve.' I was creating Greek drama back then even though the sum total of my literary experience was the Mr Men books.

When my mum was very heavily pregnant with me, she and my dad spent the evening with Eva in Barking. The Freudian wound of having had her son ripped from his birth home in untimely fashion was still gaping – after all, he had been a barely pubescent 35-year-old man when this 21-year-old temptress invader Juliet Jacobs had snatched him, Prince David, from the Kingdom of Essex. After an evening of glacial chat (both in speed and temperature), my dad had popped out to collect ceremonial fish and chips from round the corner, Mum being left to attempt full conversation with the woman who, in my memory, has been merged with that dead zombie lady from the cursed hotel room in *The Shining*.

Nanna Eva was of the generation (many of them still living) who prefer two separate rooms for entertaining, even in the smallest of houses. A dining room out back for dread-laden dinners full of silence, chewing noises and chinking condiment spoons; then a front room, parlour or living room for telly watching and sparse chat, which weaved around comforting mainstream laughs like *The Royal Variety Performance* or *George and Mildred*. My mum was part of the first knock-your-rooms-through generation. Any wall that can be smashed through was got rid of or transformed into an archway – one giant space, kitchen, tables, sofas. If she could, I think the bedroom floors would have been removed. Maybe Mum grew up allergic to the murky separateness of the fuggy front room with its permanent floating cumulus of Embassy Filter smoke. Nanna Eva's separate lounge was a room not just dark but one which sucked in light, energy; a bad star that hurt its galaxy, a cosmological entity that Brian Cox could do a programme about on BBC2. The Dark Parlour of Doom.

Mum was left there for no more than twenty minutes while Dad hunter-gathered the rock-eel, chips and gherkins. As my mum tells it, after some silence – a period of staring in the style of a Sergio Leone Western Mexican stand-off – conversation cautiously began. Chat naturally orbited around the planet that was my mum's eight-month swollen belly – speculation about the birth, what the child would be like.

'I wonder what it'll look like, Julie?'

Eva had inherited Wolffy's fetish for blond-haired, blue-eyed children. Do you realize how complex a trait this is for a woman of German-Jewish extraction? My quarter-Jew dad, of course, had been a child with locks of curly wheat-blond hair and eyes like cornflowers floating in milk. My mum was about as brunette as you can go and still tick 'Caucasian' on the passport form.

'What you gonna do, Julie? Dave would love a little girl. A fair, blue-eyed little girl. What you gonna do if it's gypsy, like your lot?'

'I dunno, Eva . . .'

She was twenty-one, remember, my mum. Back then, she was not the most confident woman. When I quizzed her on how she could tolerate being spoken to like that, she came back with the simple:

'I was young. If anyone spoke like that to me now, I'd tell them to fuck off.'

That's more like it. Once Mum found her four-lettered voice, it empowered her. But back then – when the wicked witch of the East (End) was still alive – she couldn't even manage a 'please sod off, Eva'; she just sat there and took the eugenic rant. My mum remembers her emotional weakness – hormonal and swollen. She cried in the toilets, the car, in bed later that night.

'Well,' Eva continued, 'let's hope she's blonde, Julie. Like Dave's ex, Pat. Now there was a girl. My God she was beautiful. Oh well. Oh well . . .'

If you can believe it, Eva then reached behind the sofa and

drew out a photo album. It was made almost solely of Dad-and-Patricia pictures. Pat, the blonde-haired ex whom Eva had adored. Well, she said she had adored her. It's much more likely she was a total bitch to her, and was now feigning ador-ation as a way of being spiteful to my mum.

'Look at 'em. What a figure. What a lovely girl. That's them at that Italian place down on the Broadway . . . has Dave taken you there yet? No? Oh dear.' Etc., etc.

This went on for a good few minutes until Eva put in for good measure: 'That was his true love, you know. My God, he cried like a baby when they split up. My poor David. You get one love like that, one. Except a mother's love of course. So two . . .'

Tick, tock – the old carriage clock of hers provided the background to every chat in that dank room.

After the photo memory-lane session, the conversation naturally dipped into silence again and my mum took her opportunity to strike back with love. It was a peace offering. She reached into her bag and produced the gift she'd bought when she and Dad were away in Great Yarmouth the week-end before. It was a decorative cruet set: two little Mexican men, whose heads nodded forward and dispensed season-ing. She'd put aside her holiday money all week, then bought them as a gift for her Dave's mum.

'I got you something when we were away last week, Eva. For your dining room . . .'

'It pissed down all week, didn't it? Dave should have taken you to Southend. That's where his real family is. You'll be liv-ing in Enfield, though, won't you? Over the border.'

The border?

My mum handed over the cruet set.

Without even properly inspecting it, Eva laughed and said, 'Pah . . . bloody hell . . . I won't use something like that, love. You could give it to someone else? Your London family?'

'I bought it for you, Eva. It's a gift . . .'

For a stupid second Mum had thought that might do the trick, maybe Eva would eat her words. But she just sat there, holding it, staring at it, turning it over and over; then she set it on the coffee table, gently took my mum's hand and said this:

'My Dave ripped me in two when he came out. Right from the arsehole. Nearly nine pounds.' Then she let my mum's hand drop from hers. 'Tea?' And left the room. The cruet set stayed on the coffee table and my mum never saw it again – until Eva died eight years later. They were clearing out the house and Mum found it in the back of a kitchen cupboard. One of the Mexican heads – 'The pepper, I think' – had been twisted and snapped off. Maybe it had fallen and broken but it seems too tempting to conclude that, as soon as my mum left the house that day, Eva decapitated it. Either that or when I popped out of my mum, tanned, hairy and black-haired, my nanna had dug the objects from the back of her cupboard and smashed the head from the pepper Mexican in an Aryan rage.

This anecdote is a tragic precursor of how my dad himself would receive gifts. I wonder why the pair of them, Eva and Dave, were so messed up that even someone being nice to them was somehow offensive. It was like they had to reject any step towards happiness. Any transmission from the land of the positive must be deemed suspect, so cosy were they in their grey blankets of gloom. It was another of my father's core messages: 'Most things represent hassle or aggro, boy.'

25

There was nothing done in a truly selfless or kind way. Everything had a catch or a nasty pay-off. Seems good now – just you wait. You'll fucking see.

Mum told me that, just a few months after she'd started seeing my dad (it was their first Christmas as a 'steady couple'), she'd seen a leather shaving set advertised in a magazine and saved up for it diligently from her telephonist wages. She picked her moment to hand it over, when they were on their way out for a Christmas drink. Lashings of beer and spirits, and my dad, naturally, intended driving there and back. In that era it was almost effeminate *not* to drink and drive.

He'd just collected my mum from her mum's house in Carterhatch Lane, Enfield – not by gently knocking, politely making chat, then graciously escorting my mum down the path to an open car door, no, but with a testosterone temper-tooting of his car horn. He kept doing this his whole life. Dad would defiantly leave the house first. When he was ready, you were ready. Then he would press the horn, the car swaying with his weight as he smashed down on the steering wheel. You had about two toots and five minutes before he would start beating on the dash with longer, more enraged horn wails; and you would be on the receiving end of an insult when you eventually boarded.

Mum and Dad were sat in his lime-green Ford Capri, the three-litre engine growling like a sedated bear that has not been given quite enough drugs. It wasn't Christmas yet, but Mum was so excited about giving my dad this pressie she couldn't hold back any longer: that magical, festive, bursting feeling when you know you've bought someone something amazing. The look on their face as they receive it was the feel-good hit she couldn't wait to mainline.

'Whassat?' he said, putting the car back into neutral.

'Early Christmas present. I just couldn't wait, Dave.'

'Yeah, but what is it?'

'Open it!'

He used that same line on me nearly every Christmas when I was a kid. Socks, soap on a rope, Barry White album. 'What is it?' He couldn't muster the joy to play along. What's the point in wrapping something in paper? Just give it! Or give the money so they can choose their own gift.

Mum described how he opened it in silence, slightly irritated that the quick transit to the pub had been disrupted with a load of sentimental bollocks. Something getting in the way of a planned drive – another trigger that would set my old man off. It's another example of a Wolffy rule: hard to imagine for many readers whose dads would give them lifts anywhere they needed. Not my dad. The only chance you had of getting anywhere was if he was 'going past it anyway'. Seems there are two types of driver: normal people, and drivers-for-themselves. The latter group will not deviate from their route or timetable for you. Any excuse will be found: tiredness, it's a work vehicle, the weather, the traffic. My dad was a prime example.

Of course, back then, their first Christmas, he was still straining to hold in his 'pig traits' as Mum charmingly calls them. So he gritted his teeth and took the Heineken-postponing package and opened it.

'Well?' Mum said – eyes filling already, preparing for the loving, festive hug.

'What . . . what is it?'

'It's a shaving set, Dave.'

'Why d'you buy that?'

'It's a Christmas present, you wally.'

Pause.

'I won't use that.'

Longer pause.

'Was it expensive, Julie?'

She told him the price.

'Fucking hell. Fuck . . . I hope you can get your money back.'

He handed it to her, and they drove to the pub to get pissed. Mum managed to delay her sobbing until she got into the pub toilets.

The Warren Wood, near Epping, was the pub my dad lived in every weekend. He went there throughout his youth and continued to frequent it into his middle age. It is the archetypal Essex boozer: full of hyped-up young men walking to the lavs with suspicious frequency, and dodgy-looking Hatton-Garden-robbery types. It has a conservatory where families chow down Sunday lunches big enough to give you instant diabetes.

The green paint and cream tiles, still there, take me straight back to my childhood. Me and my brother James would join Dad at the Warren Wood every Sunday. We'd be in the 'snug' with beef and onion crisps and fizzy drinks while he sipped pints and ate cheese cubes. He'd tell us stories that, let's say, weren't always age-appropriate. They often featured the word 'tits'. Whenever he said it he would hiss the S, like he hated it and loved it in equal measure. 'Lovely titsssss' – covering the area with pervy spittle as he lifted a pickled onion from the Warren Wood's bar-top.

He told me the Donna Graves story a few times. As he got older the emphasis shifted from her to the car he was driving in the story. It seems age shifts a man's focus from his dick to his shift stick. Why the link between the masculine, the middle-aged and cars? Explain that, Richard Dawkins and Jeremy Clarkson. Interesting piece of trivia: the decade of a man's life in which he is most likely to cheat . . . is his seventies. Maybe it's the invention of those cock-hardening little blue pills, or some breed of evolutionary panic making the ageing stud desire to spread his DNA one last time. Come to think about it, whenever I've gigged in Thailand there was a definite age mismatch between, let's call them brides and grooms. Whatever the reason, a lot of men seem to get one last pervy flowering. The male septuagenarian equivalent of the hot flush. Oh God, may I be spared mine.

'Donna from Basildon,' he said, his face changing quickly from leering memory to anger. 'Rude fucking cow. Never date a bird with bad manners.'

Oh yeeeeah – my dad was a right feminist too. I had, and still have, no idea what the moral of this particular tale is or whether Dad was just doing weird, sexist showing off. Donna Graves was on the scene a few years before my mum.

'Your mother was still playing with her dollies, boy. I was already out shagging.'

This line was used in a few other stories he told. It was obviously an important part of his internal scaffolding, this idea that his wife was more than a decade younger than he, that he'd 'done it all' while she was still playing with Barbies in the garden. What was that? Power? Lack of power? Or just that he liked the idea he had 'banged everything that moved' before my mum had even left school?

'I'd got it out my system. You do that too, boy. No proper girlfriends before twenty-five. No kids before forty.'

Oh, Dad. I was destined to fall deeply into a mad love with the first girl who so much as held my hand.

Dad had driven to Basildon and stopped at Donna's house, tooting the horn of his pride and joy Mini Cooper. She got in and they began the drive to Treetops nightclub, Epping. A few minutes into the journey Donna cranked open the window and spat out of it on to the street.

'Fucking gobbed out the window and on to the street, boy. A proper gozza.' A gozza is a chesty, phlegmy spit.

Dad had looked across at her, turning alabaster white.

'What the fuck was that, Donna?'

'I got a cold, ain't I?'

Dad did not speak. He U-turned the car and started driving her back home.

'Dave! I got allergies. Ain't my fault. Dave! Answer me!' She was crying . . . what have I done? etc.

'Get out.'

And he left her at her garden gate, wheelspinning back to Barking. He never saw her again but he talked about her for the rest of his life.

'Rude cow, that Donna. Lovely titssss, though.'

Germaine Greer – if you would like a signed copy of my book, please just Tweet me.

That same winter of the shaving-set rejection, Dad exhibited another disturbing car-based courtship behaviour. Either my mum was a masochist back then, or his blue eyes and muscly body outweighed the caveman red-alert signals. On one level, I'm glad, as I'm here – but on another, WTF? Maybe it comes down to a theory I have about some women between the ages of sixteen and twenty-five who suffer from a horrific condition called Attracted to Bastard disease. They walk into the pub and see a nice guy like me and think 'Bor-rrrriiiinnng'; they see coke-head Gary on the other side of the room saying, 'When I'm drunk I like to punch holes in the wall' and think, 'What a turn-on.' Many girls I knew were held back for years because they got stuck in relationships with twats and only started living when they were twenty-five and free from them and their bullying tendencies. The more sprogs the man fathered, the more the girls fancied him. Drug-dealer? *Phwoar!* Cage fighter and unstable? 'Please impregnate me instantly!' I am by no means a Darwinian expert, but I'm guessing there is some sort of evolutionary reason for girls to pass through a phase of loving bad boys, or dangerous ones, or ones who are exciting and risky. I guess my dad fell into that final category. But he wasn't just volatile and angry – he was also pretty. Slam dunk.

One of the most unlikely pieces of my dad's history is that he once modelled. Full-on, topless, pouty posing, in teeny-weeny pants. For years I could not understand how this seemingly effete profession could be on the CV of metal-smasher and doorman Dave Kane. I've reconciled it in my mind as belonging to that same central trait of 'always needing more for number one'. If I say narcissist, I don't mean Dad loved himself. I mean more that his pride and ego required constant reassurance. He longed for it, and when wounded or tested, he bit back furiously. Take my amateur psychologizing as correct and it explains a lot, including this story.

Dad had just collected Mum from Carterhatch Lane in his Ford Capri. The same routine. Toot the horn once, then bash the horn, then out she comes – scurrying down the path like a child worker on her way to make trainers in a factory. I'm sure if Dad could have found a way of taxiing alongside the house and having Mum leap in while the motor was moving, he would.

As my mum remembers it, Dad was in reasonably chipper form as they drove to the Treetops nightclub, Epping, a place for which he sometimes 'did the door' at weekends. This meant he got VIP treatment whenever he attended as a mere punter. He had slathered on his favourite Paco Rabanne shaving tonic and was bulging out of a fitted shirt, ready for a night of pissed-up female attention and masculine posturing while my mum looked on, thanking the heavens that she was the one who would be leaving with this brawny prize.

As Dad told me once: 'When I was in my prime, boy, the birds just wanted to touch me – just to check if I was real.' I was about twelve when my old man first said that to me (he said it many times after as my pathetic puberty released the minimum growth hormones needed). Aged twelve I was right at the bottom of the boy pile at school. I was in that league just above the boys who smell of wee or have disabilities or who will obviously be gay in the future. Yes, that league – you remember it now. I was with the Nearly Bullied – the forgettable, lower-ranking, pale males, whom the girls almost walked through as though you were a spirit in a ghost movie. I had nothing. I was below average height, no muscles at all, and any thought of early pubic hair had long been banished. I had a single coarse brown follicle mockingly on my chest. My chest! Why the chest first? Why not the dick or balls, cruel nature? What kind of a twisted God sends hair to the chest first? That may well have been the year I realized I was an atheist. Hairless, girl-less and with only one or two friends. Thank God (oh, wait, he doesn't exist any more) I could make the bullies laugh. I would hone that. But for now – it was nights of orgasmless masturbation, computer games and skinny rejection – and all with an alpha male dad in the same house always reminding me what a bad-ass he once was, and still is. I wonder if it's possible for a father to actually arrest puberty? To stop hormonal growth just with his words and behaviour? Science suggests it happens for girls. Dad-less girls go into puberty earlier . . . so can it not follow that an overbearing father figure could slow male development? That's what I'm telling myself. That's my excuse for the hairless acorn jutting from my pelvis well into my teens.

'I was so big, boy, my arms so massive, that girls just wanted to touch me.'

Wow. But all that brawn came with a temper, Dad . . . just like outside Treetops nightclub . . .

On that night, Dad wasn't just looking fine – he was tailored into fineness. The shirt's purchase and story had been eloquently told on the drive to the club.

'It looks lovely, Dave.'

'What?'

'Your shirt.'

'Fucking wants to, Julie . . . took half my pay packet.'

This particular shirt was extra special; saved up from 'grafting on site' all week, and purchased at the expensive department store, Pearsons, in Enfield, on the Wednesday. He'd had it adapted by Nanna Eva for his massive neck, and he probably felt even greater than usual.

The Ford Capri swung into the Treetops car park. My mum tells the sequence of what happened next like this.

As the beam of the headlights swept the eager queue of non-VIPS (not my dad's queue, obviously), disaster struck. Waiting near the front of the peasants' line was an equally ripped Essex 'foot soldier' and his 'tart'. And that man . . . was wearing the exact same shirt as my dad. What happened next would be deleted from a sitcom script as too far-fetched, but for my mum it was real life and the end of the date night.

'I don't believe it.'

'What is it, Dave?'

'I don't fucking believe it . . .'

'What . . . what?'

'That cunt there. He's wearing the same shirt as me.'

'It's similar but—'

'Similar? It's the fucking same. It's the same shirt. Checked – he's even got the top two buttons open. Pearsons wanker.'

'But you got yours from Pearsons.'

'I wouldn't, Julie, if I was you.'

'It's a nice shirt.'

'That's not the point, is it? I look like a fucking idiot now.'

'Dave – calm down.'

But he didn't. He drove the car round the back of the nightclub and into the space he normally used when working there. He got out and slammed the door. He walked round to the boot and fetched a Stanley knife from his toolbox. He walked back round the front of the car so that he was lit in double spot by the Capri's headlights. My mum had no clue what was going to happen next. Dad ripped off his shirt, the buttons spraying away from him and hitting the windscreen like chips from a Epping B-road. He stood there topless, fixating on the shirt in his hands, a mad, half-changed Hulk, eyeing the replicant garment, the foul copy, the evil twin of

34

another man's fashion choice. Then . . . he shredded it with the Stanley knife. Frantically. Tearing at it with the blade over and over till he was left holding nothing but an absurd little piece of collar, which he dropped to the floor and stamped on like a cockroach found in some Coco Pops. He replaced the tool in the back of the car, then rejoined my mum. He was sweating and breathless.

'Right, Dave. Well – that achieved a lot.'

'Felt fucking right to me.'

'And what are we gonna do now?'

'Go home.'

He wheelspan out of the car park and they did exactly that – my mum being dropped wordlessly at Carterhatch Lane (that the shirt fiasco was somehow her fault was so potent that when I sat her down to retell me the incident in 2017, she still felt it), then Dad returned to Essex at high speed in the time before traffic cameras, when Ford Capris still ruled the earth.

3.

The Castle

A shelter. My first experience of being parented. Six women, all with mewling shit machines at their sides. Women who for whatever reason had two things in common: they'd just given birth, and they had nowhere to live.

Now before we start plucking the Stradivarius violin of a blighted childhood, I should probably clear it up that my mum wasn't homeless in the romantic, Bronx-rapper sense. I wasn't slopped out into a crack den while my dad did time in the local jail for being a bad muthafucka who held up a 7-Eleven with an AK. No. If only. Imagine the rhyme-spitting hip hop star I could have become with that sort of man dem pedigree fam. Blap! No. My unmarried Mum had *made* herself 'homeless' with a purpose – so that she and my dad would qualify for a council flat when one became available. She'd calculatedly moved out of her lounge-bedroom at my great-grandma's house and put herself at the mercy of the Enfield Women's Shelter for New Mothers.

'CSA? Stands for Cunts who Shag and Abscond.'

No. Not my old man. Not one of those. He was present, my dad. But initially only just.

He visited at set times on a schedule dictated by a third party. Oh, he tried to be as involved as he could, given the circumstances, but the mixture of his hard manual 'graft' – lagging, the hardest of building-site genres, putting fibreglass on pipes in sweaty boiler rooms – plus my mum's unfortunate living arrangements at the shelter in Enfield meant not as often as he would have liked. To be precise, for the first eight weeks of his baby's life, Dave Kane had once-daily access to his newborn son (that's me, for the *really* slow people). Just a couple of hours each evening with his sprog born sprouting a freakish mane of brown hair, and no sleepovers permitted either. Come 7.30 p.m., my dad climbed back into the Cortina he was driv- ing at the time and went home, crossing the border within five minutes into the Republic of Essex. I remained with my mum, Julie, in a Moses basket, sleeping next to her in the shelter.

Just before my fifth birthday, we moved to Brimsdown (pronounced *Brims-daaaaan* by the locals). My brother James was two. Weirdly, I remember much of it with clarity. I recall where we'd moved from, too: a two-bedroomed council flat in Freezywater that we were allocated after the shelter. It was in a small block with its own car park. I have only happy memories of that flat, and when I play back thoughts I cannot find a single one where it's raining – only sunshine. But I knew my dad hated it; for him, it hammered down every day.

We had been on the waiting list for a council exchange – and my old man knew that once we were in a house, we could wield our Right to Buy. One of my clearest memories from the flat in Freezywater was when Dad pulled up out- side with pride in his brand new Ford Granada estate: BPU 787T. I've searched for the number plate. How I would love to see that beast one more time: touch it, glide my fin- gers over its indigo bonnet. A Ghia too. It was last MOTed in 1992 – then vanished.

My old man hated parking that pristine show-car in our

council-flat car park. He and my mum had running jokes
about some of the characters who inhabited the block. They
referred to the very poorest resident on the ground floor as
'Paul Getty'. Being only four, I had no idea that nicknaming
a junkie as an American billionaire was supposed to be
funny. I thought it was the man's name. I can still feel the
flush of embarrassment, saying:

'Hello, Paul Getty.'

And my dad putting in, 'Shut your mouth, boy.'

Amazing how, as a small child, you can have such a sharp
sense of having shown yourself up. I see it with Minna: the
blushing, the questing eyes searching out the meaning of the
gaffe, the tears of shame.

Brimsdown is a desolate area; too far from London to be
part of it, and not far enough to have its own heartbeat. In a
zombie apocalypse the undead would not feed on Brimsdown's residents, so lacking in nourishment was EN3 as a
postcode. In bleaker times I've toyed with the sound of it.
Brim – brimming with, and Down, down-and-outs, low, the
bottom. Who fucking named it? Who chooses Brimming
with Shit as the name for a place where people dwell?

The road we were to move to was a Thatcherite buy-
your-own-if-you-can council road. For people from my
background – former welfare kids, whose mums and dads
purchased their own gaffs – property exerts a special pull. It
has continued to do so for my whole life. I have no savings,
no pension, no plan. Just the house. That's my plan. The
faith I have in bricks and mortar is the same faith a funda-
mentalist Christian has in redemption after death. Property
is God, Your House the Son, and Interest Rates the Holy
Ghost. (Does that make my estate agent a kiddy-fiddling

priest?) Don't fuck with any of them. Pray. At retirement, you go in one of two directions: to the estate agent to redeem, or to the state nursing home with your tiny savings for a dirty purgatory with a portly nurse who hits you around your dementia skull when no one else is looking. That's how I was raised. Breeze blocks and planning permissions. These were my altars and cloths.

This was another of my dad's cardinal lessons I absorbed: that in the absence of a solid financial base, one day you could be left humiliated, with nothing. It played on his mind a lot – this idea that every job was your last, any moment was the beginning of the end; that no one will take care of you when you have nothing. Stand-ups think this feeling that their luck is about to run out is unique to them. What vain bollocks – like most of the stuff stand-ups say in the many idiotic, self-absorbed, yawn-yawn documentaries you can watch. You think because you get up onstage you're special – or that your fear of exposure is something unique? You bell-end. That's all of us. Men and women who *do* anything. Who live. And society dumps that fear on dads in double-loads. It's not a statistical irrelevance that so many more men top themselves. It's a product of the unrealistic pressure heaped on 'geezers'. Provide, or expire. And for many dads, and mums, the house, the *owned house*, is the physical embodiment of the ethos. The castle that guards against the fear.

Maybe it's hard for those of you who grew up in houses already owned or have lived in a council house their whole life to understand the fetishistic hold of bricks and mortar on my kind. I don't think it's offensive to say it's more male, more dad, than anything else. For many of these men and their sons, the outward-facing brick structure is evidence of their own virility – a 'vanishing' quality in the paranoid minds of old-school men threatened by feminism. Property is your true stamp (duty – lol) upon the world. Men like my dad Dave saw these solid castles as touchable proof they had at least made something; would *leave* something. My dad had in him a dangerous blend of *chip-on-the-shoulder 'I've failed at life' council-street working-class anger* mixed with *we're better than you* middle-class snobbery. The alchemy of these opposing energies so often produces the archetypal 'upper-working-class man': monied, but an angry bastard – and cash-in-hand ambitious. Harry Enfield's Loadsamoney character wasn't offensive to my dad. He was aspirational. It's hard to resist also folding into the mix my dad's love of muscle size and bodily power. His arms and chest were part of the construction he faced on to the world.

As soon as we were in the Brimsdown house, Mum and Dad put in the request and we bought it.

'We're home-owners, boy. We own our own manor.'

My old man's chest looked even bigger that day; his stance wider still. Many monied liberals will struggle to swallow this truth, but there were a lot of very hard-working men who'd spent their whole lives kicking against lower wages and a dim future, who suddenly had the chance to lift themselves up through the Thatcherite sale of council houses. My dad was one of those men. (Sadly his temperament meant he would soon become a miserable bastard again, and stay unfulfilled his whole life.) For a few fleeting years we were 'the nuts'. And, economically, we *remained* a 'cut above'.

'Get yourself on the ladder.'

A phrase that has kicked me forward and up my whole

life. But just when you think you've made it, there's another bloody ladder.

Once we'd bought the house, by which time I was six, I started to hear a term being bandied about, a thing that would change who we were as a family for ever.

'The extension, boy!'

Never has a noun had so many meanings for one Dave. It extended everything. His pride, his wealth, his dwelling, his confidence. It was the bricks and mortar steroids he'd always dreamed of. We had been lucky with our council house. It was end-of-terrace with a large piece of garden to the side. Dad's plan was audacious, yet simple. To *double* the size of the house. Another reception, a garage, two more bedrooms, and the finishing flourish that would make me feel like a god for the remaining summers of my childhood: a 21-foot swimming pool in the back garden.

Shit.

The.

Bed.

Works began with the foundations. Dad hired a digger and everything; burrowing into the former welfare earth himself using big machines, shovels and only taking the absolute minimum needed in additional help. It felt like the building would never be finished. Watching Dad hauling breeze blocks around for months was like watching Sisyphus.*

Danny Anderson was a couple of years older than me and lived a few doors down (along with his sister Joanie who got pregnant at thirteen by her own youth worker). He caught my

---

* He was some ancient Greek bell-end who was cursed to push a stone up a hill for ever. Like Greece's modern economy at the time of writing.

dad on a bad day of manual digging. It was roasting hot and Dad was angrily attempting to excavate a six-foot trench with a spade. After a few minutes of drooling and looking on, Danny came out with this touch-paper-lighting belter:

'Are you . . . are you digging a hole, Dave?'

I wondered if Dad might leap out and decapitate him.

'No, Danny. I'm baking a fucking cake. Get lost, would ya?'

Danny ran off crying, and an argument followed later between his mum (who ended up with the youth worker who impregnated her daughter when he was released from prison) and my dad. For years after, whenever anyone did anything thick or asked an obvious question, we called it a 'Digging-a-Hole Version' and eventually a Version or just a Versh.

'Done a bit of a Versh there, boy. Now clear it up.'

Once the extension was complete we became one of the few houses in a street of three hundred to have a garage. We also had three double bedrooms and a massive bathroom. An *upstairs* bathroom, mind you. No more commuting to a different floor for a wee in the night. No more bathing while someone washed up pots in the adjacent room. The old downstairs bathroom became the 'utility room', with its unreal ring of middle-classness. It still gives me a frisson today: a room only for utilities – for spare things. We kept the downstairs toilet, but a new rule came into force:

'No turn-outs downstairs, boy. Only slashing.'

The kitchen itself was completely relaunched – like a traveller who had been to America and returned altered and bold. We had a 'breakfast bar'. It sounded so outrageously Californian to me I almost started speaking in an American accent. (I did on one holiday. I changed accent for the entire trip.) During the week we would have dinner crowded together around the breakfast bar, the small portable telly blaring away as we munched and grunted. On Sundays and special occasions, though, the new reception room came into force. Yes: we had a dining room. This provoked me to aristocratic airs.

Covering the floors of the two reception rooms was a substance that became the Hermann Göring of the fascist regime of things that cannot be touched, damaged or disrespected: the Wilton carpet. Even today, just saying 'the Wilton' brings back rushes of fear and dread. Never has a carpet been held in such reverence. I often found myself hallucinating the face of Christ in it. At the time my mind was being pummelled by an imbecilic church school education, and the Turin Shroud was a thing in the news. I swear I saw Jesus in that carpet. Oh woeful Wilton. Oh evil police force of my shoe. Over the years that followed its laying there were, inevitably, spillages. Two occasions stand out in my mind. Once when oil was trodden through from the front garden. I honestly believed I would be executed, but the punishment was the same as always: swearwords, resentment, and referring to it constantly until he died. After the extension: no shoes, no flip-flops, barely even slippers were permitted to insult the Wilton with their filthy pressure. The incident to match Oil-gate was when my brother James trod dog shit through from hallway to kitchen. Poor James. We both had the same confidence-eroding treatment from my old man but my brother, it would turn out, had a more porous surface. He would walk a rockier path through self-confidence and mental wellbeing.

Dogshit-gate was bad. The fear. The dread. Mum got the

sick bowl* out from under the sink, filled it with disinfectant and scrubbed the shit out, while Dad did opera-level swearing in the garden.

'Everything I buy gets ruined! Everything turns to shit! Literally. Covered in fucking shit!'

'Calm down, Dave. I'll sort it. It was an accident.'

In the dining room was the only other object in the house to receive the same veneration as the Wilton carpet: the dining-room table. The solid mahogany piece, with inner leaf, was one of my dad's favourite things on earth. Both Hitler and Himmler regularly did random inspections for scratches or marks. Even the tiniest dint would result in a series of interviews and cross-examinations. I can still feel the goosebumps from the Day of the Deep Scratch. I know it wasn't me or my brother; it was probably an accident by someone who was unaware of what they'd done, but my dad wailed as though a daughter had been disfigured in a street attack.

Dad took a year's rest from home improvements after the extension was completed, and then moved on to create the thing that made me proudest of him as Dad, after him being a 'A scary cunt that no one should mess with – you hear me, boy' that is. (I heard him. By that he meant that no one could mess with *me*.) Yes, the only thing more astounding about Dad was when he re-hired all the digging equipment and started work on the swimming pool. An actual outdoor pool in the back of our former council garden. It was twenty-one feet long, six foot deep at one end, five foot the other. My brother

---

* Did all families have a sick bowl? A plastic Addis bowl that was our nominated receptacle for vomiting into?

learned to swim in it. At school I could tempt girls back to swim, and then spend oceans of time later that night having memory wanks about them in their swimming gear.

Neighbours from several houses along could spy on us climbing up the sides of the pool – it was only half-submerged – then disappearing from the horizon with a splash as we slipped into the cool waters. We were kings of the summer. I never felt more proud and alive than showing my friends that pool.

Once, when I was twelve, we went on holiday to Menorca. Our next-door neighbours, Ted and Maureen and their two kids, climbed over our fence and swam in our pool. They used it the whole week without turning the filter on. The result was that we came back to a pool full of green water, a pool that couldn't be rescued even with chlorine. It had to be drained and refilled. My dad was convinced:

'They pissed in it! They fucking pissed in our pool!'

Relations with Ted and Maureen never recovered.

Menorca deserves its own mention. It was Dad's favourite place. We were the first in our street to go to Spain. The first in our family to fly. The rest of the UK may have been doing it since the 1970s but we would be first in our area. Menorca, if you don't know, is the least-visited island of the Balearics, and this is why Dad loved it. He loved it in the way he would love, a few years later, that part of Florida where 'no morons went'.

'Menorca, boy. Not *Maj*-orca. *Men*-orca.'

'I know, Dad.'

'Hardly any idiots go there. Much quieter. All the mugs crowding on to Ibiza and Majorca. We'll have the island to ourselves, boy. Free of dickheads.'

I was twelve, my brother was nine. We didn't want quiet particularly, but the idea that we would go abroad, that we would experience an aeroplane ... we honestly felt like the richest kids on the planet.

On my first ever flight, Dad talked me through the experience like a proud museum curator. Telling me what to expect – to brace myself for the spinning in my tummy as we took off. It was hard to put my finger on at first but now I know it was Pride. The pride most of you will have seen on your dad's face, but that was so rare on mine.

'Cala'n Forcat!' Dad said over and over as we 'grafted' towards our July break, the two-week holiday where my mum's skin would roast more mahogany than the dining-room table we were not allowed to touch, and Dad would slip off with his scuba gear for hours on end, getting squiffy with German divers – and smiling. I was allowed to go on the boat once. All the German dads were lithe and beardy, and they all swigged from a bottle they called 'decompression water'.

'When you come up from the diving,' the boat's captain, Günther, explained, 'you must drink the decompression waters to help with your breathing.'

I cottoned on pretty quick that the plastic bottle was full of bad-ass rum. I watched fascinated as my dad laughed and joked along with the other divers like he hadn't a care in the world. It was so incongruous – like watching a nun pole dance.

Dad smiled and messed around a lot when we were in Menorca. He was much more like the other dads I knew. Announcing where we were eating with a flourish and then chatting on the journey there with feverish excitement, leading the way, pointing at stuff and explaining things.

'That bit of rock could fall down at any time. The sea's eroded it.'

'Erosion!' I said.

'That's right, boy.'

He felt manly and dad-like. He'd finally provided the best of the best and he glowed with silverback glory. It was like it could be, should be, back home. I've just realized this is the first time I've described my poor old dad as happy. I checked with my mum when I was writing – could I be misremembering?

'Dad seemed so sad. I'm writing about him – and he's always miserable.'

'You're right,' she said. 'But he had a good heart, just damaged by his evil mother.'

Eva Wolff. You cow.

Well, on holiday Dad was happy. In Menorca all the weight seemed to lift, including the need to lift weight. For a man so hooked on bodybuilding, I never once saw him seek out the gym on any of our vacations. We were in self-catering, too, not even the stress-free benefit of the all-inclusive, yet Dad laughed and messed around at the Supermercado as we stacked the trolley high, laughing at the brand names.

'Spanish beers, boy. It says 5 per cent on the side but it's stronger. Wahey!'

And the food. He was in his element at dinner, enthusing about *patatas bravas, paellas* . . .

'The size of the tomatoes, boy! Look at the fucking size of them! Like apples.'

Oh, Dad, if you'd just lived another few years I could have sorted you and Mum out a flat on the Costa del Sol. Mind you, you'd be moving back to Enfield after Brexit, but still. That's when he was happy. And the happiest I ever saw him (in photos he has the carefree glow of someone in absolute holiday bliss) was at El Sereno, a Menorcan restaurant. El Sereno had everything that made Dave Kane happy. Every part of this restaurant tapped into his pleasure centres, and ours. Mum loved it too. To James and me it seemed like it couldn't be real.

To get there you had to get a taxi to the other side of the island – twenty-five minutes.

'Taxis are a rip-off, boy. They milk your pesetas, but it's better than Spanish old bill.'

'What do you mean?'

'You can't drink and drive here, boy. They won't just nick you. They'll beat the living shit out of you. Haven't you noticed the way the Spanish kids behave? They don't fuck about. The old bill here, boy – they'll smash you up.'

To this day I have an irrational fear of the Guardia whenever I see them in Ibiza.

El Sereno was an all-inclusive restaurant. It worked out at £15 a head, no child prices. This was an astronomical sum – closer to the feeling of £35 per head today. But Dad didn't care.

'Do it justice, boy. We have to do it justice.'

Doing something justice, in working-class language, means using something to a greater extent than what you 'laid out' for it. The system, the people with all the wedge, are always trying to win, trying to sell you things and experiences that leave *them* quids in. But now and again the crafty among us can work out ways To Do Justice, and win. This is why the All-Inclusive is the holy grail of 'rinsing'. So long as you eat and drink and never stop you could beat odds and leave the hotel at a profit.

El Sereno was an outdoors restaurant with the sound of the waves crashing in the background.

'Let's ruin it, boys!'

'Dave! They'll make themselves sick!' cautioned a now teak-coloured Mum as we sat down to dine. The table was made of dark wood and Mum's arms and face vanished when she sat down.

'You look like a fucking floating dress, Julie!' Dad howled.

El Sereno had a unique selling point. Not only could you return to the chefs as many times as you liked, but there were *five* chefs, and *five* types of roast. All the trimmings.

'Don't get tricked by the bread, boy – even by the roasties, although they do look fucking handsome.' Dad was going full mad professor now. 'Save yourself. The meat. They don't want you to ruin the meat. But we will.' He was right. The bulky stuff was there to make sure you couldn't *do it justice*. Duck, Pork, Chicken, Lamb and Beef. The lot. We groaned in the taxi on the way back to the resort. It was the best night of my life so far. The next morning James and I invited each other into the toilet to marvel at the size of the poos we had gestated.

When we landed back in London I stupidly believed the holiday magic would carry on, but the moment Dad saw the pissed-in pool, the spell was broken.

'That bitch will love this,' said Dad, referring to neighbour Hilda. 'She'll fucking love seeing me pump the pool out.'

By now the neighbours had nicknamed our house the Castle. Dad's extension was too much for the 'true council' people to tolerate. Did we think we were too good for them? Led by widow Hilda, the scathing nickname had caught on.

It wound my dad up, to be mocked, but I think a small part of him thought, 'Yeah – it *is* a castle – fuck off!'

The low point in neighbourly relations came when we returned from Menorca again the following year to find our driveway gates stolen. While Dad was on the phone to the police, Hilda was smoking in her front garden, a Stanley-knife grin cut into her pudgy grey face. She was a vile woman, more cigarette than human – grossly fat with a tight black perm. She had always looked seventy years old.

'Pikeys must have had 'em,' Hilda said, coming over and flicking her butt on to the pavement in front of our house.

I was stood next to my devastated dad as he replied, 'They stole our gates, Hilda. Our fucking gates!'

She mumbled something spiteful that me and Dad didn't catch.

'What was that, Hilda?' he said with Ray Winstone menace.

'You wanna wash the shit out your ears, Dave.'

'Yeah . . . you wanna wash the shit out your mouth, you old cunt.'

This was exactly what Hilda had been longing for since the completion of the extension. We were no longer 'council' – and in swearing at her as he had, my dad had handed in his formal resignation from the Lower Working Class. Solidarity was over. We were independents now.

One particular feature of our extension had pushed the neighbours close to the edge, causing Hilda Black to assemble the grand council of scumbag elders and formally request our ostracism from the community. The Pillars. When Dad submitted his grandiose plans to Enfield Council, he originally sought permission for white pillars in the Greco-Roman style:

actual Doric pillars. This had been declined by the cloth-cap-wearing Enfield powers. They came back and told Dad that it would spoil the look of the council street. In the same way that sprinkling cubic zirconia on dog poo ruins its integrity, I suppose. Of course, if we'd been living on the other side of Enfield it would have been permitted. State-sanctioned class-ism maybe, but my theory is that Hilda Black blocked the planning permission.

'Greek pillars? I'm the pillar of this community!' That sort of thing.

In the end, after some haggling, the Council came back with a compromise. A square brick-built pillar. Three of them. Dad agreed, and they still stand there today. If I could use only one visual metaphor to express my dad Dave it would be those layer by layer hand-built brick arms holding our extension aloft, up to the world. Look at me: I might not have made it to the very top, but I'm something – I'm mighty.

They were unnecessary, they were all display, yet they were pure strength, effort and graft. There was something solid and sad about them too; something everyday and work-man. Those pillars, my dad. Sod you, Hilda Black. Sod you.

The Castle was the bricks-and-mortar manifestation of my dad's silverback. The house was never mine. When most kids say, 'Come over to mine,' they mean it's their house too, but my dad's gaff was his gaff. He paid, he said. No one stayed over. No one took the piss. Nothing was disrespected. Yet now and again, Dave could be persuaded into making small exceptions. As I grew up, I noticed there were two types of house logistics. The chaotic 'sleepover house' with cousins, best mates and pets falling out of every cupboard. In this type of residence you could decide you were staying at a whim, the mum would pull out a Z-bed, and you'd crash right there, maybe a smelly Labrador curled up next to you. It's the house where the parties were, the lively people; crazy, eccentric, busy parents with scruffy clothes and weird hobbies – always going on family holidays where they 'did stuff', in England. Then there was the other type of house. The 'no-visitors' house. People were invited over, oh yes, but scheduled, planned and carefully executed. Nothing was spur of the moment or untidy or impulsive. There were no mass sleepovers or cousins dropping in for a week. No dog shit in the garden, no lizards running across the kitchen top. Holidays were about the mums and dads enjoying food, going swimming and relaxing. This was a Kane house (although I was allowed to keep crickets in the shed once). Dave worked hard all week; harder than any man on the planet. Harder than an Iraqi dad dragging a water pail to a well; or an African dad walking five miles to the nearest shop. He was the most tired, the most deserving, the most sacrificing Atlas ever known. Having anyone to stay or any person over to the Castle was rare – I'd have to wait until I was with my first love for that rule to be relaxed. My best mate Michael Delaney was allowed to stay now and again, but mostly the answer to any disruption was No. Yet, on my fifteenth birthday, I managed to make Emperor Dave bend one of the iron house rules. By some miracle, I was allowed to have a party at my house. An actual gathering of teenagers. Mum and Dad agreed, but only if they could be in the lounge. I was allowed to use the garden, conservatory and downstairs toilet. People actually showed up – I could not believe it. Finally, just for one night, I was popular – even with the hard kids. And the guests were weirdly respectful too. The school bullies were more muted in their shouting and weed smoking. They knew Dave Kane was there; and while I commanded no respect at all, from anyone, the rumour of my dad's size and authority had permeated every male's mind in my year.

We had sideway access to the house, meaning guests could come and go without any Dave Kane menace. But it was this ease of getting a person into the party that led to one of the more shameful moments of my teen years. Without telling anyone, I hired a stripper – for myself. I got the Yellow Pages, phoned an agency and booked a woman. And she was a woman. Late thirties at least. It had seemed a good idea in the afternoon – a legitimate and easy way to have a real-life naked female in front of me on my birthday, but I had not thought through how hard it would be feigning surprise; plus being observed by everyone was really weird. I think what unfolded may have been one of the reasons that the opportunities with females that came later were so hampered by insecurity and fear.

The stripper arrived looking like someone's tired mum who works in the Co-op, but with a porno bra stuck on. I paid her manager in the sideway, and then I sat down in a garden chair while all my 'friends' from school shouted and clapped and formed a circle. Had this been the era of the smartphone, my life would have ended at that moment. That poor woman. She perfunctorily danced around me, stopping when she got as far as her knickers, which I begged her with my eyes to keep on. Before me were my first ever pair of boobs. Right there. She wiggled them hopefully in my face like an auntie holding up a bag of healthy snacks at the cinema. It's up there with one of the least sexual experiences of my life, and as she jangled her sorry breasts in my face, the lads of my school shouting 'Grab 'em, grab her tits' – all I could do was turn away and mouth *Sorry*. I knew in that moment it would be a long time before I touched a breast, in love. So desperate to feel like a man, I degraded myself, and became a boy for longer.

'She was fucking minging,' said Andrew Peters.

'Should have sucked 'em, you silly cunt!' said Jamie Smith, punching me.

I was fifteen. Happy birthday.

4.

My Dad the Doorman

Dad worked as a bouncer into his thirties, alongside his building jobs. I have vague memories of waiting in a Ford Granada while he bounced heads off the pavement, or maybe he just described it to me. It could even have been when someone had 'knocked him for an invoice'. Even when he stopped working as a bouncer, my dad stayed a double-hard volatile bastard. This was a point of pride for me. It was something to boast about. Where I grew up, the value system wasn't based on which Oxford college you went to. No grammar school or scholarship was coming to whisk you into the middle classes. You were fucked. Glory was how *hard* you were, or, failing that, your dad. I should have been punched and bullied a *lot* more than I was. But people had seen Dave nesting at the gates, his silver fur glistening in the 3 p.m. sun: a council/alpha dissuasion from messing with Kane junior.

Growing up as the son of a former bouncer is a particular experience. Some of you will have grown up as the children of police officers, or head teachers. Maybe you tried to come in drunk or high, or maybe stayed over at a boy's house without your mum's permission. Were you frequently cross-examined? Detected? Did they build a case against you and confront you with the evidence? Uncomfortable, I will concede. But now imagine if your old man, or old woman, worked as a bouncer. My dad did so many things like a bouncer. He answered the door like a bouncer. He answered the phone like a bouncer. Even in a restaurant:

'Does that curry come with rice?'

'No, sir, I'm sorry.'

'You sure about that? Wanna check again, sunshine?'

Anyone who came to visit me had the treatment. The initial interaction was always close-mouthed and suspicious – and for my friends and girlfriends, bloody scary too.

The doorbell is pressed: *ding dong.*

The Y-shaped meat shadow appears behind the porch glass. It opens and something from *Lord of the Rings* – my dad – stands there. The guardian of Russell, the guardian of entry and even of speech.

'Yeah?'

That's how Dad answered the phone and the door. Not 'Hello'. Not 'Who is it?' But – 'Yeaaah?'

Ding dong.

'Yeaaaah?'

It's my friend Shaun, the most confident of us when we were sixteen. (Still the most confident now. Shaun is so confident than even when he's down on his luck, or he's been bad and he knows it, he styles it out with a smile that says: 'Yeah . . . well, I'm a cunt, ain't I? I know what I am, and I embrace it.')

'Is Russell in?'

'Yeah?' Same word but with a 'what-of-it?' attached.

'Is he coming out?'

Sarcastic: 'I don't know.'

Then Dad would just walk off, the door swinging open. Is that a 'Come in'? Is Shaun's name on the guestlist? Dare he enter? Had Dad gone to fetch Russell? It was exactly like the door of an intimidating nightclub. There were rules. It was just that you, a mere supplicant, would never get to hear them.

Dad also *entered* rooms like a bouncer. Boom: and he's into your bedroom without knocking.

'Did you take the fucking bins out?'

'What?'

'Why am I seeing the fucking bin bags still in the bins?'

'It was James's turn.'

'I've already killed James. He's in one of the bin bags.' Bouncer humour. Then a fart on the way down the stairs. Always the temper fart.

All Dad needed was one of those mini-torches to thumb-click on and search under the bed and his bouncer performance would have been total. Once I hit seventeen, the drug patrols started as well. Wicker bin checked for 'skinning up' evidence, eyes examined for redness. Six a.m. ambushes as I silently turned my key in the door.

So, yeah, living with a copper for a parent might be bad. But a doorman for a dad was something else. And as bad as the authoritarian stuff was, the protectiveness, as though I were a VIP room inside the nightclub, could be even more intense. The worst was if someone attacked me. In my whole childhood (and I count up until I was twenty-five as my kid life) I managed to hide almost every single incidence of being bullied, hit or threatened. Why? I would always rather have concealed the fact of being punched in the head by the fat school bully than risk the *Kill Bill* film of bloody revenge that my old man might have wreaked. Most people's conversations with their parents run like this:

'Joshie.'

'Yes, Daddy.'

'If anyone at school ever hurts you, make sure you tell me or a teacher and we can sort it out. No need for you to get in trouble.'

Or if the parent was a little more combative:

'Joshua.'

'Yes, Dad.'

'If somebody hits you, you hit them right back. Self-defence, fair enough.'

This is how the chat ran with my dad:

'Boy.'

'Yes, Dad.'

'If anyone at that new school hits you, just tell me. I'll destroy the cunt.'

I had no idea whether this was bluster or not so I played it safe and went all the way to fourteen years old without ever asking my dad for backup or protection. I didn't want my old man going to prison for murdering a boy who took my lunch money. (Simon Priestly-Hunt.) Only once did I fail to conceal being hit. I was punched in the face on the 191 bus. Worse, I was blapped in the face just as I was getting off. The injury was fresh and shocking. There was nothing unusual about getting decked on the way home, but digged in the face – not standard at all. Bullies had a code of conduct to protect themselves from school prosecution. Mostly, punchers were quite crafty. Alan Landor and Dennis Redman would punch your arm. No one would ever witness the blackening of your biceps; the fact these boys got off by hitting weedy shits like me could be concealed. But on this occasion, when Jason Smyth primped my cheek on the bus, there was to be no hiding it.

Jason was fat. No point in dressing it up – he was a biggie. He embraced it. He was fat Jase and he was the alpha male of the bus. His reign of terror had been building over the previous few terms but he had only ever threatened me indirectly. We lived in the same street so he knew exactly who my dad was. Dad would often be in our front garden, bending metal or hacking things in half – usually topless, or in a vest, guns and pecs bulging like chicken breasts forced into a freezer bag. It kept Jason off my back but I could see it eating away at him. Me, acting like the Lord of Brimsdown, sitting there smugly with my Dave Diplomatic Immunity. The worst Jason could do was punch my arm, but he never even did that, until of course that day he lost it, the day he punched me hard in the face.

The factor that pushed him over the edge was the presence of girls on the bus. One of them was Trisha, a girl known to wank you off for ten cigarettes. She was well worth impressing. If you could get the coins together for ten Benson & Hedges, a hand shandy over Albany Park awaited you. Thinking about it now, that's actual prostitution. Thank God I was both skint and a coward. Trisha's sidekick, Disabled Dee, was with her too. Dee wasn't actually disabled – I don't think – she was just in the bottom set at Albany School and also had a wonky eye. As Thomas Lynch told everyone else: 'She shags like she hates you.' These two girls together on the bus sent Jason's testosterone into risk-taking mode. The bus arrived at my stop and I knew he was going to do one of his favourite set pieces and block my exit, hoping to impress the girls. I walked along the aisle and, sure enough, out came his fat leg, followed by his fat, breathy laugh.

'Sit down, gaylord.'

'Please . . .'

The girls laughed. He stood up and faced me, his squashed pug-nose millimetres from my Roman hook. His breath stank of cabbage. He had those stubby brown teeth that look like they've been filed down by a serial killer with a rusty tool.

'Well, gaylord, how you gonna move me out the way then?'

Recklessness swept through me. 'I'm just going to use language and politely ask you to move. That's what *humans* do.' I didn't mean it to be funny. I don't even think it's a funny sentence now, but, unfortunately for me, Trisha 'Handjob for Fags' laughed. That cackle, in support of my remark, was the last thing I heard.

Boom.

No memory of falling, just pretty grey-black stars and I was on the floor of the bus. You don't actually feel a punch in the face, it's so surprising. Jason 'helped' me up and off the bus with a final shove. They all did the wanker sign through the glass door as I stood dazed on the pavement. For good measure, Jason gobbed out of the window, but the gooey streak missed me and landed on a dog-shit bin; it was yellow like when Predator gets injured.

I tottered to my house. I had been assaulted, and I must hide until dinner.

'Ruuuuussssss,' Mum hollered. 'Shepherds pie's on the taaaaable.'

I slowly went downstairs, knowing in my guts what the reaction would be, but not the consequence. My cheek was red, my eye already blackening.

'Oh my God,' Mum said.

'You got punched,' said my brother James unhelpfully.

'Go on . . .' said my dad.

'It was on the bus. Jason.'

'The fat fucker? He's older, ain't he?'

'One year.'

'Did you hit him back?'

'No.'

'Get in the car.'

'What?'

'Get. In. The. Fucking. Car.'

Minutes later we were out in the Merc, weaving through the grey streets of Brimsdown. I think it was one of the last times I prayed and wanted God to be real. Jason always 'played out' until dark. It was just a matter of hunting. My adrenaline was pumping. What could a bodybuilding man do to a fifteen-year-old boy and *not* go to prison? I'd gone all these years without my dad getting physically involved. I was in uncharted territory of parental protectiveness. We turned down Fouracres, where one day I would snog an actual girl, and there, bowling along, cocky as hell, was the gathering of meat known as Jason Smyth. He was hand in hand with bloody Trisha. Dad slowed the Merc to a crawl, like a perv approaching a prostitute in a BBC1 drama. The windows hummed down, his at the front, mine at the back – as though to display me to a potential buyer. To this day, excepting gruesome Internet videos, I've never seen another face turn white with pre-death like Jason's did. Jason sincerely thought it was the end.

'Jason.' My dad was speaking softly. It made it much worse. 'Come here, mate.' One of Dad's arms was hanging out of the window – an animal at its cage, wanting to eat you.

Jason said nothing. Trisha hung back.

'Did you hit my boy?' Dad said softly, and then, with the unexpected thunder of a jet engine going straight to full power: 'YOU CUUUUNNNNNNT. DID YAAAAAA?'

The car shook several times. A Richter scale of suppressed violence.

The patch of piss on Jason's denim was instant.

'You even look at him again, cunt, I'll kill you. Not like a threat, not like pretend, like when you say it to your mates – I mean I'll actually kill you. You'll never see your mum and wanker dad. You'll never see your mates again. You'll never grow up. 'Cos you'll be dead. And if you tell your old man, I'll kill you. If you tell the old bill, I'll kill you. Now fuck off, son.'

Jason's hand opened and a packet of ten cigarettes dropped on to the ground. We drove off. Jason never looked at me again. I think he started getting a different bus.

5.

The House Always Wins

As I said right at the beginning of this book – no rags to anything here. I spent most of my childhood feeling like the richest kid in the school. Yes, OK, I've had to build my own stuff with bootstrap fibre but as a kid, I honestly felt wealthy.

We hit lots of firsts in my house, and one was being the first family to get a satellite dish.

'No other fucker in this street has got one.'

'It's amazing, Dad.'

'Shithole area . . . No one will get it round here for years . . .' and then Dad would trail off into a self-loathing speech about living in Brimsdown and being a failure. But ultimately he was proud of himself.

Years later, during my partying days, Dad would pounce on me in the hallway at 6 a.m.:

'Bloody hell, boy – your eyes are like the satellite dish.'

Not a satellite dish. THE satellite dish.

'Guess how many channels, boy.'

'Ten?'

'Hahaha. Ten! Ten in French – same in every other language you can think of!'

'Hindi?'

'Don't take the piss, boy . . . Italian though . . . loads of it.'

But we only speak English, I thought.

It's weird to think that just a few decades ago, cable and satellite were something Americans did, then in the late 1980s there was a glorious UK revolution and suddenly many of us had more than four channels. The choice before then was between three channels of posh people doing mind-numbing things (plus *Coronation Street* and *EastEnders*) or Channel Four, where middle-class people pretended to be working class for rebellious entertainment purposes. (*The Word* was all right, though.) There were a few gems that boys my age followed and quoted, such as *The Young Ones* (by then being repeated) and some imported action series, like *The A-Team* and *Airwolf*, etc. But mostly we felt that no one sounded like us or looked like us, and when anyone did, you just knew someone not like us had written the words for them to say.

I was too young for Alternative Comedy, and too buried in a council area (or too lazy?) to realize there were life-changing things just past my gaze, like theatre, books and the spoken word. Late 1980s telly was mostly boring. At school we heard the rumours about 'cable'; I even saw it when the Kanes went to Florida. Loads of channels. People dancing, rebelling, painting, screaming – yes, they were American, but it felt closer to my unsettled energy. I found out later, when I was nineteen, that there was one very special UK channel I had missed. A broadcast from the other side of my cultural apartheid. A radio station which, if only I'd had a relative to tell me it existed, would have changed my life: BBC Radio 4 – a stream of books and talk which proved to be the intellectual MDMA of my early twenties.

I eventually became omnivorous in my consumption of telly – everything from reality shows to documentaries about Auschwitz – but that was much later on. At this point, however, on the cusp of a hairless full puberty, the literary and spoken word elements of my unused brain would lie dormant a few more years. With cable TV, along with all the pointless European channels there would be a channel devoted to proper music. Not the shite my aunties and uncles liked. Wanky stuff like Spandau Ballet, Depeche Mode, Pet Shop Boys, Duran fucking Duran. Men with shit hair whining into microphones. Not for me and my mates. We needed anger and musicality. Punk was laughable, tuneless drivel that unemployed small men with bleached hair listened to down the pub. No. We needed beats and energy; BPMs and disaffected voices. And MTV would deliver it, from hip hop to drum and bass, if only we could see it. If only. And it was us, the Kanes, who got it first in our area.

All the more impressive that my area was smelly brown Brimsdown, on the border of Essex and Herts, the non-postcode shat out from London and forgotten. It's hard to overstate how important a postcode is, particularly to a teenager. It's a bit more in the headlines these days; gangs accrete around postcodes. SW2 will fight with weapons the mandems of SW9. You can tut and sigh and call it mindless – or you can ask why. There is an entirely natural and potentially dangerous shift at this age from parental influence to peer group. Some human groups use colours, markings, language or ritual. Londoners use postcode – anything to give form to the chaos and darkness of being thirteen. And this was the problem with Enfield. This is why I never describe it as London. Culturally it was poor-man's Essex. The Essex border was eleven minutes' walk from my front door; once over it you were in the brown-green industrial scrubland of the River Lee. You cut through the old Enfield rifle works (yes, that Enfield), over the island village, into the dog-shit-coloured fens of Sewardstone, and through the backstreets of pretty but dangerous Waltham Abbey, which has one of the highest concentrations of pubs to people in the UK. And twats. Everything non-lame my family went to was in Essex: markets, shopping; we went to our beach hut every weekend in Southend. My dad was 100 per cent Essex, and spoke about it like an exiled prince who could still glimpse the mountain range of his youth from his refugee home. Everything he aspired to was trapped there, just out of reach.

'A big house. Nazeing would be nice. One of those fucking monsters. Heated pool, gym, massive drive. I'd have an eight-foot-high fence. No fucker would see in. Six bedrooms! Six fucking bedrooms, some of them. You could have an annexe, boy. Your own room.'

The idea of an annexe was spoken about on many occasions. The mythic level of readies that allowed you to buy a house with a little house on its grounds. On more than one occasion we kerb-crawled slowly past the *monster* houses of Nazeing, Chigwell or Epping – Dad gurgling his property lust as we passed pillars, ivory lions and mature trees.

Geographically, Brimsdown, Enfield was even closer to Hertfordshire, a county which doesn't exactly shout its identity from the rooftops. Name me one Hertfordshire cultural stereotype. It just sits there, a smiling green auntie looking over London. Officially, I was told as a kid, we were in London. It always astonished me to hear it. Because we weren't.

'This ain't fucking London. It's fucking nowhere, boy.'

EN3 – what kind of a postcode was that? It didn't have the kudos of a single letter to start with, like N17, or E4 in

Chingford, just round the corner. Me and my 'crew' had a longing to make it something – to stamp something on it, and say, This is what it is. I nearly called my first stand-up show, *What is Enfield?* But Russell Howard quite rightly pointed out that no one would know what I meant. Point made again.

Naturally, being Dave Kane, he wasn't going to get a Sky dish stuck to the house like every other mug was being tricked into buying. No, we were getting the *real* satellite telly.

'Fuck no Sky cunts. Rip-off shit.'

'But, Dave,' Mum said, 'isn't Sky films and all that on the Sky dishes?'

'You gonna fork out for that rip-off crap every month? No, I'm getting the real deal. The full Monty. The absolute bollocks.'

I have no idea if the things my dad brought home in the Transit were legal or not. It certainly needed a Ford van to transport the bulky kit. This wasn't a discreet dish bolted on to the pebble-dashed back wall. This was a van-load of black metal from the future. It took two full days to set up our satellite dish on the flat roof at the back of the house, and Dad was so chuffed he only lost his temper twice.

'Cunt spanner!'

'Dave!'

Eventually, sunset on day two:

'It's done, Julie.'

'Do we need a licence for it, Dave?'

'Just don't discuss it with the fuckwits in our road and we'll be OK.'

It was dark by the time my dad drop-kicked his tool bag into the garage. Our new satellite dish was the diameter of a hatch-back's roof and it was mounted on three stacked paving slabs. Bound cables discharged from its base in a thick anaconda of confusion, winding down through the toilet, into the kitchen and terminating in the lounge, where they fed a black receiver which looked like something the Russians had developed to trick Ronald Reagan. The remote was a brick-sized hunk of black plastic with a Da Vinci code of grey rubber buttons; the manual was thicker than the edition of *Macbeth* I was forcing myself through for GCSE English Lit; but none of these was the most the gasp-worthy thing. It had an amazing feature that would draw to my house friends, cousins and, eventually, even girls agape in wonder: when you switched on the box and used the remote, you didn't just select one of the hundreds of foreign-language channels. *You chose which satellite you wanted, too.*

'Watch this, boy,' said Dad, beaming silky male pride. 'Say you wanna watch this channel. It's called Ray One. You type twenny.' He showed me on a key card. 'It's Italian. That means at night you get birds with their tits out and all sorts. All Italian fanny – top quality.' He leered like a butcher selling me some knock-off meat. I smiled politely. After all, how was soft porn in that kind of set-up useful to me? There was no way I was going to risk a danger wank in the family lounge. Not even at 1 a.m. was it worth the jeopardy of Mum's face appearing at the glass of the stairway door with a 'What you doing up?'

'Wow. Amazing,' I said. 'Italian.'

'Right. Fucking riiight. Then watch this.' He typed *20*. Nothing happened, just screen fizz. 'Come on!' he shouted, barrelling through the house. I ran after him, all the way back to the garden.

My face then was the exact face of someone in a movie when they finally realize time travel is real. Our satellite dish *was moving*. Slowly, and futuristically, the bastard thing was rotating.

'And that, boy, is what you call the fucking absolutely dog's bollocks.'

It was the first time I had heard *dog's* bollocks to describe something astonishing. I've used it ever since. The novelty of that rotating dish never wore off, and when anyone at school talked about an artist rumoured to be on MTV, eyes naturally went to me like I would have seen it first (maybe the Italian version). It was one of the many times in my childhood that my old man, as negative as he was, made me feel about three feet taller. For a man who whined constantly about his future poverty and his constant bad luck, we spent a lot of the time feeling incredibly rich. The sad thing is, he could never see it.

It's wanky, but at least once a week I make sure I take a moment out to relish how lucky I am. I've done it since I was twenty-two. Back when I had £30 a week to live on, I used to skip and jump around my room thinking about all the amazing shit that was going to happen to me that week. It could be something simple like a curry out or a film; it could be a massive thing, like seeing my girlfriend, and having actual sex with a human female. I've kept this tradition up. In the business I'm in now, the temptation to bitch about what you don't have or didn't get is a daily poison which keeps itself in a bottle labelled *Drink me*. But just like Alice, if you drink it, you will shrink, and shrink, and shrink, until the only doorways left are tiny ones. The trick is to wake up – pick some lame day like a Tuesday – sit there for five minutes and say to myself: 'Holy fuck – I have a wife and daughter I love, food in the cupboard, a dog, an amazing job I enjoy.' Then do some insane jumping and skipping. It works for me. I wish my dad had leapt for joy more often – the day of the satellite dish could have been one of those days. Instead he watched it with a grim smile for a few minutes then walked in muttering:

'I need a fucking Stella.'

A few years later, when I hit eighteen and was earning my own money, I took the unusual step of getting cable direct to my room. I don't know anyone else who did this. Feel free to Tweet me if you did.

The years of 'take care of number one' and 'I'm paying, I'm saying' had worked their financial-independence magic, and I wanted my own channels on my own telly in my own space. The result was a liberating porn-u-copia of late-night experimental European film and trashy early hours telly. The bliss of a joint smoked out of my window (draught excluder in place – sorry, Mum), followed by a French film full of pretension and hairy-pubis nudity was a midweek routine I came to savour; but, being completely honest, by the time I was eighteen and could get my own bills in my own name, the real reason for the cable subscription wasn't for the telly viewing, it was for the phone that came with it. I would be *free* at last. Free from the tyranny of Dad's Kitchen Payphone.

Defeating the Payphone was almost a pyrrhic victory. Less than eighteen months later, the Mercury one2one network made mobile phones affordable for peasants and with a tariff that gave us unlimited minutes after 7 p.m. Me and my mates would sometimes call our own landlines and leave the phones connected for the entire night, just to rinse the network properly. But in the couple of years before my first mobile, there was a glorious era when I had a landline in my bedroom. My own actual phone number. A coarse fleck of silver fur on *my* back; and I was paying for it out of my own wages. I was surprised, however, when I told the alpha male. It didn't impress him, it pissed him off. I'd been expecting a loving rub on the shoulder or a 'That's my boy – making your own way – sharing the burden of graft'. Turned out another strange thing about my dad was that even though he pushed me to get my own stuff and pay my way, he became sulky and resentful when I did. The silverback was threatened by an adolescent blackback practise-thudding his small chest in nearby trees.

'. . . gets installed next week. My own phone and cable. Cool eh, Dad?'

'You what?'

'I've only got twenty-eight channels – but I get my own landline.'

'Cable in your room? What the fuck for?' he exploded. 'You've got the satellite dish. I'm already forking out for that shit! Why?'

'It's his money, Dave,' Mum chimed in.

'Waste. Idiot. Cancel it.' But he softened his order with: '. . . if I were you . . .' A tiny concession to the fact that here was something he could not *make* me do. It was my wonga. I'm paying, I'm bloody well saying.

He walked out of my room, never referring to or acknowledging the manly steps I'd taken towards independence. I guess in his house, he ruled – and I just couldn't triumph; like the casinos in Vegas, you're welcome to try, but the House always wins. Poor Dad seemed addicted to moaning about how he paid for everything, yet if anyone dared make moves into self-funding, he was threatened by it. It's pretty messed up, when you consider it. Not that this caused me even to pause. At this point, I had a girlfriend I was in love with and I was determined to get access to a phone. I needed my own communications. The phone in our house was like a religious icon in an Inca village. Only the elders may touch and ponder it. The young and the women must stay away.

Before you eyebrow-raise at me for being sore about such a universal gripe, yes, I will concede most of us grew up bickering with parents about who used the phone and for how long. Wrangling over a bill is nothing uncommon. I wonder if today's teenagers have the same problem; the ones who aren't allowed mobile phones, I mean. But back when I was thirteen, the silverback took it two steps further.

It started with the phone lock – a small rectangle of steel acting as a miniature metal burka shielding the keypad from lust and defiling. My dad loved locking things. He didn't just lock his garden workshop, for example. He triple-locked it. Chains, bars, padlocks; understandable given all the equip-ment in there, maybe – but I always felt it was more about keeping us out of his cave than keeping the lathe and press in. One locking that was indisputably odd was my mum and dad's bedroom door. I didn't find it weird at the time. Indeed to me it seemed totally sensible that the House senators would lock their inner chamber where all the laws and decrees were made. But now I'm older, with a shit, I mean a child, of my own, I can see that locking their bedroom door was actually rather strange. Mum and Dad's door was locked a lot. If they both went to the shops, it was locked from the outside and the key went with them. If my dad had sprouted a bluebeard on my eighteenth birthday it would not have shocked me in the least. He was a locker. A locker of things, feelings, people and dreams. All securely bolted in – but now and again *BOOM*. The bedroom was locked mostly because of my dad's paranoia about his *stuff*. What if someone touched his *things*? What if someone got access to the upstairs phone – the one without a keypad guard?

Once, just before the era of the Locked Bedroom Door, one of my dad's chunky gold sovereigns went missing.

'It's probably fallen behind a unit or something, Dave,' my mum counselled.

'I left it on the fucking side. Right there.'

I've grown up into an adult whose stuff regularly disappears, but I always assume it's been carelessly lost or I misplaced it. My brain is like a bath bomb in fizzy water – never focused on keys or jewellery but on silly things to say. I get angry, but I always assume loss, messiness or being hare-brained is the culprit for my wedding ring, for example, doing a day-long disappearing act.

Not my dad, though.

'It hasn't fallen anywhere, Julie. Some fucker has taken it.'

'Who'd steal your ring, Dave? No one comes up here!'

'I don't know. But. Someone. Fucking. Has.'

And that was that. Theft was assumed. Of course, the only people who came upstairs were my friends and a few members of our family if they used the loo. Me being older, my mates were the prime suspects. Dad moaned for months, and locking his bedroom door became standard rather than occasional. Three years later when Dad was fixing a telly in their bedroom, he found the sovereign – behind the unit.

'Fuck me!' he shouted.

We rushed in thinking he had crushed a hand.

'I told you, Dave,' Mum said.

But he just did a smile that quickly darkened. 'Yeah – well, I still don't want any pikey cunts in our room.'

He definitely meant me.

Anyway, the metal phone lock meant that Dad could both prevent me from making a call, and also be menacingly present when I was granted temporary access; you know, just like in prison. However, Ben Gibbs, IT nerd from the year above me, told me how to bypass it. Turned out you didn't actually need a keypad to make a phone call. Simply lift the receiver, then use the tiny black buttons under the receiver to tap out in numerical Morse the number you needed to dial. I think I managed about six calls before Dad did an emergency audit and rumbled me. The fallout wasn't too bad – I didn't even get called 'ungrateful cunt'. The reason he went easier on me this time could have been that part of him admired the ingenuity of my fraud, but it's more likely he was glad I had unwittingly enabled his green lighting of phase two in telephone control: the Payphone.

When he first came grunting through the front door lugging the black box, I was optimistic. Surely this would be for the best. This coin collector, the size of four Hi-Tec trainers boxes, would finally quell the arguing and analysing. After all, we were now literally paying and then saying. The payphone took the old-style ten-pence pieces – the ones that got phased out in the 1990s – but no other coins. Once or twice a week, my mum, James and me would form an Oliver Twist queue in the kitchen with our pound coins and 50ps, and Bill Sikes, I mean Dad, would hand us our 'bags of tens' in little see-through money pouches. I knew within a few uses I was being fleeced. The thing ate coins like a pug at an ice-cream bowl.

'It's too expensive, Dad.'

'It's set on the standard fucking call cost – I checked it in the instructions.'

This had to be a lie. My dad was to instruction manuals what a coeliac is to a baguette.

I decided to double-check it. There was a countdown on the display so I could easily calculate what a quid was buying me. I then phoned the operator and did my own little audit. Sure enough, Dad was making 100 per cent profit. I'd be mid-way through a phone call with a mate, or even a girlfriend – and the call would end, a Nazi slap in the face with a glove. In my dad's defence, it transpired that he had indeed set it for the standard rate – but it was the standard rate for those cynical little call boxes you used to get in petrol garages. He didn't take it well.

'You're making me look a right cunt.'

'I just want to pay the proper cost.'

'Dave!' One word from Mum.

'I'm not having a go, Dad, I'm just saying. To break even so it covers the bill you need to set the rate to number one.'

I could see that using the term *break even* had annoyed him. I'd only learned it the year before from Mr McKillon in Economics. But deploying a grown-up-sounding word around my dad was never a good idea. It was another chest-thud from a lower-ranking male and you risked shit thrown in your face from the alpha.

None the less, Dad gave in and the payphone was set at the break-even rate. It was still a pain to use – and, as the old ten pence got phased out it, even worse. If Dad was working I had to wait till he got in to get some tens.

Once me and Michael Delaney tried something that went horribly wrong. It was definitely my idea. We rolled a long, thin piece of Blu-tack and stuck it to the edge of a ten-pence piece, as if the coin was on a piece of string. The thinking was we could dunk and retrieve the coin in the coin slot over and over to get infinite credits on the payphone. It worked for the first thirty pence of chatting action, then the inevitable happened. The Blu-tack string heated up, stretched and broke off from the main blob, and the coin and Blu-tack dropped inside the box. The three days waiting for my old man to find it were a special hell. But instead of being on the receiving end of his usual verbal hairdryering, I came home from sixth-form college to find, written on my desk in Blu-tack, the word 'prick'.

My dad had a gift for bestowing offensive monikers upon me: Badger, Melon Head, Bunter, Paul Getty. I was called all of these at some point. But 'Broomgate' gave me one of his earthiest.

The day of the broom is prominent in my mind not because anything objectively amazing occurred but because it's one of the few times in my life I dared to show teenage petulance in the face of Dad's authority. I was fourteen or fifteen, sat in the dining room with my mate Wayne and a few others – and Dad walked in.

'Boy. Sweep the patio, would ya?' Out of nowhere. It was a power move. Have me do a chore I've never done before or even heard of, while my mates watched.

'Can't I do it later?' A quiver of defiance in my voice.

'Now!'

I stormed outside, picked up the broom and, for the first time ever in my dad's presence, a white-hot charge of temper went through me. In the first sweep motion I smashed the head hard on the lime-green patio stones. It broke off instantly, bouncing across the slabs and landing at the glass. My dad materialized behind the pane like a flashback in a horror movie. Courage drained away. You have to understand this was the very first time I had *directly* shown any defiance or non-compliance. But again he surprised me. There was no shouting, no big tirade or speech. He just slid open the patio door in front of my pale-faced mates, who were sure they were about to witness filicide, and said, firmly but calmly:

'Wanker Kane. That's who you are.'

Such a basic roast, but it really got me. The useless wanker son. Shite academically, a stoner and unable even to sweep the floor. To my mates, it was gold. Like a Harry Enfield catchphrase it infected the school playground. I was Wanker Kane, and I would be for months, until I was Gaytan instead. And Gaytan was much worse.

6.

Steak, Not Bacon

The tale of Gaytan, which I shall set out here, involves nudity, fake tan and the desperate tears of a virgin fifteen-year-old. It's also rather funny, so funny it made the cut of a telly routine once. The reality of how I ended up bare-arsed in front of my dad, tanning mitt on one hand, the other hand cupping my tackle, is actually much bleaker and more desperate than the tale shown on the telly. It started with my dad building an actual gym at the bottom of our garden. An aluminium structure, put up with his own graft. The walls were insulated with fibreglass and featured posters of Joe Weider (the co-founder of the International Federation of Bodybuilders) and Rich Gaspari (a bodybuilding champion), along with suggested workouts and diagrams of the various muscle groups.

Muscles and body image had strutted about in my dad's mind his whole life; and I in turn would come to think about them too. Now really I shouldn't moan about body confidence. At least, that is what the newspapers and angry online forums tell me. You should not even look in on this debate if you're simply an averagely slim man, like me. Straight too. I drew the triple dud card in the world of body-image-rage debate. So, up until recently, I kept my mouth shut, when on telly or radio. After all, who wants to hear someone not struggling with their weight and who has never been shamed or verbally abused commenting on such an incendiary topic? Yet, come and see me live (please do, I have bills to pay), or just keep reading, and you'll see that in a theatre I can't keep my fat-free jowls shut. Why? My guess is I'm not alone when I reveal just how profoundly body image, and male physique goals, have affected my every year, meal and mouthful. What the hell is body image anyway? For a bloke, I mean. My dad had strong views.

'If you look like a defrosted piece of bacon, you're gonna end up ketchupped . . . Life will hit you, you need to hit back. Steak, not bacon, boy. Steak, not bacon. That's the fucking mustard.'

But I was training my head muscle, my brain – surely that would make me immune to life's abuses? In theory, yes, if I'd lived in a well-to-do neighbourhood (free from Jason Smyths), or gone to a posh school, or been skimmed off by the morally evil eleven-plus exam. But I did not. I lived on the borders of London and Essex, in an area of hyper-masculine, dare-doing, comprehensive-school terror. Muscle-building and fighting would have been on our flag, had we had one. Who can you hit? What drugs have you tried? Have you lost your virginity yet? Being punched, a lot, simply for being in a higher set for English was the norm.

Not only did I have peers making me feel small, but I had an old man who actually used to compete in bodybuilding. Before I came along, he'd entered a few of those competitions where you have to slather yourself in orange tanning fluids, oil up, and do that weird sideways bicep clench, one hand on top of the other, like you're resting on a flirty cane. Strangely, he never spoke fondly of the competitive side of bodybuilding. He praised muscle-building his whole life, but actual standing on a podium . . .

'It was just for the queers it turned out. Most of the geezers are sausage jockeys – they were after me. I wasn't comfortable.'

I'd be willing to bet that my dad was using homophobia as a smokescreen for the fact he did badly, never won. That, and as another excuse to let me know how everyone thought he was a god and wanted to touch him. Lol.

Anyway, the poor inglorious Adonis Dave Kane got me for a son. Russell, the genetic clone of his mother, minus the perm (plus being a boy). At aged sixteen I was eleven and a half stone, five feet ten. Up until two years ago my body was still exactly the same dimensions. (Anyone doing dick jokes in their minds, please cease and allow the professional to continue. You'll only make a *cock* of *yourself*.) This is why I have an opinion on body image. I think it's sad that we live in an era where only those who are offended get the loud-hailer. Any issue, particularly sociological ones, should welcome robust constructive chat from all sides – but urgently so here. This affects nearly everyone. And boys too. I'm not interested in some limp manifesto about men and men's minds. (Not interested enough anyway.) I just want to throw it out there that these days a lot of men, particularly the younger ones, are totally screwed up when it comes to body shape. Worse, they are confused and scared in secret. And eating chicken. They're eating so much boring steamed chicken. Sod that.

We make the mistake of confusing what's reported with what's happening. We only hear about female body shaming, eating disorders and paranoia – so we assume girls are much more affected. Doubtless they are, but my guess is that the gap is smaller than you think. Pick any seventeen-year-old lad living under Lord Instagram and speak to him. You'll be surprised.

Steroids: we know the dangers now, much more than my old man did. Yet male 'body dysmorphia' (wanky phrase but a real thing) is almost an epidemic. And it's way worse among boys who grow up poorer. I'm guessing that making yourself physically big is a way of getting power over your surroundings. Apologies, hardly Richard Dawkins levels of insight, but there it is. Muscling up is an achievement that can be controlled and *willed* into success. Wealth – mostly you have to be born into it. We're so busy worrying about girls getting too skinny, we've not noticed the weird bastards inflating into meat balloons next to them.

Steroid use is at an all-time high, and if you switch on any of the nourishing reality shows that drench our screens and minds, you're as likely to see a chemically induced X-Man with abs as you are plastic boobs, arses and botoxed *Lion King* faces. We are heading for a massive heart attack epidemic among these men once they get into their fifties. They either don't know the risks or don't care. It's pretty shallow, live-in-the-moment vanity:

'I'd rather be able to wear a Topman muscle-fit T-shirt than watch my kids grow up.'

That's priorities. Maybe it's just delusion, or youth. How can the same generation that so thoughtfully voted Remain – thinking carefully about a healthy economic future – so readily think YOLO at the same time. The co-existence of YOLO and Remain. What the fuck?

Bigorexia they sometimes call it, one of those worthy, clumsy coinings that make you reject the term and the notion.

Most blokes do suffer from something I call Beckorexia – the desire to have the reasonably toned body of David Beckham. Nowadays, me and my mates all slip off our T-shirts at the beach that little bit more slowly. Grown-arse men, planning Vegas trips in February rather than May just so we can avoid the pool parties and the pressures that being wobbly, scrawny or pale will bring. Ab-awareness cannot be switched off once activated.

My training in male body image was more extreme than most other boys. My early memories play like a cine film of solid muscle, strength, weightlifting and gyms. It's interesting speaking to the people who knew my dad before I was born. He would enter the room the way a glamour model fresh from a boob job would. Absolutely hell-bent on absorbing every gaze. He wore tight clothes, injected steroids and lived down the gym. It was the central part of his identity and he knew no better than to try to pass that on to me.

'You look like a milk bottle with hair on, boy. No bird will touch you.'

Yet when I tried to get into his world, I always got it slightly wrong.

When I was about fourteen, me and my friend Michael Delaney decided we wanted to get ripped. Michael was my first and oldest friend. Our mums had given birth in hospital just a few days apart. There have only been forty-eight hours when I have not known Michael. We had sat next to each other in infant school, junior school, and although aged eleven he'd moved seven miles down the road to Woodford Green, Essex when his mum got remarried, we had bikes and kept the partnership going. All my best, innocent, pre-fourteen memories were of staying at Michael's house, and he at mine. After around fourteen, although we still stayed at each other's houses, things had moved on and it was all about the partying. We made comedy videos on his camcorder. Our longest-running series was our *Laugh-a-maniac* series. Four 'feature-length' (six-minute) films, which comprised the same scene over and over: me killing someone, then doing traditional horror film laughing all over the body. We had discovered that by pausing the camera on its tripod we could make me 'teleport' and reappear roaring my crazy laugh in various silly poses – hanging out of cupboards, head popping out of toilet, that sort of thing. We made adverts together too. They flashed on during *Laugh-a-maniac* movies. This one, from when we were fourteen, is the only script I could find, mercifully, and I present it here in its entirety.

The Remington Bollock Scratcher
Russell Remington (American accent) stands scratching his nuts.
Russell: Gee – my bollocks sure are scratchy – but
    fingernails just won't do it.
Michael V/O: Try this.
A small gardening fork is handed to Russell. He scratches.
Russell: Wow. My bollocks are no longer itchy.
    THANKS Remington.
V/O: Don't go to Venus to scratch your penis. Get the
    Remington Bollock Scratcher for just $999,999,999.

Not exactly the burned works of Kafka, is it?

That particular Sunday, Michael and I had spent all our pocket money on bodybuilding magazines. We were particularly obsessed with 'striations' – that's the sinewy muscle surface you see showing through the skin of bodybuilders,

My dad, the silverback.

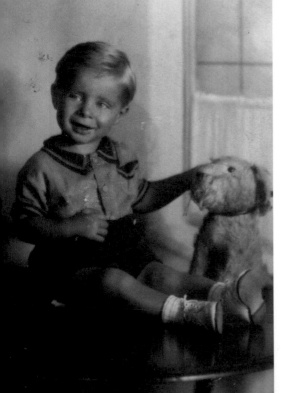

Above left: Great-granddad Benjamin Wolff (my dad's grandfather) – author of the Wolffy commandments – outside the beach hut in Southend.

Above right: One of the few photos I have of my dad's dad, Sidney. He's still with Nanna Eva here, but it wasn't long before he absconded with another (happier) woman.

Left: Even the silverback was a baby once. Dave with one of the toys Eva said were taken by Sidney 'in order to fund his elopement'.

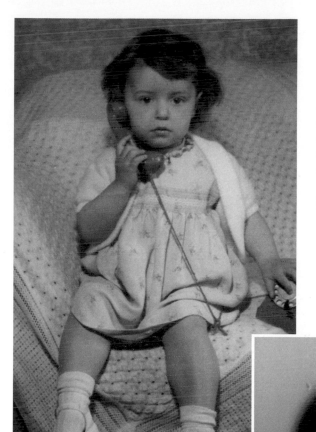

Much to Nanna Eva's disappointment, my mum's side of the family are dark-haired and have dark complexions.

Left: Mum aged two.

Right: Mum again, this time shortly before she was up the duff with yours truly.

Fancy gyms were 'just a fashion show, boy. You just need an old bench, a bar and some weights'.

Below: Here is my dad's favourite exercise, the front squat. It is one of the most painful exercises to execute (the bar sits on the collarbone). My dad loved it.

Golden Virginia, the natural tobacco to smoke.

A surprising fact that didn't fit with the rest of the man: before he got his 'proper job hands' my dad was a model and actor.

Above: This photo of us always shocks me. I can never quite imagine the silverback cradling his young.

Left: Me, ready to go home to the mother and baby shelter.

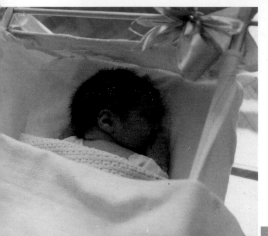

Below: On the left of this photo is the amazing Connie, my great-grandma, who raised my mum in the absence of my crazy nan, Joyce, who's on the right. Nanna Eva is holding me. Notice how she's moving her head away from mine.

Above: The Castle. The pillars symbolized Dave Kane strength, effort and graft.

Below: The finishing flourish to the Castle's building work – the swimming pool that made me feel like a god.

Above left: Finally we owned our own place, even if it was a council house.

Above right: I joined the Cub Scouts even though I lacked any hands-on skill whatsoever. I was eventually thrown out for making a crude joke as they raised the flag. I won't go into detail, but it involved the words flag, erection and the Queen.

Left: Not saying we were poor, but when we'd finished eating crisps, we'd play with the box.

the actual rippling of the rippling muscle. We had all the mags spread out, workouts highlighted – and then my dad walked in. He'd been for his four pints at the Warren Wood and was back home for Sunday lunch. I was certain he would see the magazines and be impressed that we were finally taking seriously his orders to get down the gym he had built and start our 'training' in earnest. I was wrong. Again.

'What the fuck's all that?'

'*Muscle & Fitness* magazine, Dad.'

He smiled. 'You idiots! That's what the queers buy. Fucking hell . . . Julie! *Julie!* You seen what these two have got? Gay mags.'

He laughed till he cried. And was still giggling as we all ate Sunday lunch. Michael was as embarrassed as me. This meaty body thing was more complicated than just size – it was an attitude.

It's an odd word for a type of exercise: training. Surely training means learning a new skill, or honing one for a competition? What was I training for? My feeble barbell curling was going nowhere, nor was it meant to. My training was perfunctory, its purpose more to tick a mental box than to build muscle. I still get asked it now. If I'm enjoying a bit of lamb skewer in Sheesh, Chigwell, blokes will come up to me:

'Looking fit, Mr Kane. Do you train?'

Not exercise.

Not work out.

But train. As though there is a goal or a qualification at the end of it. A fight, an exhibition – a standard to be achieved. Training.

Having a bodybuilding dad put me on conflicted path

that I've been on ever since. Sorry, fair reader, but I have no juicy tales of bulimia or anorexia to slip in here. I've just spent a lifetime going from one fad to another, always chasing what my dad set out. It was only recently I realized what bollocks it all is; and that without steroids I will always be a 'peperami with hair on'.

I wish I'd realized when I was younger that the number of women who actually desire a massive, muscly, bouncer-sized man (and one who lives in the gym) is tiny. In fact, I rarely meet any. Well, my mum, I suppose. Of course, we all want to date someone we find attractive, someone who takes reasonable care of themselves – but an actual mountain? Are there really women who desire that? Real ones? These days? Women who actually want a man who looks like he might shit himself if he turns his neck too rapidly?

'Darren?'

'Yes, darling . . . damn it! I turned my head too quick and followed through into my Calvins!'

The number of women who want an *X-Men* man must be tiny. Ask them. There are so many reasons why not. 'He lives down the David Lloyd'; 'He looks like a caveman; it grosses me out', etc. But speak to the men, listen to my dad back in the day, and:

'That's bollocks, boy. It *is* what a bird wants.'

Yes, Dad, sixteen-stone, acne-backed, shrunken scrotum and an unpredictable fiery temper. I bet Michelle Obama wishes she'd met a real man like that. Poor Dad. It wasn't just that his defining trait was brawniness. It was more he had found a way to be noticed, adored. (Oh Christ. I just realized that is also the description of a complicated stand-up comedian.)

Dad couldn't bear the thought of being old or frail, of not

being a supreme specimen. Once he got into his fifties – which now, at my age, seems absurdly young – he began talking about death and nursing homes. If he was in a really low mood he would launch into his set-piece monologue about demise.

'I won't make old bones, boy. I'm fucked.'

'What do you mean?'

'I've worked too hard putting a roof over your head . . .'

I swallowed the guilt. Selfish me and my love of roofs.

'There's nothing left of me, boy. I'm wanked out.' (I've always felt 'wanked out' should have gone more mainstream as a phrase for being exhausted and washed up.)

More than once, even when I was quite young, when *he* was still young – he would dwell on what his final years might be like, urging me to join him in making macabre pacts.

'Promise me, boy – I don't want you to actually do the deed, but promise me . . .'

'What?'

'If I'm old, dribbling in a chair, if I'm so wanked out I've lost my marbles, shitting myself, and all that – just hand me the sleeping pills and a bottle of whisky then leave the room.'

'Right. Got it.'

I think I just agreed to an illegal assisted suicide. Never mind – off out over the park now to play with my mates. I'm not being flippant here: it really did seem completely reasonable, even preferable, to me at the time: it made sense. Why be old and shit when you can just hit the off button? My great-grandma Connie (Mum's nan) had just started her descent into the cave of dementia around this time. Who would want to exist like that – locked in the past and losing control of your body functions one by one? Yet, I realize now as I set it down here,

Dad making his assisted-suicide plans when he was in his early fifties (and I was fifteen) demonstrates award-winning levels of pessimism – even for Dave Kane. I guess once you have achieved the pinnacle of biceps and brawn, there is further to fall. And the fall for him was unthinkable; correction – it was undoable. He was addicted to thinking about it. Mostly, men of my dad's generation have a reputation for being no good at putting things into words, for holding it all in. My old man was the opposite of that. Even the tiniest possible bad outcome would be verbally explored and dwelled upon.

'What if I die in poverty?' That was a classic. 'I'm scared, boy. What's gonna happen when I can't graft any more? We'll end up with nothing. If I break a leg, we starve.' And: 'Our area is turning shit . . . the house is losing value . . . see that foreign couple moved in . . . we're fucked . . .' You could judge him for being negative or celebrate that at least he had the courage to speak up about his fears. It's more than a lot of blokes are capable of. Yes. Every negative thought and concern was voiced at length – except one.

If he knew about his coming heart attack (and as the years have passed, I've come to suspect he might have), then he deliberately avoided treatment. Maybe this phobia of infirmity was the reason why. He didn't just ignore his symptoms in the regular geezer-ostrich way – he did so with a firm resolve. Let's not dress it up. I have to consider the possibility that Dave would rather have died than weakened.

In 2002, the year before Dave Kane ceased to be, he said something portentous to my great-uncle Ivan ('Uncle', as I call him, without any name). Uncle finally told me this in 2007.

'You know I could die at any moment, Ivan.'

'I'm sorry?'

'Yeah . . . I'm a ticking time bomb. Matter of months: and boom!'

I found this out over a decade ago – but it's taken me until recently to understand the implications of what the silly bastard might have meant. Was he *just* guessing? Was he having a sixth-sense premonition about his cardiovascular health? Or had he been told and hidden the facts from us? Was it fear, suicidal impulse – or plain old working-class-male head-in-the-sand? Of course, he could have just been being negative and dramatic for effect, he may have known nothing at all about how close he really was to death – but it's bugged me for a while.

He'd had one appointment at the hospital after getting 'chest cramps' at work one day in 2001. No one knows what was said in that meeting once emergency scans were done. He reported back to us that the doctor had told him it was nothing to worry about for a few years – and just to have regular check ups. Which is the truth? Did the doctor say that, and Dad was having one of his melodramatic over-exaggerating days when he said what he said to Uncle (in which case the NHS gave him incorrect information which cost him his life), or was it that he changed the report and only told the truth to Uncle in a moment of wild confession? Maybe something in between. My guess now is that my old man was told, at least to some extent: have heart surgery in the next year, or drop down dead. But Dave Kane went down for no one; he missed the gym for no one – and the idea of not grafting: unthinkable. He squatted, pressed, lunged and lifted – always had, always will – and fuck anyone who told him different.

'I'd rather die than sit in a home shitting my pants.'

Yeah. Maybe he chose the former. Stay the silverback, and go out with a bang.

Perhaps you're thinking: yeah, Russ, but heart surgery – come on, that would make most of us think twice. Agreed, but the aortic valve – the one in my old man's heart that was malfunctioning, is one of the simpler bits to replace. Mechanical or pig (he'd have liked a pig one), it's an off-the-shelf fix, with a 95 per cent success rate. Ninety-five! Who focuses on the 5 per cent? It's ironic that a man who prided himself on an inside knowledge of valves and joints may have died for fear of replacing one of the simplest in the human heart; one damaged by the chemicals which had given him the body of his dreams: steroids.

Back to *my* muscle journey.

Michael Delaney and I decided on regular workouts. The regime was simple: three sets of ten with two-minute resting intervals. Monday: chest and shoulders; Wednesday: back and legs; Friday: arms. No cardio.

'Jogging is for cunts,' Dad sagely advised.

Dad became fairly involved in setting down our regimen. I have no idea how much of what he said was true, or whether he was simply trying to inspire us.

'Eggs, boy. I used to eat a tray on training days. Thirty eggs. I was eating so much protein that there was only certain khazis I could use. Know what I mean? Needed a wide U-bend. I wrote off a few toilets, boy. That's how much protein I was eating. You talk about cable – the cable I was laying, you could get Sky Movies in the toilet.'

He was suspicious of 'fancy equipment' too. Most people in gym culture obsess over training shorts, gloves, special belts, angled bars – not my old man. He didn't even like the machines like the leg curl or lateral pull-down devices. He found it all suspicious.

'That's just a fashion show, boy. It's all bollocks. You just need an old bench, a bar and some weights.'

The more basic and underground-looking the gym, the more *real* you were. Rust on the bar seemed to equate to hair on the chest. This was crushing news for me and Michael – we'd spent hours reading muscle mags and obsessing about different brands of lifting grips and protein shakes.

'Protein powder! Fuck's sake. Just eat some chicken, you silly fuckers.' Sometimes he'd say this while maintaining eye contact as he picked up any nearby meat and ripped into it with his gnashers.

So we went for it: as much to impress the girls as to get my dad off my back. On more than one occasion I cycled the seven miles to Michael's house on my Raleigh Euro, topless, and oiled. Yes, for one sweet summer I didn't hate myself; I was an Adonis who actually loved himself (I never experienced such supreme body confidence again). But still, even after working out for *weeks*, the girls refused to fancy me. There was one last thing to acquire on my ascent to studdom: an Italian-looking tan.

In my school the boy whom all the girls fancied was an Italian lad called David (pronounced *Dahvid* – even though he had a scumbag accent like me, not an Italian one). He was tall, dark and handsome – the three things that the keepers of boobs and fannies kept mentioning. Well, ladies, I could control only one of those – dark: my tan. Dahhhvid (seriously, just call yourself David, you penis) was one of those boys who hits the ground running during pubescent body change. By thirteen he had a hairy tree-trunk cock that he swung around in the PE changing room like he was dowsing for my insecurities. He found them, and not very far beneath the surface. He was also five feet ten before he was fifteen. The boy was a total disaster for me and the Bald Thimble brigade. (The Bald Thimbles were the boys who had not yet started puberty – the name referred to our pathetic, hairless manhoods.) In Communion, I often thanked God from the bottom of my dead atheist heart that at least there were a few boys worse off than me. In the communal dressing room the No-Cocks took the heat off the Bald Thimbles. There was one who was so thin, he looked like an extra from the concentration camp docudrama we'd been forced to watch in Miss Oldman's History class. There were two who were both so grossly fat we couldn't actually tell if they had hair on their dicks or not, or if they had dicks for that matter. One had it slightly easier as his protective older brother was heavier than a physics lesson and good at rugby. But the boy who had it worst in the changing rooms was Oliver Caron. He had a French dad, too, which made him totally hated. It seems we're born with ironic racism against French people preloaded. But Oliver wasn't just 'part frog' – no, he had the smallest willy in our year. The frog had a tadpole (not one of my jokes; only senior bullies had the privilege to coin new insults). I cringe at the awfulness of what happened to the poor bastard – even if I was mostly just a spectator.

'Caron, Caron, he cannot get a hard-on. It's so petite, he has no meat, Caron, Caron,' they sang. And:

'Caron Caron, he sticks his tiny cock in Dijon . . .'

'The frog-tadpole, can never fill a hole . . .'

I make myself feel better by telling myself he had a late developmental spurt – or that he was a grower. Hopefully he now lives in Paris with a beautiful woman called Amélie, and he's as well hung as an Elizabethan criminal.

Unbelievably, while I was proofreading this book, I saw Oliver Caron for the first time in over twenty years. He was working in a shop, and I was buying crayons for my daughter. I have no idea if he recognized me, but the fact I was buying 'mini crayons' with tiny nibs ripped a traumatic guilt gust through me from my guts to my eyes. Horrible. I really hope he was a late bloomer and is now packing more sausage than the Wall's factory.

The changing room of any secondary school is horrific but those of us boys and girls who had no cubicles and shared showers had it worst. I would be interested to know if that's still the case – is it even allowed any more, forcing people at the most vulnerable stage of their bodily development to be naked around their peers? Most of the fourteen-year-olds I know are writhing in self-analysing pain just from another teenager's Instagram post where they 'look a bit fit'. Imagine real-life Instagram. The real, perfect body and genitals of the dominant male or female. Yep, PE changing times were a hothouse for body dysmorphia and fear. You never do fully recover from being punched by Dennis Redman or Alan Landor while naked; the hard hit on your arm, your silly little cock shaking with the impact of each blow. And all the time, sat in his throne watching, his hairy dick and bollocks tumbling over the wooden bench like a bag of wool and sausages, David (*Dahhhvid*) Eposito – the Italian Stallion. I knew I would never have his body, but I could enhance my meagre gifts. Yes. I could definitely make mine browner.

On the back of my bodybuilding confidence surge, and fuelled by my envy of David Eposito, I decided to take that next step: fake tan. You need to be of a certain age to remember the first generation of self-tan; I think it came from Boots. It was in a blue and white box with complimentary mitt and paper thong. If I could only get the skin colour of the Dahhvid, all the girls would fancy me. This theory was entirely groundless. I had no foundation to build on. I didn't even have a blueprint for the building. I had never kissed a girl. Not even on the cheek. Nothing. In fact, I would leave school without having lost my kissing virginity. A virgin plus. That's almost an achievement where I come from. Most lads are dads by the time they're twenty, but I couldn't even manage a snog. Yet in my head, entering those school gates next day with a bronze Italian glow would create a punani tsunami (maybe outside Geography, perhaps in the chemistry lab . . .).

I'm not talking figuratively here. Anyone easily offended or who enjoys finding things sexist, please skip over this next bit. I put it in purely so you can try and understand how some teenage boys' brains work. Me and my virgin friends actually believed/fantasized that it was possible to become so attractive to the opposite sex that you could die being smothered by their nether regions. This was dreamed of, sought for – a death-fuck fantasy straight out of Freud. Maybe we'd been affected by a set piece in Monty Python's *The Meaning of Life* where Graham Chapman chooses the manner of his own death and is chased down by naked girls and off a cliff, or maybe it's more common than we realize, but we honestly believed that if we just drove the females into enough ecstasy of attraction, they would disrobe, corner us and suffocate us in a squelching pelvic attack; and in my tiny hormone-ruined wreck of a brain, I thought fake tan might be the crucial step towards turning this sweet death fantasy into a reality.

You have to understand the punishing, incessant cruelty of the teenage boy's sex drive. I'm not suggesting girls aren't pervy-surgey-urgey at this age too; I'm just arguing boys have it worse. The wanking starts and it does not stop. Function wanking, like brushing your teeth or cleaning your shoes, is something to be done, to be got on with, just to empty the tank and proceed with your day. Not like posh masturbation once you're older – and you might treat yourself to some HD material, scented candles, a flute of champagne, maybe a silk glove. No, in the teen years it is a rotten, repetitive illness, and everything is arousing. Imagine masturbating so frequently that you experience the impossible feat of both being bored and wanking at the same time. You could leave the house and the tiniest thing will set you off; you'd have to run back for an emergency tug.

'Oh great – a daffodil! The flowery slut! Now I'm going to have to run home for another hand shandy.'

It was a living masturbatory hell. If this act did, as rumoured, cause blindness, I would have been Helen Keller by the time I was nineteen. On the contrary, however, a recent report I read suggested masturbation increases health and prevents cancer. Excellent news: teenage boys are now immortal.

With this relentless compulsion, any scheme to make myself more attractive to the opposite sex was worth a punt.

After all, I was the son of a man who sold the myth of male perfection and female susceptibility to it. Yes, Dad definitely fuelled things: his constant descriptions of women losing their self-restraint and stroking him ''Cos they didn't believe I could exist, boy' made me truly believe that girls might be pushed over the edge of self-control simply by looking at a boy they fancied so long as he was fanciable *enough*. And a tanned version of me might just be that boy.

The gym Dad had erected at the bottom of the garden was intended for tricep extensions, squats and bench presses; and initially Michael and I really did try. But understand – I now had a private space at the bottom of the garden where I couldn't be seen or heard, and a door that closed properly. It was harder for Dad to burst in on me. He had inadvertently created a safe space where I could lounge, skip, dance – do camp things I would never have gambled on in my easily stormed and eavesdropped bedroom. I had my tape recorder down there with me, and at last I wasn't afraid to play my own music. It might be 'chart shit' – it might be seven show tunes. Dad hated nearly all my music; oddly, he loved Barry White. He was cremated to Barry White.

'Shagging music, boy.'

I didn't love Barry White. Once we had that rotating satellite dish my music tastes went all modern American. Down that shed I played the music of MC Hammer and tried to learn the dances. In my head I looked super-cool. In reality I probably looked more like that picture of Katie Hopkins when she was on ketamine in South Africa. It was during one of my dance rehearsals, torso glistening with sweat, when the plan came to me. I would use my paper-round money and go to Boots. The next day I would slather myself in fake tan. Low risk, maximum gains.

For what happened next you have to hold in your head my dad's homophobic paranoia that his son might be gay. Or as he termed it when he once caught me learning a dance and wearing a headband:

'You're not a fucking turd burglar, are ya, boy?'

I suppose he was piqued by the combination of me never having had a girlfriend or generating any female interest mixed with all the weird skipping and dancing I did, which sadly I have not grown out of. I've had a few punters pull me up on it.

'Why do you do all that camp prancing shit? You're better than that, mate.'

Well, mate, let me say this once and for all – I'm not doing it on purpose. I've done it my whole life – the more excited, the more nervous I get, the more I move. It's like a whole body twitch.

The day my dad walked in on me self-tanning in the gym shed, I was fully naked, except for the complimentary paper thong, and rubbing myself all over with the mitt. I don't remember exactly which tune was playing – but I know it was something from a West End musical. Maybe a Liza Minnelli. It was the worst possible intersection of false flags for my old man to walk in on. I was so immersed in my girl-capturing scheme I did not even notice the shed door creaking open. The first indication that my ashen-faced Dad was stood behind me was the sensation of fresh air on my buttocks.

'Fucking hell . . .' he whispered.

I cupped my bits, and made things worse by looking over

my shoulder at him rather than facing him. I accidentally took on a more coquettish, Marilyn Monroe posture.

'Dad . . .'

'What . . . are . . . you . . . doing?'

'Tanning.'

And next he came out with a contraction of all his thoughts into a single word, a new word, which became my nickname.

'Gaytan!' It came out of his mouth like a minimalist Japanese poem. It expressed all his fears and observations in two syllables. Gaytan. The label stuck for years afterwards.

'Gaytan, get in the car.'

'Gaytan, pass the horseradish.'

(Gaytan was eventually replaced by Badger after I attempted my own blond highlights.)

It was at this point I realized where my dad's head had gone. I saw what he was seeing.

'No, Dad, no. It's not that. I'm tanning for the girls. I'm doing it for the girls.'

What he came out with next is impressive for its literary provenance. I didn't think he'd retained anything we'd read as kids but it came out of his mouth, one of the all-time top Dave zingers.

'Girls???! Bollocks, son! You're so far in the closet, you're bumming Mr Tumnus.'

And he strode off.

If you're wondering, the fake tan did activate. Oh, it certainly did. It took hold rather too well. I got on the 191 bus more orange than an angry Belfast Protestant. I told myself, against all evidence, that I had the Italian glow I'd been going for. I walked in through the gates, positive visualizations tumbling through my mind – but I wasn't more than fifteen metres into my comprehensive when Alan Landor shouted:

'Ha ha – orange cunt!'

It wasn't until he added, 'Everyone, look at this . . .' that I knew I was doomed.

Michael Delaney's stepdad – Nigel Hampton – was one of the thinnest, most insecure men ever to have worn a knitted waistcoat. Anything male that came near him had to be challenged or pushed. There was immediate tension between Nigel and my dad. Nigel just couldn't handle the fact my dad was large, and his discomfort manifested itself in ways that were a danger to his own physical safety.

'All right, Dave!' he'd say, and then do a combination of jokey pummels of my dad's arm, but they were just hard enough to reveal the real emotion in Nigel's touch. He enjoyed hitting my dad.

'Please, Julie,' Dad said later one night, 'let me just knock the cunt out.'

'No, Dave, he's my best friend's fella.'

Nigel Hampton was one of the most confused examples of testosterone I've ever known – and his daring around my dad was spectacular. When the two came together, I made sure I had my popcorn. They were from different man planets. If you were to draw right now the archetypal weedy, bald Englishman from every sitcom ever, you'd draw Nigel. Yeah, OK, he did the right thing by Michael and his family, sharing with them his lovely home in Essex, but something wasn't right. Nigel didn't look at you right. He definitely didn't look at our female friends right. He felt threatened by everyone, yet at the same time maintained an absurd strut.

He would sometimes suddenly show off his masculine prowess in socially inappropriate ways: pull-ups hanging off a tree in the garden during a barbecue; jogging in only his underwear around the garden – stuff like that. He had a Dobermann named Hatler – and when my mum was over he would gee it up, pretend he was about to let it off the lead to set it on her and laugh as Mum cowered behind a door. He liked power, and seemed to dislike women. If I tell you that Nigel eventually divorced Michael's mum and disappeared into Thailand, I think you can draw your own conclusions without me running into legal problems. The two most entertaining things Nigel ever did were these.

It was New Year's Eve and everyone was stood around talking. Michael I were fourteen, so allowed to stay up with the adults. My dad walked into the kitchen freshly showered and wearing a skintight black shirt that showed off his full ape size. It was too much for Nigel. In a roomful of people not yet that drunk, he dropped, almost on reflex, to the floor and began doing one-arm press-ups. The room fell into an awkward silence. It was the exercise equivalent of David Brent's dance. It's one of the bleakest attempts at attention-seeking I've ever seen – and I'm friends with stand-up comedians.

The other incident – perhaps better for its piquant mixture of menace and danger – was when Nigel got carried away telling my dad a story. Nigel and Dad were sat on the breakfast bar stools in the kitchen.

'I couldn't believe it, Dave,' said Nigel, standing up and adjusting his knitted waistcoat. 'I was minding my own business in the Warren Wood when this geezer comes up to me and does this . . .'

Instead of describing the slap around the face in his story, Nigel actually executed one. A solid, meaty, ringing slap on my dad's cheek.

'Can you believe it, Dave. Like that it was, Dave. Like that.' *Thwack*. And he did another, lighter slap.

I was four metres from my old man but I could clearly see each hair on his neck bristle as his body went into combat mode. The frisson passed, and Nigel wandered over to our kettle, visibly buzzing from the thrill of having struck the alpha male with impunity.

'Tea?'

Nigel never knew how close he'd come to becoming a wheelchair user.

7.

You Don't Need Friends in Life, Boy

When it comes to friendship, I've always had an attraction to nerds. Maybe it was Dad's hyper-masculinity, or maybe I just genuinely like role-playing games and science. Of all my friends, Steven Epsom is the only one I can fully nerd off with. Most of my other mates do manly jobs and like manly things; they are sparkies and tilers, one sells cars, and even my more arty mates have a bloke's energy. Me too, and so does Steve – but he also has a strong dose of nerd. I happily live in both worlds. Growing up with Dave for a dad, I had to become fluent in Geezer – but thanks to Steven Epsom, I also know that a twenty-sided dice is needed to create a wizard in *Dungeons and Dragons*.

'What the fuck are you lot doing round his gaff?' Dad asked me once, convinced I was in a drug cult.

'It's called *Dungeons and Dragons*.'

'What? Sex shit?'

'You know those little figurines on my shelf – we pretend . . . to, er, be them.'

'You're seventeen, boy! I was nuts deep in Jack and Danny at your age. Birds everywhere. What you playing with dollies for?'

The relationship Steven Epsom had with his dad was on a totally different plane to the one I had with mine. His dad had hobbies: Roger Epsom painted watercolours, he did bonsai, he liked discussing difficult moral problems with Steven and his mates sat around him – a working-class Socrates with his salon in Enfield Lock instead of Athens.

'Why is euthanasia OK, Roger?' one of us could have asked.

'It's about individual freedom,' he would have rejoined in that voice of his that was cockney yet nasal and nerdy – halfway between Boycie from *Only Fools and Horses* and Jason Statham.

Roger Epsom would talk to you about wanking and sex in a matter-of-fact, informative way that made it sciency, instead of giggly and taboo. Roger was also a *Dungeons and Dragons* player . . . in his fifties. If you've never played, it's not as mysterious as it sounds. You simply create a character using dice, then sit around a table in an elaborate role-playing game controlled by the games master, or dungeon master, as he's properly known. The dice decide everything, but you're free to be as theatrical and geeky as you want. I loved it. I still do. I would play now if my diary didn't look like a chimp has thrown some glitter at a sticky grid.

It's worth lingering on Steven Epsom, with his dusty blond hair and massive chin. Steven features in a few key moments of my teenage years; and my old man is never far from each scene.

The most trouble Steven and I ever got into at my house also involved Michael Delaney. We were all fifteen, and one day we came up with a proposition while watching my brother James firing his cap gun in the garden.

'Is it actual gunpowder in a cap gun, Steve?' I asked,

assuming the scientist among us would know. He did not disappoint.

'Not quite,' he said, stroking his Bruce Forsyth chin. 'I believe it's fulminate of mercury – ignited by force or flame.' His voice had the same Boycie/Jason Statham edge as his old man's.

Michael laughed – we were fifteen and obsessed with things exploding and burning. He was thinking what Steve and I began thinking at the exact same moment.

'What if,' I said, casting myself as the Guy Fawkes of the situation, 'we went to Jennings and bought all the caps they have . . .'

'Dig out the fulminate with a screwdriver?' said Steve.

Michael laughed again. 'Let's make a bomb,' he said.

I went to Jennings that day and cleared out their stock of caps. One thousand five hundred of them. I also swiped a magnesium strip from a Chemistry lesson on the Monday. That would be our fuse.

We reconvened the following Saturday with a genuine tingle of purpose and daring. We might not have girlfriends, but we would show the world we were men. We spent a good hour levering out the tiny patties of explosive from their capsules. There wasn't a massive quantity of fulminate – just enough to fill the lid of a hairspray can. We were so sure the explosion would be modest that we didn't even wait for my mum and dad to be out of the house. Dad was in the front garden waxing the cream Merc 190E and listening to soul music. Mum was in the kitchen inventing cleaning jobs that didn't need doing. My brother James, thank God, was safely indoors.

'My suggestion,' said Steve, just a white coat away from

being professorial, 'is that we sink it into the mud of the flower bed and then balance the magnesium strip on the brickwork edge.'

'Will that give us enough time to run?' asked Michael.

'Ample,' said Professor Steve.

All three of us scooped earth from the flower bed and packed the lid in tight. We inserted the strip, rested the end on the surrounding bricks, Steve lit it with a match and we ran. Then there was a problem.

'Shit!' said Michael.

The magnesium strip went out just 2cm from the bomb.

'It's OK,' I said. 'There's still a bit left.'

And this was the poor decision we made.

In our impatience, the three of us lit matches and crowded in around the remaining stub of magnesium strip. The last thing I remember was looking at Michael's match thinning into a black spike and its glowing orange tip breaking off. The hot end dropped into the lid, and physics quickly took over from chemistry. I have no recollection of the bang itself. I wasn't knocked out, but I was completely deaf as I sat stunned in the smoke, three feet from the flower bed with cartoon black hair and face. There was mud and small stones everywhere. Steven lay on the lawn in the other direction, staring up at the sky, blinking. Michael, although standing, had it worst. His face was embedded with tiny stones that were dropping out one by one like horror film popcorn, leaving measles-like red spots on his face. Miraculously none of us was seriously hurt. We were trying to talk to each other but sound was returning too slowly. I saw my old man bounding through the smoke like an ape in a documentary about

Rwanda. I thought briefly of Sigourney Weaver, the gorillas, but snapped back into reality when I saw the mute spittle flying from his face.

'What the fucking hell was that!?' he mouthed. 'The whole house shook – the double glazing nearly came out, you silly cunts.'

'My flower bed!' screamed Mum. 'Are you OK?'

Two bricks had actually blown out of the flower bed. The mud was scattered like black champagne over the garden.

'The peat's fucked!'

We were marched into my kitchen. Mums were phoned, Savlon applied. Michael's cheeks weren't getting any less red.

I looked at Steve.

'It might not have been fulminate after all,' he said. 'Could have been straightforward gunpowder.'

My dad never really trusted Steve after that – even though it was more my fault than his. Mind you, that made us about even as just a few weeks before I'd been marched out of Steve's house for 'stealing' a computer disk.

'Get him out of my house, Steven!' Roger had screamed. And I had walked ashen-faced past a man I admired. No point protesting my innocence to an authority figure like Roger. Roger found the disk a few weeks later and normal relations resumed, but I was always tinged with the air of a would-be thief, even though the crime had been imagined. Dads: once they think something, it becomes the truth, even when they find out it isn't.

The other main event at Steven's house also centred around his computer. Roger Epsom had always been light years ahead with his Amigas and PCs. And to see a Commodore Amiga Advanced in action was a thing of beauty. Sometimes

Roger ran the computer for days doing 'fractal imagining' – a process where a machine hums away on its own, generating weird pyramids and shape-scapes.

'I want to create the whole hobbit world on my Amiga,' Roger had announced to us boys, who all then had simultaneous geek-gasms. So different to my old man, who wanted to bend and dominate bits of the *real* world. Change lead pipes, alter pieces of wood, dig into things, break things with a hammer. I never heard Dad curious about anything cerebral. Maybe it could have saved him if he'd got obsessed with, say, military history – or even the history of cars. Just something. But Dad's list, even when he hit sixty, remained the same: metal, meat, cars and tits. An Essex man of pure pedigree. Still revving his car and gawking at knockers – even with a bus pass beckoning. You know, I can't even visualize my dad on a bus. Is that normal? Can you imagine your dad on a bus or a train? I'm trying but I just can't see it. He was a man who travelled alone, the wheel firmly gripped. He did get the Tube once – to a job in South London. Me and my brother were stunned.

'Your dad's in a bad mood,' Mum had warned. 'He's on his way back from Tooting and he's had to get the train.'

'The what?' Me and James at the same time.

It was like imagining your nan on the dance floor or Prince Charles in Asda – too incongruous to be possible.

Later that evening, over steaming piles of chilli con carne, Dad described his experience.

'This geezer touched my arse. Not on purpose – well, I dunno. But I was thinking – touch me again, and I'll fucking knock you out.'

I could imagine Steven Epsom's dad on a train. I saw him

on the train. Roger used to jump on, wiry and primed for his day, at Enfield Lock – one stop before me when I was older and working in London. Roger was one of the first dads to have a mobile phone. It was called a Rabbit phone and you could only use it where you saw the Rabbit logo. So not a mobile at all really. Still, Roger enthusiastically used his. He would get off his train, pointlessly head out of his way to the Rabbit transmitter logo and dial.

'On my way home, dear. The train was on time,' and then walk the four minutes home. It was just for the boyish joy of using technology.

My dad, at first, repudiated mobiles.

'Waste of fucking money. What's the point,' etc.

But then his lagging and building clients kept asking for his number. He caved in around 1999, just three years after giving me absolute hell for getting a mobile myself. He bought a Nokia, which he reluctantly nursed, an overpriced electrical tumour. About a year into his phone ownership there occurred another excellent example of Dave Kane's pessimism. One of the finest. It was a Sunday morning; by then I was at university and had popped over for a roast dinner. I knew straight away there was an atmosphere – something had happened. Although, actually it hadn't.

'We had a close one this morning,' Mum said solemnly. 'Tell him, Dave.'

'We went to the market . . . and I left my mobile, on the dash, in the car park – right on fucking display . . .' He paused.

'Shit . . . did you catch them at it?' I said, putting the story together in my head.

'Who?'

'I thought you meant the van window got smashed . . . your phone?'

'No,' Dad said. 'I realized when we were in Tesco. We ran back to the van. Got the phone.'

'From who?'

'I mean – some fucker would have had it.'

'Close one,' added Mum.

In their heads what could have happened was as traumatic as it actually happening. Dad had kicked off at an imagined crime and was still stressed about it three hours later. Impressive levels of pessimism. As I say, a hobby was what he could have done with.

When I was about twelve Dad did undertake something close to a hobby – although its end result was illegal weapons being sold down the pub. Dad had worked out that, using his lathe and woodwork skills, he could make amazing nunchucks. At the time, all the villains down the Warren Wood were obsessed with martial arts and Bruce Lee – so Dad's nunchucks were very popular. Sometimes I would be sat in my window doing the voices of an Action Man doll, or leafing lazily through a computer magazine, and Dad would be in the garden, in tiny blue swimming trunks, doing nunchuck practice – catching each baton under his arm and making traditional karate noises through his nose as wood impacted on armpit flesh. We were different, me and my dad. But what a geezer.

Anyway, back to Roger Epsom's Amiga.

'Check this out,' Steve said one Sunday to me and Malcolm. Malcolm was another nerd friend. We were all good at the same things: films, vampires, *Dungeons and Dragons* and being virgins.

'What is it?' asked Malcolm, as Steven loaded the disk into the Amiga.

Steve's mum and dad were away for the weekend but we had been allowed in their bedroom as that's where the Amiga was located.

'*Party Games*,' said Steve.

It was the first time I saw a moving pornographic image on a computer screen. It only had two frames. A guy was shagging a girl and you had to waggle the computer's joystick to make the man shag faster. It would be nothing more than a duotone GIF these days, but back then it was filthy wizardry and sublime spectacle. It was also very funny, rather than erotic. We all cried laughing, then grew bored of it and went downstairs to watch *Star Trek*, a more arousing proposition.

Later that day, Malcolm charged Steve and me with going to the shops to buy tea and biscuits for that evening's *Dungeon and Dragons* session (I know, what a rock and roll teen I was). We got 100 metres out of Steve's house when we remembered that the shop closed at 3 p.m. on a Sunday, so we turned back.

'That's weird. Malcolm's gone!' Steve said as we walked into the front room.

'A spell!' I said, never missing a moment in which a *Dungeons and Dragons* reference could be dropped.

'Oh my God,' said Steve, pointing towards the creaking ceiling.

'What?'

'He's in my mum and dad's room.'

'Mal—' I went to shout, but Steve put his hand over my mouth.

'No,' he whispered, giggling.

We crept up the stairs and positioned ourselves outside the bedroom door.

'Ready?' whispered Steve.

I nodded.

Steve slowly pushed it open and we saw exactly what we were expecting, only better.

Malcolm was supine on the bed, furiously wanking. But the thing that made this so much funnier was that his left hand was also engaged. He was waggling the Amiga joystick – diligently trying to score *Party Games* points while at the same time pleasuring himself. It was the purest blend of nerd and perv I have ever seen.

'Get oooooooout!'

But we didn't. We pointed and cried with belly laughs. We still laugh about it now. Sorry, Malcolm.

When I spoke to Steve recently, he reminded me that I still call him the Chin of Ecstasy. I had misremembered where the nickname came from. I thought it was from our clubbing days – when I often picked up Steve from a hard-house dance floor, looking like a gurning Bruce Forsyth. But that wasn't why he had been nicknamed the Chin of Ecstasy. It came from a camping trip that he, Malcolm and I took when we were all sixteen.

We had decided it would be fun to get intoxicated around a campfire. So we got permission from the mums to go camping for the night. Camping is another thing I could never have imagined my dad doing.

'Lying around in mud. Fuck that, boy. All-inclusive. Luxury.'

'It's nice for a short break though,' I said to him once.

'Short break?' And he laughed derisively.

Both my mum and dad rejected the 'short break'. It's another upper-working-class rule. You graft your tits off all year, don't take any breaks or time off at all, and build towards one *massive* holiday. Two weeks or even twenty-one nights was the gold standard – all-inclusive, everything you need in the resort, and out to explore for a couple of nights here and there. And of course the most important thing: you know your final bill in advance, no surprises. Don't get me wrong, I love a long holiday too; I adore an all-inclusive with Moron wristband – lolling around a pool by day, and gorging at a buffet by night. Yet the thrill of two nights here, three nights there. As I type these words I'm on a train out of Edinburgh after three nourishing days poking around castles. I've always enjoyed stuff like that. I must have a mutant gene. I would quite happily travel eight hours for a three-night break; the giddy adrenaline of a tucked-away three-star hotel, your Lonely Planet guide in your grasp, and no real plan. What a buzz. Not for Dad.

'Transfers to and from the airports. Pre-paid, boy. It's a holiday. I want to bloody relax – not ponce about like Phileas Fucking Fogg.'

'I have to have an en suite,' puts in Mum.

Totally valid points. But I do find it relaxing to investigate side streets and hunt out the restaurants that the 'mainstream' tourists have missed. And I love camping.

The events of that July evening took place when we were all sixteen, some of us still clinging tenaciously to our virginity while pretending a deep and intimate knowledge of female anatomy. Malcolm had been smiling and doing weird pervy hints with his eyes all that week leading up to it. This would not be the usual camping trip.

'He's up to something,' I said to Steve.

'Do you reckon, Poirot?'

'Well, what?'

'It's obvious. He's invited a girl.'

'Who?'

'In my opinion, it'll be Abigail.'

Two days before the trip, sure enough, Malcolm revealed: 'I've invited Abigail.'

'I fucking knew it!' said Steve.

Abigail was a posh girl from Surrey with whom Steve had dallied. At this point any of us who had touched a girl in any way was a legend. It was never clear exactly how far Steve had gone with Abigail, or when, but she was a big part of his life, all our lives, for a short while; without Abigail I never would have met my first love, Jessica, a few months later. Steve had met Abigail on the school trip to the south of France. It was the big final school trip before we left school; and it was one I did not go on.

'Sorry, boy . . . can't afford it!' Dad had said slathering on his Paco Rabanne and getting ready for dinner out. 'Hurry up, Julie, we'll be late for the Warren Wood!'

In France, the boys from our school befriended some posh girls from Lady Margaret's Independent Day School in Surrey. The regular school bullies and alpha males came unstuck when faced with girls who wanted actual conversation. Some of the girls were stuck up, and spoke French so they could mock the common boys in earshot. Others were intrigued by Steve and his bright but odd-sounding friends. It meant the nerds and kooky lads got a look-in. That's how the Jimmy Hill-chinned lover of science Steven managed to get off with Abigail Hemsworth.

'Steve got hold a of a bird in France,' Malcolm reported to an astounded clique of geeks.

'French?' asked James Opal, dribbling.

'Better,' shot back Malcolm. 'Posh.'

Steve walked in, a soldier, fresh from battle: 'Full tongues . . . And when I touched her fanny . . . it was *dripping.*' The silent listeners grew reverent. We were a long way from goblins and dragons now. 'Absolutely sodden . . .' This detail added not in a laddish, sexist way, but like a scientist reporting on the miracle progress of cress in a sunlight-less lab. On hearing the last particulars me and the other geeks all thought the same thing at the same time: how quickly can we run off somewhere private and have a massive wank while imagining the scenes Steve described?

The rest of the geek squad met Abigail and her friends a few times in the term after. We found ourselves invited to Saturday-night parties in Surrey; staying over with our mums' permission in big houses with loose rules. Posh people managed to be more buttoned up but also freer – a paradox we could not comprehend.

On one particular visit I was set up with Abigail's friend Gina. This wasn't simply a possible shag. I had actually received a letter from her in which she called herself Shagger Gina – and said she was 'Definitely gonna take my V'. There was a countdown chart so I could cross out the remaining days till I got my 'willy wet'. Malcolm and Steve laughed and clapped as I read that last promise: they were happy for me.

'Not even you can fuck this one up, Kano,' said Steve on

the day as we trained it to Surrey. We stopped at Epsom train station and I bought some condoms, trying one on for the first time in my life in the station toilets. I was awful at it. I rolled half of it on and the teat flopped about like a depressed baby elephant. This was a concern. What if she had AIDS? Everyone had AIDS back then. What if I got a girl pregnant and my dad found out? I would instigate a philosophical event: creating life at the very moment mine would be ended.

'Get a bird pregnant, boy, and your life will be over,' Dad warned through gritted teeth. 'Wait till you're forty, boy. Even that's too early.'

I tried another condom, this one rolled on inside out: 'I can't do it,' I whispered despairingly under the toilet door.

'Don't worry,' shouted Malcolm indiscreetly. 'She'll roll it on for you with her mouth.'

'Yeah, like in *Sluts Four*,' Steve put in, referring to a VHS doing the rounds.

Steve and Malcolm ran out of the toilet bellowing, leaving me to face the other patrons when I came out of the cubicle blushing.

We partied in Surrey that night – and, inevitably, Kano did fuck this one up. I spent the night avoiding Gina, scared. Turned out, at nearly sixteen, I was not ready. I was also deeply paranoid about my skin. I had three massive spots which I had attacked with Rimmel cover stick.

'You don't need to put that on your face, darling,' Abigail had said, being kind but inadvertently letting me know that everyone had noticed I was a boy wearing make-up. I drank elderberry wine till I found myself hugging the toilet and – the finishing touch – sobbing. The crying, vomit-stained virgin. Not even Shagger Gina could let her standards drop that low. She gave up around 11 p.m. and got rodded sense-less by someone else. I would remain cherry intactus for another year.

'I've got someone else for you,' Abigail had consoled me the next morning as I mournfully walked to the train station slathered in cover stick. She was telling the truth, but I would have to wait to meet Jessica.

So Abigail was coming to Epping Forest on our camp-ing trip. It would be cosy. A bit too cosy. We were already three boys in a small tent. Four of us? We were just young enough not to be weirded out by it; more concerned with practicalities.

'Won't it be a bit crowded?' I said.

'Exactly,' said Malcolm, pervy smile.

Steve laughed.

'Seriously, where will Abigail sleep?'

'Maybe she won't,' said Steve like a porn stud, even though he was built like a milk lolly and looked like Texas Pete from *SuperTed*.

We set up the tent on a sunny afternoon, built a fire and waited for Abigail to arrive. We were all topless and in shorts – still collecting insects and killing them, the traces of boyhood not yet fully expunged from our hormone-ruined minds. We were halfway between *Lord of the Flies* and *Kevin & Perry*.

'Hello, boys!' we heard being shouted in posh. And there she was. Abigail, guffawing and galloping across the grass, part Enid Blyton character, part buxom wench.

We loved Abigail because she was exuberant, middle class and carefree. No girls like that lived around our way. By the time they were fifteen, our girls had hardened suspicious faces. They knew the rules – boys would use you; life was tough; girls got 'up the duff'; work was coming. Our girls had older sisters and mums who sat at tills beeping people's shopping; who stacked shelves, washed dinner plates, wiped the arses of richer, more successful women's brats. Their mums were grey, lumpy women who cared for other people; enhanced other people's fun. Our girls went down Walthamstow Market and bought pretend versions of posh things to wear on nights out where boys with fake IDs drank Bacardi Breezers, sniffed 'gear' and acted like idiots, fighting and jumping off things. By fifteen, our girls knew what was coming, and they were strengthening themselves against the impact.

Abigail was different. She pronounced transport 'traaansport'. She had a dad who was a barrister and a brother who played rugby for England under-18s. No one round our way had a detached house or a Siamese cat called Matisse. The girls at Lady Margaret's School didn't get pregnant. Why? What was magic about their wombs? They seemed to like sex a lot more than the Enfield and Essex girls, but it was the girls from round our way who vanished from lessons with swollen bellies. How can the posh girls be doing it more and be less at risk? The answer was the same then as it is for those adult women today, all these years later. Confidence. Feeling you have a right to speak and be heard. Class is a real gag – I mean that it's both a joke and a mouth-blocker. Abigail and her friends could hold a condom packet aloft and holler:

'Right, stick this on your todger and we're good to roger!'

And the boy, bemused but eager, would obey.

Girls from round our way would be sheepish, maybe not have the facts, maybe not have the gall to say what they want, what should happen. Lower class means lower volume. You have to be taught to shout. Being near Abigail meant being close to a portal that was hidden from working-class boys: the secret door into middle-classness. There is a key, of course, a key anyone can use, so long as you can find it in the dark. To pick up that key you must go through comprehensive school invisible, even being bullied, and then live like a hermit, digging through A-levels with your nails, despite the fact that no one in your family reads, has fancy books or ever went to uni. The chances of grasping the portal key in those conditions, with that as your background, are very low. Check the statistics if you don't believe me. Yeah, OK, I got lucky three years later, but for now – Abigail was the sweet wind from a mountain we could never ascend. Even though she was 'well fit' – and any one of us would have loved to shag her – it really wasn't sexual. To be honest, if she'd been an interesting, posh boy-nerd, the effect would have been the same, socially speaking. But she wasn't a boy. My God, she was not a boy! We were a generation where the grunge look became fashionable for both girls and boys – being skinny, looking dirty. Small boobs were all the rage – Kate Moss riding high. Abi was not like this. She was voluptuous and loud, voluminous! I even once wrote her a letter addressed like this:

'To Abigail – the firm-buttocked stunner!' Actually on the envelope.

She had found it funny, and so had her dad. Imagine writing to a girl round my way like that.

'What's that supposed to mean? I'm not a slag!'

We spent the afternoon and sunset cooking marshmallows and telling funny stories. It was clear she was here for Steve. But before we went to bed, she made a suggestion.

'Why don't you and Malcolm take turns giving me a massage?'

'Huh?'

'Just back and shoulder.'

Looking back now, it was a weird afternoon. If we had been twenty-six instead of sixteen, we probably would have broken into some morally corrupt orgy. But instead we calmly took turns giving Abigail muscle rubs. She lay face-down, unclipped her bra and looked serene – genuine spa face, nothing erotic for her, at least that she betrayed. It's trickier for an adolescent boy to hide arousal, and I *wish* I could report the same clean mind for myself, but give me a break: I was a sweaty virgin massaging a girl, astride her bum, exactly as one would ride a horse. I tried everything to stay neutral: thinking of football, my nan naked, of my pets dying in the road – nothing worked. My boner jutted humiliatingly from my body like a Dalek's arm. Not being able to masturbate was like fasting in a patisserie. I ran into the woods to 'collect kindling' as soon as the massage was complete.

Later that night it got much worse.

Me and Malcolm were trying to fall asleep in the darkness with the sounds of Steve and Abigail snogging in the middle of us, that repetitive squelchy kissing sound that we're all used to now thanks to reality TV programmes with lapel microphones. The sound of white glue being stirred with a stick. After thirty minutes' close-quarters petting, a full moon hit the side of the tent and broadcast to me the outline of the lovers. Abigail and Steve had no idea I was following their porno in silhouette. I found out later that me and Malcolm were both wanking in clockwork synchrony with the paramours.

Things heated up, and Abigail disappeared under Steve's sleeping bag, slowly moving down over his belly. His sleeping bag looked like when a snake tries to swallow a deer, a mass moving downwards. Steve's head was frozen in anticipation, backlit by the moonlight. And that's when the Chin of Ecstasy happened. The moment Abigail tugged down his boxers and made Steve's day, his head spasmed off the pillow and jutted his chin at forty-five degrees. It honestly looked like Bruce Forsyth was getting sucked off. The tableau of Steve's massive chin pointing towards the moon meant he would be called Chin of Ecstasy for some years afterwards.

'You don't need friends in life, boy – just drinking partners. Contacts. Nothing else.'

Anything stronger might fall foul of rule number 4. *Never rely on anyone. They* will *let you down.*

Dad did have the odd friend over the years, but even with my detailed recall I can only think of a few.

There was Bob Fitch. A short, pervy-looking man – bald too. He had a fiery relationship with a taller, larger, blonde lady who looked like 'Diana fucking Dors', or Gemma Collins for younger readers. I'll never forget Bob coming round one night and showing my dad his balls in our kitchen. Bob had argued with his girlfriend and she'd kicked him in the nuts so hard that his knackers had turned black.

'Fucking hell, Bob. Get down Whipps Cross now!' (That was the hospital near Woodford Green.)

Then there was Roger and his wife Gay. That was Dad's diving friend with fuzzy hair and gaping smile. Inoffensive.

There was William Kenton. He was a mystery friend. Like a recurring offstage character in a soap opera, he was referred to but never seen. He was vaguely connected to Dad's metal-work and drifted out of our story with a few Fucks and Cunts one year after a query over an invoice.

My dad was close to my Mauritian uncle, Uncle Norbert, who was married to my mum's sister Nicola. They went on fishing trips together. When my dad died, Norbert was the only one who went to see the open casket at the funeral home.

'I don't want to see him like that, Mum,' I had said.

'It's part of Mauritian culture. They visit the dead before they bury them.'

Norbert went and paid his respects. I can't decide if it was cowardly of me to refuse. Should I have gone and said good-bye? When my beloved Tonkinese cat Wayne died in 2015, I did go and visit him one last time at the vets. I didn't find the body cold and disturbing. I actually found it really comfort-ing to have a little sob and bid farewell. Maybe that's what visiting Dad would have been like. I've often wondered. I still can't shake the irrational thought that had I gone to visit him post-mortem, he'd have sat bolt upright and said: 'Wanker Kane, looking at a corpse. Prat.'

Later on, when I was in my twenties, Mum and Dad formed a friendship with Paul and Janet Phipps from Loughton. It was an uneasy alliance, and whenever I dropped in for a Sunday lunch there was sure to be beef, not just on the plate, but from the night before, related in some way to the restaur-ant's final bill.

Paul Phipps had started off like my dad – an Essex wide-boy who fell into a decent living with first vents and then air con. The difference was, Paul got lucky. He got into the office air-con boom of the 1980s and 1990s. He ended up with one of the most profitable firms in the south-east.

'King of Essex, i'n he? Typical, boy. I picked the dying trade, he picked the one full of wedge. The Kane Curse – it'll follow you through your whole life.'

Paul Phipps was a lean man with slicked-back silver hair and the radiant year-round tan of the working-class wealthy. He would often throw wildly expensive recommendations at my dad: 'Try the Seychelles, Dave. Me and Janet loved it.'

And then Dad, later, at home: 'Fucking Seychelles! Cunt! Menorca is rip-off enough. He's taking the piss out of me, Julie.'

'To them it's nothing, Dave,' my mum would put in, accidentally making it worse. 'Like buying a cup of tea to them.'

The Phippses also had a mockingly large mansion in Loughton, part of my old man's former Essex Kingdom, in which he would have loved to be able to afford to live.

'Detached an' all. Imagine, boy. No fucker either side of you. Free. And we've got the cunt Black.' Hilda Black was our nosy, fat, pensioner neighbour who spent her days hanging off her front garden gate like a meat bauble, smoking and spitting venom about anyone who dared to do better than her. Which was everyone who could move. Somehow, though, she had control of the gossip telegraph. Dad hated her. He hated that we were only semi-detached, that we were joined to Hilda Black.

'The fucking Phipps mansion . . .' and the cherry on the cake of jealousy, their eldest son Kyle: '. . . he's gone into the City, boy. Stockbroker. Why can't you do something like that? Obscene wedge . . .'

Becoming a stockbroker was the standard cash route out of our ghetto. Most Essex mansions you drove past back then housed some sort of wheeler-dealer who worked in the Bank area or Fenchurch Street. Crass cockney alpha males in two-grand suits and coke bogeys hanging from their noses. They would fill Liverpool Street Station on Friday nights, snogging Debbies and Helens by the Burger King, shouting into mobile phones and pissing against shop windows in full view of CCTV. They were like football fans in Prada.

Kyle Phipps made as much in one Christmas bonus as I could earn in a decade. He coined well over two million a year, and drove a glistening new Ferrari.

'Fucking Ferrari, boy!'

At the time, I was driving a Corsa. I would never be Kyle Phipps — you could see it in Dad's face.

'Paul won't die on the floor of a boiler room'— one of my dad's favourite death fantasies — 'Kyle'll take care of them when they're older. Paul could retire now if he wanted.'

'Rolling in it,' Mum would put in.

'Like a dog in fox piss,' Dad added.

I've never understood working-class comparisons where the thing people want is something no one would want. 'A pig in shit' is another. Who wants to be covered in shit? 'The girls were round him like flies on a turd' — surely it should be flies on a cake?

This was the root of the conflict between Paul Phipps and my dad. Paul had the money, the happiness, the peace of mind — but, worst of all, he didn't share it around: *a tight gnat's arsehole.*

'They split the bill down the fucking middle every time,' said Dad one Sunday, venting like a New York manhole cover in winter. 'Minted — Imelda Marcos — and the fucker rinses us every week.'

'He doesn't do the driving, she does,' Mum put in, like Janet was a bitch for being able to drive. The smug cow with her licence! What Mum meant was, the Phipps were crafty – Janet would do the journey, freeing up Paul to guzzle down premium liquid like Kyle's Ferrari at Epping New Road services.

'Yeah,' exploded Dad. 'She fucking motors it, all right; then he does the bill for double brandies, cheeky cunt!'

'Dave!'

'What? He is!'

'It's true,' said Mum, philosophically.

In the Warren Wood, Phipps had been nicknamed 'Paul Pockets', because he was always in the loo when it was his round. Before that, and I can't imagine why, he was known as 'Paul Sauna'.

A note about that 'Kane Curse'.

Dad fully believed that a curse followed around all those who bore our name. From the tiniest incidents to the largest risks, the mark of Kane was pernicious and persistent. If, for example, we bought an electrical item, it would be the only one in the whole of Argos with a vital part missing from its box. Meals would arrive cold from a restaurant kitchen. All car journeys would begin in a freakish delay.

'Two minutes earlier, we'd have missed the crash – now we're stuck in it. Fuck! The Curse, boy. The Curse.'

Any big job my dad estimated for, he would be pipped at the post by another contractor. My dad went through life waiting for the Curse to strike him down.

'The Curse. Get used to it, Wanker Kane!'

As atheist and down-to-earth as Dad was, it seems

sometimes it's just easier to blame something bigger and more mystical than yourself.

Apart from this compact list of oddball friends, Dad had boiled his network down to 'drinking partners', manly fixtures who spent their lives perched on tired bar stools, his mates whenever he went to the Warren Wood or the Izaak Walton. Dad would always arrive at the Warren with his two plates of home-made snacks covered in foil – rollmops and cheese cubes – which he would place on the bar, his gift to the drinking team. Some of the men were just broken old hard-workers like him, roaring into the bleakness of middle age, treating Monday like an enemy to be punched. In the Warren you also got a few gangsters and dodgy types, now suspiciously retired with lots of liquid capital. The crooks were always happier and more lively than the honest men.

Anyway, maybe it's good that Dad inadvertently trained me in self-reliant friendship. Even at age eleven, when the moment of my leap into senior school arrived, I was ready to fly friendless if need be. True, I had a brother but, although we're only two years eight months apart, and we apparently have 50 per cent DNA in common, we shared not one common trait. I was outgoing, indoorsy and cerebral. I liked intricately involved games with convoluted characters and precise family trees, and acting things out in dramatic voices. My brother was shy, loved animals, trees and plants, and was not into boring books like me – he was musical, instinctive and wild. We played, but we fought more. I was vile to him, as was my duty as his older brother, but I regret it now. I was always much closer to Michael Delaney than I was to my brother. It's part of the reason I doubt I'll have a second child myself. Lots of people say this: 'Have a second . . . they'll play together.' But it's not guaranteed, is it? Plus, I could end up with two mental balls of energy stalking me around the house. Fuck that. One is enough. Half would be enough – a torso I could love and dote on, but with no noisy mouth. Is it wrong I just wrote that?

8.

You'll Be All Right, You're Clever . . .

I don't know how lucky it was to be born what Dad called
'bright'. The problem with a comprehensive school in a
poorer borough is what to do with that 'bright' brain. Yes, fair
Guardian readers, the ideal would be to go to a lovely, properly comprehensive school and naturally rise to the top.
Sadly, that model of progress only exists in the mind of do-
gooding bells who have no idea what working-class teenage
existence is really like. That 'comprehensive' system doesn't
cater for shallow, attention-loving freaks like me. Let's be
really clear to all the Pollyannas who say:

'Comprehensives are the fairest for all, Tom. I mean,
we've sent Lucian and Oliver to our Notting Hill comprehensive and it's fantastic!'

Yes, it's just something well-off people say, or lucky people
who pinballed through the system. They say it to feel better
about our fraudulent education structure, which *is* pegged to
wealth. Face it: the better your income, then the bigger your
house, the nicer your area, and with this the higher the quality
of your local comprehensive. It's not a bloody 'comprehensive'
system at all. It's a 'how posh an area can you afford to live in'
system. It's unfair as fuck. The social advantages or problems
of the surrounding area enter the school. The two things are
inseparable – but bless you for pretending they aren't.

Enfield had one saving grace, though. Yes, most of it is rougher than the first draft of a Brexit negotiation, but it had one nice corner: Enfield Chase. If you could get into the Church School, there might be a few posh kids there to take the heat – for to be posh was the greatest crime of all. Much worse than being clever – although cleverness was also a fast track to black and blue body parts. The schools in the rest of Enfield – Bullsmead, St Alban, Edmonton Grammar (not a bloody grammar) – were hell on earth. You'd be smoking weed minimum by the time you were thirteen, and if you weren't, your arms would be sore with the punishment you got for not 'being cool'.

So, to my school: I want to state (pardon the pun) quite clearly that my school was a good school. In fact, it was one of the best in Enfield. If you told people you were at the Church School, you got an 'Ooooh' and they would press their noses up, as though you were aristocracy. But Church was still crap for me, and the highly strung boys and girls like me.

At primary school I had always been one of the brightest, maybe the cleverest in language and creative lessons, but I was afflicted with a shallow need to show off, and an even greater love of not being repeatedly punched. I read comedian Robin Ince's brilliant book recently in which he discusses how most people who go into comedy are younger brothers and sisters. Most people who learn to be funny, show off and survive punches are the smallest or youngest. Well, not me. But I was born in August. I was always the youngest in my year. Maybe that's what caused my extrovert/please-don't-kick-me genes to express themselves. Survival and stand-up are linked. It's not coincidence bad gigs are called death. You must survive, and in a working-class borough, cleverness won't do it.

Up till I was eleven, this was not a problem. Adults dictated the rules. Teachers at primary reward the well-behaved, and this is generally backed up in the playground by prefects, then at the gates by parents. But as soon as the hormones kick in and peers take over, it changes; and from the first day of comprehensive school, I knew I was in the deepest shit. A decision had to be made in my first year of secondary, year seven as it's now called. Calling it year seven makes no sense. It implies continuity with year six, the final year of primary. That's like saying your all-inclusive holiday has continuity with your first day serving in the army. It's year one. It's the first year of secondary school. It's hell. And the choice I had to make came fiercely upon me: stick to my academic guns and soar in History, Literature and Arts subjects – or cross the playground and become jester to the popular kids, the tearaway bad boys who got all the girls and none of the punches. You might think: why not do both? Sadly, the entry card to the opposite side of the school playground is lack of academic achievement. Once we were 'streamed' into sets . . . well, God help you if you were in set 1a for Maths. What kind of 'pussy-denying' loser correctly executes a quadratic equation?

There's no doubt that a school being fully comprehensive is infinitely kinder than what happened to my parents, my wife, my brother-in-law and most people I know from Kent/Trafford/Southend: fail an exam and get dumped into the bin of a Secondary Modern. I don't come from stock who passed their eleven-plus. It is awful to tell a child at eleven that they have failed at education and they must wear a sort of *Handmaid's Tale* dunce cap for the next six years. Plus, nearly all the evidence suggests that even when bright kids from poor families *do* pass an eleven-plus, it's those from the stable and better-off poorer families, meaning grammars do nothing to balance social inequality.

All this may be true, but I can only tell you that when you place a lively adolescent child in a melting pot of temperaments and abilities, no matter how clever he or she is, the number-one mission becomes *survival*, not being really good at Shakespeare or trigonometry. In fact, if you dare to excel in any such subjects your life will be a living hell of arm punches and being flobbed on. You will spend every 3 p.m. scrubbing dried spittle and chalked-on swearwords from your blue blazer. You will join the No Cocks during PE, or 'Games' as it was misnamed, and your life will be a testosterone-driven hell. I plummeted from being a very bright and forward eleven-year-old to a naughty rogue jester with no powers of concentration. But I didn't care, the hard kids liked me, and the girls thought I was funny. The learning part of my education went on pause for six years. I walked away from that place with one nugget of learning: the oxbow lake. (Google it.)

My mum worked hard to get me into Church. We researched it together, and I supported the choice. I can still feel that fuzzy adventure feeling in my belly as I chose my big school. Dad was useless in the process. Any appeal for advice led to a dramatic story about his own shit Secondary Modern and what a waste of time his education was.

'What do you think, Dad? Church School gets the best results.'

'Don't ask me, boy.' He was in a melancholy, put-upon

mood. 'I'm just a wanker builder. I left school when I was fourteen, boy.'

He wasn't, though. He was a highly skilled sheet-metal worker and thermal-insulation engineer.

'OK.'

'My school, boy. Waste of my time. I was shit at everything. In one lesson I couldn't spell *phosphorous* – so do you know what the teacher did?'

'No.'

'He wrote it on my trousers, in chalk, on the arse, then took me to the front of the class and caned me until the chalk disappeared.'

My God. I wonder if this one was true. How did that teacher connect arse-thwacking with absorption of spelling? My dad's handwriting was like small, ground down teeth. Written language came out of him like stones from a kidney. It was as though he detested it – the medium of an elite class who'd rejected him.

'You're clever. You'll be all right, boy.' A rare compliment, and that was it – admin was passed back to my mother.

At first – and even though I was only eleven, I had looked into it – I wanted to push myself and try the entrance exam for Latymer,* a sort of special school for clever-clog show-offs. It's weird that one of the best schools in the UK should be not just in shitty Enfield but in the shittiest part of Enfield – Edmonton, a stabby, grey place where we would sometimes shop as kids. Architecturally, I never recovered

* The Latymer School is a selective, mixed grammar school in Edmonton, established in 1624 by Edward Latymer. According to league tables, Latymer is one of the top state schools in England.

from Edmonton Green, the word 'Green' bled of all meaning by the grey, sick-coloured buildings of a place that was like the set for a zombie movie. Mum and I were in the process of going through with the Latymer application when she was put off . . . by none other than the Cheese Lady at the supermarket. Yes, in one of the weirder spins of life's wheel, the woman in charge of cold meats and dairy fancies at our local shop decided my educational fate.

Cheese Lady was a large woman called Lesley. She was also the founder of the local amateur dramatics group the Lyceum Players, and responsible for my first foray into theatre. When I was ten she gave me a part in a local panto where I played a doomed giant spider king, who got massive laughs from an extended death-throes scene. I can still remember the lines:

I'm vile and evil, twisted and terse
You've heard of King Richard the Third,
   well I'm worse!

Then I got stabbed, and began my laugh-harvesting writhes.

When I was a toddler, Cheese Lady Lesley would surreptitiously hand me cubes of cheese, which I sucked on as I was pushed around the supermarket in my buggy. She gained the nickname Cheese Lady, and it stuck to her like Brie to a blanket. Over the years, she and my mum formed a sort of friendship, so naturally my mum knew that Cheese Lady's very camp dancer son, Mickey, had gone to Latymer. She asked her about it.

'I wouldn't recommend it, Julie,' Cheese Lady warned, handing Mum a chunk of Cheddar. 'It's a pressure school.

Mickey has struggled with it.' I can't summon one memory of Mickey where he is not in lilac leg warmers and counting in eights.

And that was that. There was no way I would be a Latymerian. 'Pressure school' sounded terrifying to both me and my mum. I don't remember Dad commenting, but surely Pressure, Stress and Struggle were well up his street – all the ingredients that the Curse loved. We could have harnessed its power, used the Force. Thinking now about Latymer School, it's probably exactly what the precocious eleven-year-old me needed: a hamster wheel to run on for six years. But in the end it was Cheese Lady's fully matured warning that sealed my scholastic fate. I would go to the next best thing Enfield had, the Church School. And Cheese Lady had one last favour to impart – a letter from her husband that would get me into Church.

'My Peter knows some of the board. It's a religious school, selective. He'll write you a recommendation,' she said, pushing forward a small plate of chive-infused Red Leicester.

Yes. I was to become a Godder. All Church kids were known as Godders, with good reason: Communion morning and afternoon, plus assemblies. I was to endure five years of having pointless and intense RE pushed into my rationalist head. Church was a better school than most others in Enfield, so I joined the Bald Thimble gang and would leave at sixteen not properly knowing who Jane Austen or Oscar Wilde were, and without having been touched by a girl.

When I try to remember my schooldays, no connected stories come back, just flashes and set pieces. I have more joined-up memories of being nine than I do of being fourteen. Eleven to sixteen years of age should be when you change the most, and most profoundly, but I can honestly say it was the most I've ever stagnated. OK, my body changed a bit (not frigging enough). I grew . . . a bit – but overall I was in stasis, in a holding pattern over the runway of my manhood. You see it in nature sometimes. If the conditions are wrong, an animal stops growing, arrests its development, or changes gender. Actually, am I thinking of *Jurassic Park*? Anyway, if the environment is hostile enough, a creature simply waits it out.

My secondary education was more like a medical procedure, something painful to be got over with. I didn't know it then, but for me there was only one way I could learn or achieve anything: on my own. Self-driven. One of Dad's cardinal rules had evidently penetrated my cerebrum. I had to become a *self*-teacher – the proper word is *autodidact*.

'No one will do anything for you, boy. If you want something done, do it yourself.'

It sounds as bleak as his other rules, but it could be useful. Languages, books – they have fixed components, grammar and structure, and if I just went at them with enough solo dedication they could be solved. But that came later. My education would begin, it turned out, when I turned twenty-one. At school I was just uninspired.

For example: we only learned German. No matter which teacher, no boring German verb went into *mein Kopf*. I could not be engaged on the robotic, unromantic language. Yet when I found out Dad was taking us to Spain on holiday, I began teaching myself Spanish from a library book with cassettes. By the time we went to Menorca that summer, I was having basic conversations with hotel staff. But when I went to Bonn, Germany, with the school, I could barely conjure a

Guten Tag or a *Fick mein Arschloch* (don't google that one). In the end my mum came into the school and asked my head of year whether I might take on Spanish as an additional language. He said no. *Gracias*, motherfucker. *Hijo de puta*.

Your birth is the best predictor of where you'll end up. Sadly, at the time of writing, this is even more solidly true than ever. If your mum and dad are both ground-down manual labourers, if there are no books in the house, you'll probably end up on a building site or, worse, doing nothing. Gordon Mellor from Church School comes to mind. He came from the toughest family. Particularly prominent in my mind is the day his elder brother, who had already left, sneaked into school and pissed against the headmaster's office while the current year's thugs cheered him on. I don't remember having one proper conversation with Gordy Mellor in the five years we shared a form class in Hamble House, yet he's there on the edge of every memory: pacing, spitting, smoking. Gordy wasn't as enthusiastic as Redman and Landor in punching people on the arm for no reason, but he was without doubt the hardest in the school. He was wild, angry, remedial in every subject and amazing at rugby. He could do the longest spit dangle, managing to get the flob from his mouth to his non-regulation shoes before sucking it back up like a cockney running a Dyson over jellied eels. Gordy knew about ganja, girls and good cars. He wore glasses but he didn't give a fuck about anything. Once he had a tussle with a Chemistry teacher and found himself suspended, but still he bounced back. I think he got away with more because of his rugby skills. Church needed him – we were county champions.

I honestly believed Gordy was immortal. He was the boss, the daddy of our year. I found out that not long after we all left, however, Gordy got into dealing, then using. And it was the drug my generation had roundly rejected. *No one* did heroin. No one *knew anyone* who did heroin. That was for people's dads and old losers down the pub with greasy hair who had got addicted before the powerful television campaigns in the late 1980s had terrified me and my peers.

'At first you'll be sick, but then you'll come back for more . . .' No thanks, Heroin.

But for some reason, Gordy Mellor – one of the most dangerously alive people I have ever known, fell hard for the golden-brown goddess. He ended up living in Germany for a bit when things got hot, then, aged twenty-five, hanged himself in an apartment somewhere in Kent. Whether it was debt, the old bill or addiction I do not know, but Gordy Mellor went to the earth young. Where you're born, and who you're born to, matters.

Rugby stalked me from toddlerhood to age sixteen. As well as all the other crushingly manly things Dad was good at – bodybuilding, metal mastering, fighting and meat cooking – he had also played semi-professional rugby for Essex County. Rugby Union was the only sport we ever had on the television.

'Not football, boy. That ain't a man's sport.'

'Everyone at Church wants to play more football,' I said, informing Dad of the protests from younger boys about the absence of soccer.

'Ain't a real sport. Bunch of turd burglars kicking a ball about and pretending to be injured. Put them on the rugby pitch, they'll last five minutes. Girls.'

Some people think of rugby as posh but to my dad it was

a purer, more masculine sport – closer to the ultimate game, which was boxing. Rugby is football with the bullshit removed. No football on in my house, ever. I have grown up into a football illiterate. At school, I parroted the things my dad said and enjoyed saying them. Even the bullies found it hard to argue with.

'Oi, Roger Rabbit,' shouted Redman (RR was my nickname until my teeth were corrected), 'do you support Arsenal or Tottenham?' His fist was hovering, ready for the incorrect answer. There was no correct answer to his question: he supported West Ham.

'My old man doesn't watch either. Football's not violent enough for him. We watch rugby.'

I still got punched, but there was no fire behind the blow that day.

Football was a once-a-term treat. Every other lesson on that accursed pitch was Rugby Union. Having a football-hating, rugby-loving dad was just one of the crueller ironies of my schooldays. I struggle to fully describe the hell of being an undeveloped eleven-year-old string-bean of a boy walking out in icy mud towards his first session of licensed kicking-in-the-face. That's all rugby was to me: diplomatic immunity for the school thugs. A game where you were allowed, encouraged even, by Mr Bloom, to throw each other into the filth, trip one another up and then, one day, learn a move called the face-off. Yes. Smashing your open palm into another boy's face.

Games became something to wiggle out of. I prayed for Spanish flu, amputation even.

Dad wasn't much help.

'When I played rugby at school, boy, I didn't need to run

a try. I just picked up the ball and walked with it. Slowly an' all – just looking at the other lads, daring them to touch me.'

I struggled to reconcile the two school dads in my head. One a rugby god, the other a victim having *Phosphorous* beaten off his buttocks.

'I was captain in the end.'

Dad had been a rugby gladiator but I was a piece of crispy bacon trodden into the grass. At the start of my third year at Church, things got worse. Mr Bloom gave us official playing positions. I was now a flanker. Have you any idea of the fate of someone with buck teeth whose primary sport role rhymes with wanker? But even that social damnation was nothing compared to the day I was given my dad's old rugby boots. On my fourteenth birthday, Dad produced a musty parcel from the loft.

'I've been waiting for this day, boy,' he said, filling up with a mixture of fatherly pride and a reliving of his own glory days. This was incongruous. Tender movie-dad language from my father. It disturbed me. Robin Williams mixed with Ray Winstone. Like seeing your nan in a bikini – possible, but not right.

'Fucking open it then, Melon Head!'

Ah – that was more like it. As a nickname, Melon Head ran from when I was twelve to about fifteen. I had – still have – an unsightly, bulging cranium. No hats fit me. When I graduated from university I had to have my mortar board specially adjusted.

I unwrapped the brown paper and opened a shabby red box. Inside were a pair of professional rugby boots: black and understated, confident in their low-key menace, like Mike Tyson's shorts. They were used and ancient and potentially shame-making.

'Wow. Thanks, Dad.' Did my lip quiver?

'These have stamped on some fucking faces, boy, I tell you,' he said warmly, as though remembering a fine meal in a nice hotel.

I suppose it was sweet, really; a nurturing fatherly thing, passing me the rugby boots with which he had once dominated the playing fields of Essex. But these leathery relics looked every day of their thirty years. They looked like war shoes – pieces of fabric found in a trench that had belonged to a gunner called Arthur.

'I could have climbed the peak of Everest in these, boy, and still knocked out that cunt Edmund Hillary when I got there.' I didn't dare point out my dad would have been a child when Hillary had reached that summit. I hardly ever dared correct my dad. If I did I would get a repeat performance of the 'Yeah, that's right, take the piss, I'm just the thick wanker builder' routine. Sometimes, when I was in my twenties, I would test the water, see if he was softening with the advancing years. He wasn't. He never did. One evening Dad had managed to get hold of some young chicken – poussin (*poo-sahn*) – for dinner. He was a little tipsy and taking great pleasure in educating me.

'*Poisson*, boy! That's what we're having. They're called *poisson*!' He was saying *pwa-sohn* – relishing the hardness of the *pwa* – and perhaps I should have my kept my ungrateful mouth shut. Who cares that *poisson* actually means fish? What difference did it make? Dad was happy. But out of my show-off gob came:

'I think *poisson* means fish?'

'No, boy – butcher told me. It's a baby chicken. *Poisson! Poisson!*' *Pwa! Pwa!*

I got my French dictionary and showed him. *Poisson* was fish; he meant *poussin. Poo. Poo.*

'That's right, boy – I'm just the fucking idiot who *buys* the meat . . .' and that was the end of that meal's atmosphere.

Worse still was when we were watching *Who Wants to be a Millionaire?* I was at least twenty-five by then, but age makes no difference when you are eternally 'boy' in your dad's presence.

The question slid out of Chris Tarrant's mouth like liver from a jar:

'California borders how many other US states: one, two, three, or four?'

My dad had been to the USA several times. He'd been to California with my auntie Brenda and stayed there for weeks. This was his question. My brother and I looked to Dad. He was already forward in his seat:

'Easy. Two. I even know what they are: Nevada and Oregon, boy. Vegas and Portland – been to both.'

The contestant guessed three.

'Hahahaha. Silly cunt. It's two. I've been!' Dad was loving it.

Then Chris Tarrant: 'Three is correct. You've got yourself £16,000.'

There wasn't even a moment of self-doubt. 'It's wrong. It's fucking wrong! Call ITV. It's two! I've been there!' Dad was shouting so loud I missed Tarrant listing the three states.

'It must be three, Dad.'

'Shut up, boy. It's two. It's wrong.'

I went to the shelf and pulled down the atlas. I was flicking towards North America when I saw the thunder go across Dad's face. He angled his head away from the book, and this time I left it. He would go to his grave denying that Arizona also borders California.

My dad was right about everything. How could I tell him his old rugby boots were unwearable?

I had hoped to bring the execrable footwear out of my sports bag unnoticed; a vain longing. My sports bag was enough on its own to draw unwanted attention. Both my mum and I are over-packers. I easily had the biggest school-bag in my year. The brand was 'Head'. Early on, someone had written the word 'Dick' in Tipp-Ex above it. My bag was so big that the bullies once emptied it out and made me get in. I fitted. Easily.

I lifted Dad's old rugby boots out of my Head bag and tried to slip them on discreetly but within seconds I heard Mark Spein's whiny voice and saw his manically pointing finger.

'Haha – what the fuck are those?'

'Pikey cunt!' Keiron Gray shouted.

'Bobby's boots!' someone else put in. It was a reference to a TV series. A poor kid from a council estate gets a beaten-up pair of football boots which turn out to be magic. He becomes the lead scorer for his school. It was a twee, awful programme that we all mocked, and I was now styled as its lead character.

'Bobby's boots!' many others said, laughing. The name stuck. For a whole term I didn't just get pushed over and stamped on. I got pushed over and stamped on wearing 'Bobby's boots'.

I can't overstate the importance of the footwear hierarchy in the life of a teenage boy. Trainers were, and still are, currency. Treads, creps – the slang changes but the pressure remains the same. If posh boys greet each other they take in each other's accents or shirts or ask about schooling. Working-class boys look straight at each other's feet. It's not a look up and down, it's just a look down. *Nike Huaraches? This guy has some dollar* . . . etc. My proudest changing-room moment came after I had been to Florida for fourteen nights and managed to spend not one cent of my holiday money. I waited until the final day, then went to a mall and bought Reebok Pumps for $120. They were so new you couldn't even get them in the UK. Boys actually fell back in stunned admiration as I unveiled my white leather grails. Even Redman and Landor, who were quite capable of flicking ink at them and ruining them, just looked on from a few metres, like put-out alpha males in a David Attenborough film.

'All that money on a pair of fucking trainers. Disgusting,' Dad had said, way too loudly, in the American sports shop.

'It's his money, Dave.'

It had been an easy holiday on which to save my spending money.

The 1990s was the decade when the first batch of working-class Brits could afford a Florida holiday. If you came back to school in September having been, you joined an elite who knew what Disney was really like. I'd spent the previous few years ogling Steven Epsom's family pics of Florida. His dad in a silly Donald Duck hat, his mum waving and queuing for Thunder Mountain; all five of his family holding chicken wings aloft and saluting the camera in some sort of Tudor-themed restaurant, cheeks pink from sun-kissed adventure. It didn't matter if you were fourteen and too old for Disney. It wasn't about age, it was about saying you had the Disney tag, that you'd been to the States, worn baseball caps, tasted burgers, been to a mall, seen the actual *Jaws* shark, seen *ET* – you had touched the American Dream and had fries with it. That's what it meant to a teenager; and you had the smell of it on you when you returned to school.

My dad's announcement that *we* were going to Florida came when I was fourteen, and there was a massive giddy high followed by sinking despair, all within the space of ten minutes. We were going to Florida, but we were going the Dave Kane way.

'I'm paying, I'm saying, boy.'

'Cool, Dad.'

The factor that had tipped my dad over the edge into paying out for family transatlantic travel was that Auntie Brenda, his alcoholic sister, she of the blonde flowing locks and white sneakers, had moved there from California. She lived opposite some beautiful apartments on a paradise beach – and could get decent prices on a three-bed condo for the fortnight.

'Right. Good news, boys. We're going to Florida.'

James punched the air, and we actually hugged. It's one of the few times I can remember showing my brother affection rather than fists or mind games. Mum looked on warmly but the smile looked a little forced. I dropped into a half smile. I sensed the kicker, or – should I use rugby lingo? – the conversion.

'Brenda's moved out there – we're gonna stay opposite. Beach's like the fucking Bounty advert, boy.'

(The Bounty advert was the gold standard for beach comparison. If you haven't seen it, it's basically two minutes of a model sucking off a chocolate bar on a Formentera beach.)

'The sand looks like the *inside* of a bloody Bounty bar . . .'

'Turquoise sea!' my mum put in.

'Absolute fucking heaven. Nothing to do but roast every day, and feast every night.'

My first alarm bell rang. Roast every day . . . but . . . but . . . How would we sunbathe *every* day? Maybe a couple – everyone likes the beach. Well, mums and dads do. That's fine. But no need to roast at Disney.

All I managed was: 'How far is Brenda from Disney?'

'Disney!' Dad burst out laughing. 'Fuck off! You winding me up? Queuing like wankers? Mugs? No way.'

'But . . . how far *are* we from Disney?' I felt myself whitening – plans to cab it to Disney on my own forming vaguely in my mind.

'Seven hours. No chance, boy. Further than Edinburgh to Devon . . . Fucking hell, Julie – you hearing this? Ungrateful little shit.'

'Are we gonna meet Donald Duck?' asked my eleven-year-old brother James.

I suppose it does sound a bit ungrateful. I was lucky to be going on holiday at all. Many at my school never went on holiday; didn't have a dad. The problem was we were flying to the actual place where Disney was, and not going – on purpose. Torture. Like sending someone on the Atkins diet into Greggs and expecting them to smile about how lucky they are to buy lunch at all.

'Boys. Listen. We are going to paradise. Sand like baking soda. Roasting fucking hot every day. Not a single fucking tourist. Not one. Imagine that. Unspoilt. Disney? Pah! You got any idea what that would be like? The queues. Hours of it – and every fucker in there. Packed with gullible wankers being ripped off. It's what the peasants do. We're going to the real Florida – not the rip-off wanker bit.'

'Pensacola,' said my mum.

It sounded like a lame drink from Costco.

'Steaks, catfish, cocktails – and 90 degrees of heat every fucking day. Bliss,' said Dad.

'Your dad works hard, Russ.'

It was true. Poor Dad had worked his knackers off every day, 6 a.m. to 6 p.m., crawling around in boiler rooms, shards of fibreglass raining down on him as he fitted insulation on pipes. He needed sunshine on his tired bones. I was lucky to be seeing America. I should keep my mouth shut and go.

And that's what I did. We flew to Orlando, then got an internal flight to Pensacola. Fort Walton was indeed a stunning powdery beach with lukewarm crystalline waters. It was also the most boring holiday of my entire life. I turned fifteen when I was there (just prior to the stripper disaster party). Within twenty-four hours teenage petulance kicked in and I resolved to spend the fourteen days watching American cable (which, to be fair, I loved). Of course, James and I played on the beach a bit. We also got to meet our Hitler Youth-blond American family. There are some good memories but the overriding sensation was poisonous boredom.

On the day of my birthday, Auntie Brenda bought us a fantastic coffee and chocolate cake, but she spoiled the day by drinking neat vodka and ice from 9 a.m. and becoming offensive by 10.30. Dad drove us to the mall to get some food and beers for the beach, and on the drive back we could hear the sound of cans being surreptitiously opened in the back. Brenda couldn't even make it back to Fort Walton without guzzling. I could see the hairs on my dad's neck prickling with suppressed temper but his sister was one person he didn't shout at.

We had an awkward lunch in the apartment, then went to the beach. Brenda by now was completely sunk in booze; she was a cotton-wool pad soaked in ethanol. She wore obscenely small shorts, white sneakers, a yellow T-shirt and a green poker-player visor. Her long blonde locks blew around in the Gulf of Mexico breeze. She looked like someone's grandma had taken meth and dressed as a Disney character. I was used to my nan, my mum's mum, and I naively thought I could have the same fun with Brenda.

'How long have you lived here, Brenda?'

'Forever, Pipsqueak.'

Pipsqueak? I wasn't outraged at all. I was playing, and I thought she was too. 'I would rather be a pipsqueak than a hip-creak.'

Not my finest work but it ignited Brenda. The face thunder rolled in quickly and I knew I'd misjudged her drunken banter skills. 'What did you say? You calling me old, you little shit?'

I doubled down, thinking she'd laugh. 'You are over the hill, Auntie Brenda . . .'

There was no laugh. She sprang like a cat with chilli on its anus and went for me. Physically. I ran around the beach with my auntie Brenda chasing me. At first it looked as though we were playing. People smiled and pointed – look at the young lad with his aunt, frolicking on the beach, but then:

'Come here, you motherfucker!' Parents were covering toddlers' ears. 'I'll kick your butt. I ain't over the hill, you motherfucker!' She picked up a can of beer and threw it at my head. It missed my head by millimetres and landed in the sand, a violent comet of boozy hate. I looked at it and all I could think was: I should be with Mickey Mouse right now.

'You're fucking lucky, motherfucker. I ain't over no hill!' Brenda walked past me, picked up the can and cracked it open. She stood there necking it, breathing hard.

'Go back to the apartment, boy,' said Dad coolly.

The flight back home with my new trainers couldn't come quick enough . . .

That was the last time I saw Auntie Brenda. She came over to the UK once more when I was in my twenties but I missed her. By that time her and my dad's double act had a sombre edge – like Laurel and Hardy's final tour. She was fun, though. Yes, Brenda was a dark, messy, violent, drunken crone of a woman with an evil streak. Yes, she bullied my dad and scared him so much when he was little that he used to piss the bed in fear. But she was also big, brash and American. She seemed freer than us. I prefer to remember her visits when we were younger. *She* was younger, for that matter, and didn't yet look like something that had fallen out of an Egyptian coffin at the British Museum. She came for a two-week stay when I was eight and James was five, and every night at bath-time would run really deep baths for us. The water went past the tap. James and I called these 'American baths' for the rest of our childhood. She also made beans with sugar in. She was a marvel to us – but she was an alcoholic and by the time of my non-Disney Florida holiday, she was lost.

We landed back at the beginning of that September and I couldn't wait to take my pumps into school, all the time pondering how different the previous year had been for me, footwear-wise.

9.

Valentine's Day

The most famous incident from my schooldays is also steeped in masculinity and heroism. I mean famous in its proper sense: Church School, for one day, became known nationwide. It became famous in the horrible, front-of-every-newspaper, 'glad it didn't happen to one of my kids' way. The morning after it happened, we were the front of the *Sun*, the *Mail* and the *Mirror* – and I was within a dog's hair of being one of the headlines.

It was the day before Valentine's Day, always one of the worst days of the school year for boring virgins. It went without saying that I would get no cards whatsoever; it was just a case of waiting to see how many mocking things got left in my desk instead – made-up cards, socks with fake spunk in etc . . . I'd be sending a few items, of course; I always did. Becky, Samantha, Helen – all would receive blank cards. No point in writing in them, as only four boys in my year had brains, and it would be instantly obvious who had written any card in which the words weren't Neanderthal. On Valentine's the year before this shocking day, we had a German girl on exchange: Lottie. Of course, I fell in love with her. She was plain, boring and didn't ever look at me: aphrodisiac to a teenage boy with low self-esteem. Thanks to the dodgy porn tapes going around school, there was the tacit belief that girls from 'Europe' were much more likely to shag you than the fortress-knickers, tea-drinking horrors of our own country.

That year Church School ran a delivery and read-out Valentine's service, carried out by smug sixth-formers. Sixth-formers were a bizarre cult who had their own special section in the Canterbury Wing behind a glass door. You could watch them lounging in their 'common room'. The year before they had been scum just like me, but one summer holiday and they started speaking a bit posher and saying random things like 'badger' and 'tofu', and thinking it was really funny and creative to do so. My poem arrived in the hands of fat, camp seventeen-year-old Gavin Harper, whose acne face looked like my nan's Artex ceiling. It was during the worst of all lessons, Maths, so the atmosphere was already the enemy of romance. Lottie was approached and Harper banged out my poem in a theatrical way to much raucous laughter.

> 'My wonderful from Deutschland,
> My Käse Brot from Bonn,
> Your sexy German accent,
> Really turns me on.'

She went red, and any chances of her ever speaking to me vanished.

Yes, Valentine's Day was always awful. But the year when Church School went famous for the day was the worst ever.

I was fourteen years old. Anyone who knows me will tell you, I'm one of the most punctual people you can meet. But on this particular morning, while building a vertiginous quiff in the bathroom (in a desperate scheme to get Becky

Simpson to notice me), I had spilled bright blue L'Oréal hair gel on my school shirt. It looked like a Smurf had ejaculated on me. The few minutes' delay caused by changing the shirt meant I missed the 191 bus. There would be no time to walk to school so I had to do the unthinkable: ask Dad for a lift – a *favour*! There is a certain type of dad you do not ask for a lift, and my old man was one of them. Any favour he granted would be accompanied with a tirade about sacrifice and tiredness. I wouldn't have been surprised to discover him nailed on a cross, moaning about what a selfless leader he was, absorbing our pain and sin. No, asking Dad for a lift was always a bad move, but on this particular morning, I had no choice.

'For fuck's sake, boy, get in the Merc.'

Not too bad a response.

We drove to Church School in a simmering silence punctuated only by my dad shouting the C-word at any bad drivers who looked female or brown – even being Cypriot was enough to set off his Alf Garnett Stone of Rage.

'Fucking Greek cunt!' We pulled up outside school. 'Right. See you later then, yeah.'

'Thanks, Dad.'

He drove off . . . slowly. I always found it odd that my dad was not a wheelspinner. He had the air of a tyre-screecher, a thrasher, but in the years I lived with him, I only ever saw him pull away elegantly. Chances are, he loved his Merc too much to cane it. The cream 190E disappeared into an Enfield side street like crème fraîche into a stew, and I turned to walk into school . . . but wait, something wasn't right. Maybe if I hadn't been distracted analysing the silverback's motoring, I would have noticed earlier the very odd thing beyond the school gates that morning. Silence. Exactly how late was I, for God's sake? I checked my watch – seven minutes. Yet not a soul could be seen. I walked up the school drive and into the yard. Still no one. Now that made things really eerie. Had I come to school on a Sunday? No. Dad had not been in pub mode (smiling). I looked in through the classroom windows I was passing: empty, but with books on desks, opened and abandoned. Yard: still silent – and then I saw someone. A girl, banging on the Chemistry lab window. *Thud thud* – she was trying to get my attention.

'Get inside,' she was mouthing. 'Get inside quiiiiiiick.'

What the bloody hell was happening? Chemical spill? Serial killer? Had Gordy Mellor gone mad like an American and begun shooting up the school with his Black Widow catapult?

Then I saw Mr Fuller the brawny Maths teacher running through the yard, roaring and holding a basketball hoop complete with stand. He was using it as a weapon to chase something big and black. It was a motherfucking Rottweiler. I saw two more dark blobs. There were three of them. Not moving like normal dogs but like they'd been injected with some sort of horror-film scrum. Three slavering, slasher-movie Baskerville bastard dogs. Big dogs seem to run in slow motion when you think you're about to die. I didn't move. I didn't scream. Not even a jet of wee came out. I didn't really feel anything except a blank curiosity as these three massive deranged dogs ran across the yard and round the back of the Orchard Wing, Mr Fuller giving chase. When the yard was silent again, my legs kicked in and I sprinted through the first door I could find. I ended up cowering, along with the rest of the school, in the main hall while we waited for the police and fire brigade to bring the situation under control. The one time I actually thought of God was when our religious assembly was cancelled.

The dogs, it turned out, were from a house opposite the school. Three pure-bred Rottweilers, poor bastards, that had been kept in a tiny council garden. Unwalked, unstimulated, untrained, until one day they just snapped. The biggest one of the pack had torn the back gate down, and the three dogs had become mad with a spiteful and vengeful freedom. They ran as a killer pack around my school, attacking anyone and anything. Fortunately no one was killed. My mate Liam Ward's younger brother was pinned to the floor and his ear ripped off (stitched back on later). Others were mauled, rolled or pressed against walls and dribbled on while one dog decided listlessly what to do with its quarry. Many Church kids were in counselling for a long time afterwards. Mr Fuller, legend that he was, turned the tables and heroically attacked the dogs. He was still going full Highlander when the old bill arrived. Fuller the Puppy Pounder – he touted the nickname with pride, until he got another one. It was a surreal day of my late childhood, but the best thing was, no fucking Maths lesson.

A note about the surprising Mr Fuller. I only had one close encounter with him. He was an ex-rugby player with a squashed face, a big tash and, even though he was white, an incongruous 'fro of brown hair – like Michael Jackson in 1980. He had ended up as a Maths teacher, and now and again covered for the boring robot that was Miss Dearlove. Miss Dearlove was my teacher. She taught Maths like a trainspotter gives oral sex – I'm sure correctly, but with no joy, relish or any stimulation whatsoever. One lesson we were with Fuller. I was coping with the torture of quadratic equations by writing filthy poems and throwing them across the room to Becky Simpson. She laughed. Her laugh went through me with prickly excitement but I knew she would never touch my willy. I was delighted when she sent something puerile back. It was fun. Fuck you, quadratic equations, banter is more fun.

'What's this?' said Fuller, appearing like a rash when you're on holiday.

'Er . . .'

He opened up my poem and (suppressing a smile, I was pleased to note) barked, 'Detention, Kane. You too, Simpson.'

It was the weirdest detention of my schooldays. He made me and Becky Simpson draw the human genitals and describe sexual intercourse in prose underneath. At the time I thought: clever punishment – humiliating me and making me realize how immature I was to treat sex as a joke. The punishment fitted the crime, and neither Becky nor I found it weird or inappropriate. It was only years later that I formed a different opinion. Mr Fuller left our school sometime after that detention. It transpired that he had moved to another school, and, in 2006, was convicted of abusing multiple boys in his care there. Suddenly, that detention took on a bit of a different meaning for me.

10.

The Car is the Man

I left Church School one day in July with a white school shirt covered in blue ink signatures, swearwords and cocks with dashes firing from them to represent semen, or jizz as it's more properly known. I don't remember when I sighted my first traditional school cock-and-balls drawing, but the last one I saw was on the back shoulder of my fifth-form shirt. I expect many of you still have your leaving clobber and now and again look at it, reliving the innocent banter of your final school day. I binned mine, blazer and all, within eighteen months – not through bitterness, just apathy. It meant nothing to me. Church School, apart from those few strident memories, was a neutral, blank time. A few reunion-party invites have popped up on my Facebook over the last few years. I never felt the urge to go. The idea of it scared me a bit. What if the Cinderella carriage of my post-twenty-one education were to transform back into the ugly pumpkin of my teen years? The spell might break. I'd be a lonely virgin again. Too much of a risk. It's almost as though my birthdays went nine, ten, eleven, then straight to sixteen years old. Church School, Ofsted loves you – I didn't.

Maybe I should have gone through that glass door and into the sixth form. Miss Hanbury, my English and fifth-form teacher, had told me they wanted me – she even dropped a hint about head boy possibilities. They saw something I didn't. Worse, the idea of doing well at A-level, of climbing the ranks to head boy, seemed silly and effeminate. The alpha males had done their work on me well. Head boy? Pah! I now believed that to do well at A-levels, in academia, was the same as being gay/weak/virgin/shit.

At home, it wasn't that I had been discouraged – at all. Anything I did was supported by Mum, and even Dad in his weird way, sometimes. It's just that graft – real work – was king of your destiny. And I knew I would never be a man until I had blisters on my hand and soot in my lungs. At sixteen, however, as much as being a goody-two-shoes was unappealing, the idea of work was repulsive – so I had a plan.

After Church, I decided on drifting – for eighteen months if I could swing it. Not easy when you live with the Gestapo of Graft. I *pretended* to do A-levels at my local college in Essex, which was more of a training camp for people who want to smash through baggies of recreational drugs. Oh, I *was* officially enrolled. It's just that the place was such a dump, I didn't have to apply myself. Even being totally shit and not trying I was still in the top tier. The tutors liked me, and lessons were cosy and warm, like smoking sheesha under a blanket. My English lessons were pleasant enough, but passive and dreary. I certainly can't tell you a sodding thing about my other Arse-level – Social and Economic History 1750–1914 – but I definitely remember the first time I heard jungle and hard house, and the first time I saw Disco Danny break a White Dove pill in half and share it with a girl called Simone Fletcher in the refectory. She didn't make it to college the next Monday, but when she sat down in Media Studies (my third Arse-level) on the Tuesday she looked different. She was now a 'raver'. I fancied her to the point of boner cramp. I hoped she might be the one to take my V but, predictably, she went from a bright, three-A-level student to failing and getting pregnant by a car mechanic called Lee Pinks, who lived in Stevenage. I online stalked her recently. She looked more like my one of aunties, as though each baby she had birthed by each of the men she'd mated with had sucked the life force from deep within her.

What is it about cars, dads and sons? What's the animal kingdom equivalent? A chimp inspecting the nut-cracking rock of his gangly adolescent son, then tossing it aside with derisive hoots before throwing shit into his face? Here's a newsflash – some people, some of us even men, are not interested in cars. I know! Take me to the vets and have my nut sack removed for I, even as a newly licensed seventeen-year-old, did not give one solitary shite what I was driving. Do not misunderstand me, by seventeen I wanted a car. I desperately wanted a car. I had a girlfriend, blonde-haired goddess Jessica, and she lived in Surrey – bloody hell, I needed that car to drive the thirty miles for rumpy-pumpy, teenage declarations of love and shite poetry about mutual suicide and elopement. Oh God, yes. It's just that I didn't care what I drove. This came as a shocking blow to the silver-back. Only becoming vegan or having him walk in on me having full bum-sex with a mixed-race boyfriend could have destroyed him more.

'It's your first car, boy. The most important thing you'll ever buy.'

'What if I buy a kidney one day?' Oh, if only I'd spoken that clever riposte out loud, but then I enjoyed being alive so instead I said: 'I know, Dad.'

'We need to look under the bonnet, make sure it's not a fucking ringer.'

I'm still not completely sure what a ringer is, but it's possibly a 'cut and shunt' since my dad was in possession of the violent conviction that at least 50 per cent of cars are in fact two different cars welded together.

'They get two write-offs and stick them together to make one car. A car that you will die in.'

It was one of Dad's favourite epithets: deathtrap. Could be a car, could be a holiday, could even be the piece of chicken you were eating in a curry house (any curry house that wasn't his sacred Akash, Potters Bar). He'd do a survey of the thing, look up and declare: 'Fucking deathtrap. You'll die in/on/eating that.'

But two cars welded together? Surely it's easier just to sell two shit cars than weld two together, but Dave was convinced. 'There's nothing villains love more than a fuuuucking ringer. Fucking cut and shunt, boy. They take a car written off at the front, another one at the back, and glue the cunt together. You wouldn't know a thing about it till you hit 70mph, then that's it. Boom. Deathtrap.'

For every car we inspected, I too would be required to kick the tyres and look at sticks with oil on. I couldn't bring myself to tell him: I will never in my whole life change a tyre, check oil or pour any fluid into any part of any car. I can't think of anything more boring or annoying than fixing a vehicle. I will admit, I've very recently grown to appreciate a 1980s ironic classic, a Ford Escort or BMW 3 Series – maybe out of some nostalgia for my dad's golden period of motor lust. In fact, my next tour will be in a 1989 Mercedes 190E. The exact same motor my old man drove, the same year – shit, just realized that. But to maintain or tweak any part of that car, to shop for parts and wear mucking-in overalls – fuck off! I'm one of those who would sit shivering under a silver foil blanket at the side of the motorway waiting for an RAC person, someone else's dad,* to come and change a tyre for me. Either that or meet a woman who can do it instead. How's that for a night out? A nice dinner, then a girl changes my tyre. Not a standard fantasy, but one that appeals immensely.

'You gotta learn this shit, boy. Your motor needs to be reliable – then you need to save for a proper set of wheels. A fanny magnet like I used to have. Like I've still got. The Merc is a proper cock swinger.' (To swing one's genitals in a display of dominance or attraction.)

I looked at the B-reg Vauxhall Nova Swing I'd chosen. Swing, as far as I could tell, meant it had a sunroof. A simple pane of tinted glass was enough to equate my three-door with the all-American music from the 1930s. The Nova Swing. Was it not a fanny magnet? And why would I want to magnetize fanny anyway? After all, I had Jessica. Oh Jessica, sweet, virginity-cancelling Jessica, well-spoken and celestial. Love, love, my love. Yes – we were seventeen, but we were going to die together, shagging inside a castle made of rose petals when we were eighty. Our grandchildren would sob at our graves, the perfection of our love too much for them to bear, and one day when—

* Or mum.

'. . . you see, boy. A car is the man. Don't buy Jap crap like Toyota, boy. Be patriotic. That's why I've got a Merc.'

German? The height of patriotism. I said, 'Right, Dad.'

'When I was in my twenties, I had a Mini Cooper . . .'

Dad only ever had one car crash his entire life, and it was in his beloved Mini Cooper. He chose to tell me the story of its demise when I had just passed my test.

'I was driving along, boy, fucking lovely car – it took off at roundabouts. When I put my foot down in it, it left two types of skid mark. Terrifying acceleration, boy. Should have got nicked in it – never did, though. Quick as fuck. Anyway, I was driving, and saw this blonde bird standing on the corner with some skinny geezer. The Bristol Cities on her. I took my eyes off the road for one second and bang. That was that. Wrote it off. Racing green. Fucking lovely motor. Let that be a lesson to you, boy.'

'I always keep my eyes on the road, Dad. I'm really careful.'

'Not that, you prat. That's not the lesson.'

'Er, what is?'

'Women. Be fucking careful, boy. Be fucking careful.'

My first night out driving that Vauxhall Nova Swing ended in cross-parental fallout and my longest friendship estranged. It put a wedge between me and my bestie, Michael.

The whole crew was at Jeremy Wright's house. Jeremy was the cool DJ one among us. Obscure house record collections, pensive face as he pincered each vinyl from a well-ordered record bag like a surgeon selecting a steel tool for heart surgery. Jeremy is still a cool DJ type in 2019. These days all his friends have high-fringed Shoreditch haircuts and look like kind vegans. At any moment you expect a pop-up shop to begin, selling soil or solar plates. Back then Jeremy was just as hip, but still lived with his mum in shitty Enfield like the rest of us. Being cool in Enfield was like being in love on a lads' holiday: admirable, but no point in being there. That night, the full gang numbered about eight, and with Jeremy's mum out we had the gaff to ourselves. It was a massive novelty that one of us had wheels outside. Non-drivers will have no memory of what it feels like to mix being so young with suddenly being able to drive. You've just finished seventeen years with a tiny range of travel. Your total journey possibility was how far you could walk, or maybe the bus, or a shitty Toyota Prius with an hour's range at most before, beep beep, your mum at the wheel summoned you back. Passing your driving test was one of the moments of change that wasn't gradual or creeping. It was one specific day. The day before, your parent ran you to the shops, or you jogged to your mate's house. The day after: anything.

That's what it felt like the first time you turned the key: like you could drive all the way to New York or Australia – like you could just keep going and no one could say anything. For me: Surrey, Jessica. I was a driver; with a little bit of fuel I was free. I feel sorry for people who never felt that. I reckon it's possible as adults. That's why self-selecting non-drivers annoy me so much. 'I don't need to drive – can you give me a lift?' Fuck you, Social Prius. Fuck you. I became a bit of a man, an adult, that first day I drove to Jeremy's, parked – and walked in like a don.

OK, Mum, I'll admit it now, that night most people had cans of Tesco lager in their hands. Some were even smoking 'ting' (as we called it) in Jeremy's garden. But so what? And me? Hell, *no*. Nothing on earth would make me jeopardize my love taxi, my Vauxhall Nova which could take me to the nova-like constellation of Jessica's knickers. A starburst of lust and love was bound up in the B-reg hatchback. Just the word 'knickers' could glaze my eyes for an hour. My love, my Jessica. I'd die for her, but not drink and drive for her. I was razor sharp and clean – sipping only tea and arsing around, doing wrestling jumps on to the cushions with Michael Delaney. Nothing could induce me to impair my five-minute drive home. And none of my mates would have allowed it. Warren Evans, the mum of the group, would have chinned me out cold rather than let me drive intoxicated. Our generation was very anti-drink-driving – it was a thing racist old crusties did. I was a man now. I had driven myself out, and for the first time ever I would drive myself home. Swing.

The problem was, unbeknown to us, Michael's mum, sat at home, was stewing, imagining me and Michael in a tiny steel box driving at 70mph off our tits on pills and booze. Drive home? She wasn't having it. She whipped herself up into a conviction that I was high and ready to smash us both to our doom. What if we all piled into my car in a test-passing, drug-fuelled celebration and died in a fireball? I suppose it wasn't an entirely irrational fear. We all liked to party. But so far as me, she was wrong that night; and in the middle of our gathering at Jeremy's, the doorbell rang.

Ding fucking dong.

There was no panic, no wafting away of fumes – those smoking had smoked in the garden. Michael's dad, harangued by Michael's mum because he lived closer to where the party was that night, had driven over from Essex to Enfield. He was the opposite of my father: spiritual, unshaven, softly spoken – kindly . . . but on this occasion, totally wrong, and now he was at the door asking for me with the calm authority of a special needs teacher.

He put out his hand, and I shook it.

That handshake was the undoing of mine and Michael's friendship. I've never had a firm handshake; still don't. When I meet men who have a crunching or, even worse, hand-flipping handshake, I cringe for them a bit. Imagine if you've got to a place in your head where all you have left with which to assert your manliness is how hard you grip another man's hand. That really is some monkey shit, some unevolved basic stuff. I go for the soft handshake followed by using my brain to establish who I am. Back when I was seventeen, I was more used to a fist bump than the formal hand-shaking of proper adults.

Michael's dad withdrew his hand, aghast.

I found out later the reason why. He'd taken my limp handshake as evidence of drug abuse. Funny now, but not at the time. It led to the falling-out of Michael's mum and mine. I was 'a bad, junkie influence', a Jim Morrison leading the pure monk Michael into an acid party at Glastonbury. What bollocks that turned out to be. Out of all of us, I was the one who ended up knee-deep in books at Nerdsville. Michael, it played out, was a talented guitarist destined for dreadlocks, African music experimentation and young father-hood. And this was the moment our paths split, our mums driving in the wedge off the back of Michael's dad's report of a handshake.

I drew my hand back, like whipping a hot sardine from a grill, and placed it in my pocket. I knew something was badly up.

Michael's dad barged past me into the lounge and took us all in, one by one.

'Hey, guys,' he said, doing the understanding, gentle hippy smile; the youth worker who wants to remain on side.

'Hi,' I said.

'Look, man' – did he just say *maaaan*? – 'I get it. You like a smoke, bro' – *bro?!* – 'that's great. If you want to have a smoke, man, that's great. But if you want to drive too – well, hell, bro, that's just crazy. That's crazy talk, compadres.'

We sat in silence holding in our laughs like a curry fart at the end of a first date. We were working class and thus had no facility for real conversation until the age of twenty-five. Michael's dad took Michael and left. We all knew what would happen next.

'We've got about five minutes till his old man rocks up,' said Little Mike (more about him in a bit), pointing at me, enjoying the thrill.

Even confident Scott looked nervous. 'Fuck sake, just go home.'

But it was too late. Dave was already en route. I heard the burr of the Mercedes diesel, then my dad's Christmas-ham-fist banging the door.

'Boy. Out here. Now. Fuck sake.'

I think one mate climbed over the garden fence just at the thought of my dad coming in.

But my dad didn't – he called me on to the street.

'Do I look stoned to you, Dad? Do I look high? Seriously,' I pleaded, taking my volume as high as I dared.

For a second he looked at me like an equal. We were in a situation together. Just once, I wasn't a tadpole, and then followed something that had never happened before. My dad believed me. He took my side. I was stunned.

'Fuck sake, boy. No, you don't.'

There was a silence where he looked at me once more, then he said, 'Why do your mates smoke that shit? How much is it?'

A hesitation, then I thought, sod it: 'Fifteen quid. For an eighth.'

'Fucking hell. I used to get a lump the size of an Oxo cube for a fiver when I was twenty-one.'

Then he got in his car and left.

Michael and I didn't speak for four years.

11.

Graft Detective

Essex Regional College for Further Education. I studied something when I was there, but it wasn't academic. Miraculously, I did complete the A-levels in English, History, Media, but got a D, an N and a C – like someone was spelling DUNCE during a game of hangman. And I was hanged.

Did you know N was a grade? It was then. 'N' stood for all the words meaning nothing, nil, none, niente – or, worst of all, its actual meaning, 'nearly passed'. I'd rather have got a fail. After my pitiful GCSE performance at school (A, B, C, C, C), I'd barely scraped into this weed house. Even the building could turn you to drugs: a soul-eating edifice a few miles from the stunned beige mass of brick known as Cheshunt. Cheshunt, as a town centre, has less soul than a racist's playlist and is particularly unsuited to collegiate progress. For me, if I hadn't slipped into partying, this college would have meant two years of being bored shitless, surrounded by gangsters and wasters (I was in the latter group) before, in year two, steadily transitioning from lacklustre study into simply killing time. Killing in the true sense. Murdering every moment with the will not to be anything other than baked on resin. Arsing about, it turned out, was more fun than literature, media, and social and economic history.

The reason I didn't drop out of my Essex Regional

A-levels altogether was fear of Dad's reaction. I knew he was waiting to pounce on me for becoming the Do-nothing he had prophesied.

'Working hard at "college", boy?' he said over a steaming mound of shepherd's pie.

'You are, aren't you, Russ?' said Mum, bless her.

I knew I wasn't. Dad, Graft Detective, knew I wasn't – he was on to me. I was on to myself.

I finished the stupid A-levels with the cocky abandon of someone failing on purpose. My exam results came through that August – on my birthday, in fact, and so, aged exactly eighteen, I had failed precisely in the way my birth had predicted. I was the idiot my dad had predicted. I had, as he sensitively put it:

'Fucked it! Now – you get a trade, get a job, or fucking well get out.'

Turned out that within twelve months I would select option C, *fucking well get out.*

I feel I should explain my Essex College failure a little more. Two factors led to my A-level shocker. One was me. I *enjoyed* being popular and dicking about on the mean streets of Cheshunt. I admit to my love of loafing and signing on. I did not apply myself, and I bloody well loved not applying myself. But secondly, what was the point in trying? My dad had told me, explicitly, that I could not go to uni. Funds would not permit . . .

When I was nearly sixteen there had been a short conversation between me, my mum and my dad. After perfunctorily filling out my UCAS form a few months previously (the first year that the UCCA and PCAS forms merged), I'd raised a question: what if by some miracle I did do well at A-level? I *might* end up with a university place – you never know. My dad, although not enthusiastic or encouraging in any syllable, was at least not scathing or mocking – itself surprising. There was an interval of a few weeks while my mum and dad filled out various documents to find out what financial help or benefits I might claim, were I to make it to uni. This, remember, was the period when student grants were coming to an end. The annual grant was down to £2,000 a year. That two grand had to pay your rent (which was exactly two grand), buy your books and enable you to live, eat and breathe. In other words you needed to magic an extra three grand a year at least to survive. That was my calculation. Five grand a year to get an education, unlock the secret portal to the middle classes and claim my hummus.

The decision came back from Enfield Council. Nothing. Another 'N'. That's what benefit and help I was entitled to.

'Sweet FA,' said Mum dolefully.

'You see, boy, because I dare to work and earn a decent wage—' Dad began.

'Because your dad isn't a lazy fucking ponce like everyone else round here,' my mum put in.

'Yes. Because I graft and earn a living, I'm just over the threshold, you see. So you get nothing.' Not 'we' – you.

The forms were tossed aside. The door, shut.

I wasn't upset. I was maybe even a bit relieved to have an excuse to not try. Whatever I felt, I definitely agreed with my parents. They pay, they say. And that was that. The end of the debate. I could not go to uni. The idea that my old man might make a few sacrifices and give up some of his dosh and pleasures to put *me* through college was never even raised or discussed. And, being totally honest, I never thought it myself. Not for second did it occur to me that my dad might have less of his stuff to fund *my* uni education. Why? Why would he? Why *should* he? That could only be for a 'lazy ponce who wants handouts'. So in fact my thoughts and those of my parents' were in synergy. We were on the same finished page of the same closed book.

'We can't send you. So if you get the grades, you're paying for it yourself, son.'

Good. Fucking. Luck.

If you're screaming at the page, 'Why didn't your parents give up more so you could go to uni?' you are forgetting two vital facts. One, my dad was in charge. And two: the rules. No, not the usual golden rule: Treat People As You Wish To Be Treated Yourself. These ones, remember?

Never rely on anyone. They *will* let you down.
Take care of number one, and fuck everyone else.

When I was eighteen, I had faith in those rules the way an Islamic scholar believes the Quran. My dad had developed a few others to support them over the years. There was the Law of Least Effort: that everyone around you will do the least possible and exploit you to the most. Be on guard. Look out for lazy fuckers. Then there was the immutable:

I'm paying, I'm saying.

He was the breadwinner. He called the shots. This, with its ring of martyrdom, was his favourite.

School was done. I had as good as no A-levels, pitiful

GCSEs and was almost in the same socio-economic group as my parents – but lower. My mum, after all, as well as a cleaner, dinner lady and shelf-stacker, was a qualified child-minder. My dad was a skilled labourer trained in the difficult art of metal shaping and insulation. I was, simply, a nob. Once, my dad fashioned a flower from an aluminium sheet and presented it to my girlfriend Jessica – another of the many confusing things that didn't seem to fit with being a true silverback. Dad, though broken and tired and worn into submission, had a trade, a craft. I was just a ponce (if you're northern, a 'cadger').

Where we lived took my prospects down another notch. Brimsdown, Enfield. This was the 1990s. The era of the rave. A few doors one way, I could buy trips, mushrooms, speed and, of course, the cranial travelcard of my generation: MDMA. A few doors the other way and I could get skunk and 'solid', its resin form, liberally toked on Friday nights while watching *The Word* and eating pizzas bigger than lorry wheels. Drugs all around – but sorry to disappoint: no tales of addiction grace these pages. Just class-B leisure usage – fuck me, lots of it, but none the less, always in control. Annoying. Rehab would have filled a whole self-scrutinizing chapter of juiciness.

The rave scene was something me and my friends dipped our toes into. We were too young to experience the really big raves, but we caught the tail end of them – and for me, I think it was as much about peace, loveism and racial unity as it was about searching for the most opposite thing to Dave Kane I could find. Me and my mates spent our weekends queuing for Roller Express – a warehouse in Lee Valley which would fill with sweaty teenagers dancing to hardcore, hard house or jungle until the sun came up. It was our hippy movement. We spent the night hugging strangers, affirming that we live as 'One Family' (cracking tune, YouTube it). People were mostly off their tits. Police didn't matter, rules didn't matter. Structure could fuck off. Structure is what held us back. All this was fun, until 7 a.m. when I had to put my key in the door at Brimsdown. The closer the night bus got to my house the more absurd my grey reality seemed. Here was my gate, my house – only it wasn't, it was his house. His gate. It all looked so normal and so weird. Would I ever even want to eat again?

'Fucking state of you!'

They were early risers, my parents – always up, ready to do an 'eye inspection'. I was normally soaked in eight hours of dance sweat, hair down to my shoulders, and by now had Jessica in tow. It was like someone had medicated mental-health patients just enough to get them to the shops.

Those were our weekends, then back to Essex College in the week. I can't lie, there were awful hangovers. I must dispel the falsehood that you don't get hungover when you're young. Why do people say that? Sometimes I was still crawling on the Tuesday. I feel almost nostalgic for my days of sobbing in the toilet. It wasn't pleasant at the time but it's a vital reminder of the golden days of youth.

D, N, C. My A-levels.

12.

Work No Matter What

At eighteen I'd come to the end of my educational flip-flopping but I still did not want to work. Raving was too much fun. I was so in love with Jessica – why couldn't we bum about like rock stars? I found myself about to break one of my dad's deepest sociological taboos. Were I a conservative Pakistani bride, this would be the equivalent of pole-dancing on my hen night.

I took the Job Seeker's Allowance. This tore my Brimsdown household in two with seismic shame.

The upper working class is a specific socio-economic stratum with solid rules to which you must strictly adhere. The most important is: you work. *You fucking well work*, no matter what. Vomiting, bleeding stump, pregnant, depressed. You work. If you're *not* working, then you better not say it's 'bad luck' or 'hard times'. *Mug. No.* It's choice. This is why the people moaning about the policy of austerity are mostly the 'liberal elites' (like me). Most people where I'm from don't look at out-of-work people, down-on-their-luck people and think, 'Damn you Conservatives and your austerity.' In fact, down-on-your-luck is not even a thing. You're 'down on your effort'. This was how Thatcher made the Tories a working-class party. You might not have anything right now, but you yourself, and how you use the free market, are in charge of how you change that.

'Boy, there is always work if you want it. Sitting on your arse is a choice.'

Admit it, Gary/Dave/Lee/Scott/Wayne/Kelly/Donna/Tina. You have chosen not to work. Laziness or employment – these are the only two options. *On your bike, buy your home.* Tebbit and Thatcher, Jesus and God – and anyone who deviates, an infidel.

'If I *had* to, boy, I would scrub the skid marks from the local shitter for a pound an hour rather than sign on.'

Would you really, Dad? Or was it just something you said to shame the non-grafters? Actually, I think he would have. I think he would have done anything rather than sign on. Including die. Maybe that's what was going through Dad's head when he was diagnosed with the heart problem.

Yes, I could have it done; 95 per cent survival rate. But then I'd never go to the gym again. I couldn't work for a year. I'd be a ponce. No. Death please.

Dad certainly didn't want me to scrub skids from an Enfield turd house. No – that's not *upper* working class. What he wanted was for me to get a trade, specialize, earn 'good wedge'. A stockbroker like Kyle would be the dream. Italian sports cars for father and son – bosh.

Upper-working-classness: a bit of cheeky cash-in-hand is OK. You buy your own council home (Thanks, Maggie) and get a half-decent car. Dad wasn't anti-university as such. He just found it dangerous to the finances. Potentially, an expensive waste of time. Upper-working-classness says higher education is *probably* bollocks, but if you want to go, good on you, as long as you pay for yourself and go on to do something remunerative. You're paying, you're saying. Upper-working-classness: Spielberg films; getting pissed on birthdays; extensions and conservatories – and a violent hatred of the lower working class, gays, skivers and cunts (and more recently Eastern European migration). Oh yes. There is a list *this specific* of things. But the absolute cardinal no-no was to *not work*, and below that, the absolute *Daily Mail* spit-on-you-in-the-street horror: signing on. Job-seeker, weed-smoking, stealing-off-the-state, waste-of-space *mug*. Mugging yourself. Robbing from yourself, your own pride – assaulting your own self-worth.

Ponce.

Ponce. It's not a word used everywhere in the country but it's one of the most derogatory in my manor: to leech, to not make your own way but to attach yourself to something bigger than you and suck away. It would not matter if people like David Cameron or Rupert Murdoch were to do speaking tours and craftily not pay any tax. That's fine. They've used their ingenuity to cheat the state. Plus, it's off the back of their *graft* and therefore excusable. But if anyone in our street was faking a disability (or beefing one up, like Philip Gray at 189 with his little toe missing), then they were not just stealing from the state or the system, no.

'It's like they're going into my wallet, boy. Robbing me.'

To Dad it was pure theft, but worse. One could grudgingly respect the out-and-out villain. He is what he is, and that's that. But the ponce . . .

'He steals without telling anyone. Crafty. Bit by bit taking stuff off you. Never ponce, boy. Never ponce.'

And to the people who did sign on:

'Liberty-takers, the lot of them. There are jobs. They just want me to fund their fucking idleness.'

It was my old man's vision of the world – people coming

at you like those nibbling fish Chinese people get to eat your feet in the beauty salon, except they would keep nibbling and you would be the mug walking to work with bones for toes.

None the less, when I got to eighteen, I had become determined to drop out. I signed on and took grief from all sides of my free-market, Thatcher-loving house. I was quite good at signing on. I didn't mind it. I was strangely adept at having nothing. There was something liberating about getting my £80 for the fortnight and knowing that was that. I've still got the diaries for those years with little charts about what the money would go on. Fiver for petrol, money for fags, stuff like that. I felt independent. This was my money. Mine. I'd never had any before. I'd been living off my mum and dad. It might not be much, but the eighty sheets were all mine and I intended to enjoy them.

'You've got three months,' my old man warned, backed up by Himmler, my mum, his fingers-to-the-bone Co-op-working lieutenant in the background.

'Don't take the piss, Russ.'

Three months till what? Would they throw me out? I didn't give a smart remark in return as I wanted to remain alive. I also wanted the grace of doing fuck-all with no goals for a few months. It was a novelty. I had gone my whole life, from toddler to man, without once ever – and I mean never – answering my father back. No sarcasm, no raised voice; I wouldn't even question him. So I took the ultimatum. Three months of doing nothing. That actually sounded OK – three months is a long time. That's twelve raves. Shit. That's quite cool.

I was heading into my nineteenth year and my relationship with Jessica was coming to an end. A new man was emerging.

A self-elected, proud dropout. I had consciously decided that I would smoke, bum about unemployed, party at the weekend, and die young. This isn't an intelligent boy killing time until the real world of elitism beckons, this was the real deal — proper council-road nothingness. I saw the abyss — and quite fancied it. Was that so wrong? Why would anyone want to be forty? Imagine the tragedy of being that age and still *trying*. I'd seen the balls of my older uncles in the shower on family holidays. Actually, what am I saying? I've just done the maths. My oldest uncle was thirty-five at this point.

(A note about ages in my family. It can be confusing. My great-grandma was in her twenties when my nan was born. My nan was sixteen when my mum was born — and went on to fire out five others. And my mum was just twenty-two when I was born. That means I grew up with a nan in her forties, and uncles and aunts in their twenties and thirties. It's odd when your youngest aunts and uncles are into the same stuff you're into. Even weirder when you can remember your mum's fortieth birthday and were able to get drunk, legally, in celebration.)

Being forty looked steaming shit to me. What was there to live for? By the way, armchair counsellors, I wasn't depressed, I wasn't on a downer. Quite the opposite — I felt invigorated and excited, like when you decide to blow all your euros on the third day of your holiday. Fuck it — why spend the week counting the pennies when you can be a legend for three days and go home early. That was my plan. Go. Home. Early. Clock out before my saggy-bollocked fortieth. I actually voiced it to my friends, to my daily toke-mate Little Mike. This isn't me in 2019 going back and saying, 'Wow, I'd lost it.' Understand: I wanted it. I wish more skivers would own how they enjoy the open spaciousness of not giving a solitary fuck. Lazy nihilism. I found it enjoyable lounging about in a cannaboid haze, not working on purpose. It was actually fun, I guess, because it was chosen. Three months.

Of course there was one teeny-weeny downside. I was skint. Little Mike and I hadn't caught the thieving bug so virulent in Enfield, so it was brassic for us. Many people in our peer group dealt bits of weed here and there, sold on electrical or dodgy white goods. We were always broke. Actually, can you be broke when you had nothing to start with? There was nothing to break. Most of mine and Little Mike's fantasies revolved around the simple things. Imagine being able to afford an ounce of Jamaican homegrown, 'like Bob Marley used to smoke'. What about food. Imagine eating the set meal for two from the Akash, one double meal for each of us. Me and Little Mike sometimes filled whole afternoons fantasizing about the takeaways we could not afford, smoking heavily and playing a game we called Almost-free Curry. We would take it in turns to read out the Akash takeaway menu while the other *imagined* he was eating the dish described. It was 'almost' free – because whoever was listening would eat a slice of Happy Shopper white bread (10p a loaf), filling up while allowing the glorious descriptions of bhuna and masala to feed the ears.

We watched the same things every day. *Countdown, Fifteen to One*, and the best of the painter Bob Ross. Man – we lost hours watching that old hippy create a snowy mountain range using titanium white. Well worth a google if you've never heard of him.

I've often wondered: was this weird, brief, uncharacteristic period of my life a late adolescent reaction to the upper-working-class tyranny of Dave? David the Work Martyr; always on his cross in the evening waiting for his cuts and bruises of graft to be admired. The graft monk; the prophet of labour.

'Proper job hands, boy. Look at 'em.' His fingers like ruined sausages, split and hurt from the sacrificial money-earning. Was I supposed to feel guilty? Did my existence, my selfishness at being born, mean he had been enslaved to the boiler room? Without my being there, what might he be doing? Running through fields. Seeing the world. Acting, modelling.

Unsurprisingly, my memory of those three months is sketchier than Picasso's notepad, but the thing that saved me, that got me back on the path to graft, was not my dad's workaholic philosophy winning through, it was my natural restlessness. I have an unusual amount of energy. I've been that way since I was born. I was examined by a specialist a few hours after my birth because my hands were clenching and my body writhing like a salted slug. I've continued with that writhing, jumping and pacing at every stage of my life. I'm not doing it to be annoying or affected – I just can't bloody sit still. At one point my mum thought there might be something properly wrong with me, so I had everything scary-sounding measured: endocrine, haemoglobin, adrenaline, pituitary – all normal. (Apart from my manhood, which is unusually large and I am currently seeing a specialist about a reduction. I'm under the same consultant as that African meme guy with the massive wang. I am obviously joking. This may be the last year of dick jokes being morally permissible.) Seriously, though, I am genuinely wired fast. Don't get me wrong: I get knackered, tired and as ready to drop down into bed as the next person. But once I'm awake and caffein-ated, I'm off. Boom! Red hot, visceral and messy as fuck. Like someone stamped on a tube of chilli paste. This is part of the reason I've never messed with hard drugs. I was born buzz-ing. It's a sad comment on our times that men always sidle up to me after gigs nudging and winking.

'How do you do it, mate?'

'Coffee and adrenaline.'

'Yeah . . . bollocks . . .'

First few times I just laughed, then I pondered the tragedy of these men's lives: that if they see another man lively and interested in things, they assume he must be on drugs. How flat and empty is your internal life that you can't imagine someone being awake and vibrant just from a book or a film.

Sometimes I wish I could slow down. It can be exhausting. My whole life people have been telling me, starting with my dad, to make the most of it, that you'll burn out one day. (They say it even more now.) 'I wouldn't carry on like that if I were you.' Yet, in 2019, it's worse/better than ever. I move chaotically, am more hyper, my brain careens around corners; I'm a MacBook Pro plugged into an incorrect power source which is self-typing *The Da Vinci Code*. Yes, most of it is shit, but it's coming out anyway. I'm always roasting hot, always rushing, sweating. Always *awake*. Whenever I'm in a room alone, if there is air con, I turn it to sixteen degrees Celsius. Paradoxically, being constantly full of energy is bloody knackering. But time and time again, at my lowest ebb, this wrong-wiring has been the trait that has saved me; at my highest ebb (can one ebb upwards?) it's been the thing that has made me. If you have average intelligence, average ability, average height, average body (not manhood – wait, I've done

184

that lazy joke already), if all of you is nothing special, then all that's left is energy. Effort, and energy. So that's what I went with. Without realizing it I went on to put into practice every-thing my old man had taught. The Law of Least Effort would be beaten. I was saying, I would pay with work. I would rely on myself and no one else – anyone might let you down.

Restlessness saved my arse. Just in case you have never spent more than a month smoking, let me tell you this: being stoned is boring. It's *fucking* boring. There, I've said it. Drugs are boring. Oh, they're interesting for a bit, but for me they are not compelling enough to form a habit for or to get hooked on. They are less engaging than a book by Gertrude Stein, not that I knew yet who Gertrude Stein was.

A quarter of a year sat in Little Mike's lounge was enough. Dad's maxims had got through. I had to get a job. The time had come, and by the time I mean horology. Watches, and a world that in Essex has the feeling of a religion: Rolex.

The moment of change came as I was walking home from Little Mike's across Albany Park one night, smoking my pre-dinner L. A pre-dinner L was mine and Little Mike's favourite part of the day. You get to about 5 p.m. (post-*Countdown*, pre-*Neighbours*) and you know you're within one hour of a real, hot, home-made meal. The ritual, to properly prepare one's palate for such majesty, was two king-sized Rizlas glued into an L-shape to make an extra-long, fat, coned bifta. It's a special sort of stonedness, just on the bor-ders of the Republic of Catatonia, but enough inside Lucid Park that you could still feign basic cognition in front of a vehemently anti-ganja Dad. Puff and weed represented something lefty to him, so he hated it.

'Why would you want to smoke that Jamaican shit, boy?'

The L skin would send me into red-eyed gourmand mode, eager for shepherd's pie or chilli con carne with chips on the side, followed by two rounds of Gales honey sandwiches afterwards. I could eat. I could really *really* eat. I know all eighteen-year-olds eat a lot. I know people talk of the munchies, but my intake was legendary. It was spoken about, debated – and tested. I'm not the biggest lad so this made my calorie-intake skills all the more impressive. Eating vast amounts was a point of pride; it was also partly defence against my slightness, the slimness my dad found so astonishing.

'What happened to you, boy? When I was your age I needed planning permission to take my top off.'

'Leave him alone, Dave.'

'He looks like a fucking straw!'

Yet my dad could not out-*eat* me. That's my only alpha-male achievement. Growing up with a Dave for a father, you more or less give up on ever feeling manly in any department. According to him, Dave, my dad, was the biggest, baddest, hardest-working, most in pain, most experienced, most put-upon gorilla ever to drag his proper-job knuckles through a building site. But I could eat more than him.

Once, when we were fourteen, Michael Delaney and I took our bikes and cycled thirty miles through Epping. All the way to the forest and back, over the border into London, in one afternoon. It felt massive. The odometers on our red Raleigh Euro mountain bikes did not lie. I made sure we were standing glowing and sweaty in the garage when my dad came home from work. Michael and I were faking some sort of bike-chain maintenance just to be there when he walked in. The garage door opened, and there we were. The Glazed

Warriors with 31.8 miles packed into our meaty thighs and glutes. How about that, Dad?

'Thirty miles, boy? I used to cycle fifty a day. To work. Fuuuuuucking hell. Now move the bikes – I gotta put a real vehicle away.'

There wasn't irony in it. He wasn't saying it to make a joke. (Although it is bleakly funny reading it back.) It was a straightforward jet of Dave-hot dominance piss across my weedy attempt at a boast. We never spoke of our cycling achievements again.

'There's something queer about cycling anyway, boy. The benders love it.'

'Dave!' said Mum.

'They fucking do! All the Lycra – and where do they go every year? Brighton! I rest my case.'

No case was ever rested. Merely stored for louder unpacking later on.

Could it be that the more I grew up, the more camp and bookish I became in reaction, in defence? Steven Epsom's dad used to grow bonsais when we were teenagers. If you place a canopy over a bonsai but leave gaps of light at the side, they will grow widthways. Sure, they'll still be a contorted, miniature version of the real thing, but they will find a weird sideways route to express themselves. That was me. An emotional bonsai. Dense and shrunken, yeah, but at least different, and growing. For me: books, skipping, feelings, poetry, wine – and eventually the theatre. These were the elements of rebellion. These were the daggers with which I poked at Dave.

When I was eighteen, there was only one knock I could make on the alpha male's concrete ceiling. That was how much I could eat. I genuinely had a freakish appetite. Veraciously voracious. An ability to chow down twice as much as Dave Kane, even though I was half his weight. I could rise up from the sacred Sunday lunch table, or curry-house platter, and be *the Man*. Yeah, OK, my body looked like someone had painted nipples on a flute, but for a few glorious hours a basketball tummy stuck out – a bulge of victory. And Dave acknowledged it too. Being fair to dear old Dad, when he was out-alpha'd, he didn't become defensive, he didn't put you down. Sometimes, on the rare occasion when my manliness was acknowledged, he would wear one of his reluctant half-smiles and a very small compliment escaped his tight white mouth.

'You're a fucking animal, boy.'

It was the highest praise. I *too* was an animal.

Speak to any of my friends now. Ask them. I was the biggest eater. And the biggest farter and pooer too. If, dear reader, you have had a life where the arses of your friends were not a staple of your entertainment, I salute you. But the fact cannot be changed that I held the record for the number of farts done in a single evening. It was off the back of three Fray Bentos pies and some sprouts in a Welsh cottage. One hundred and twenty-six, if you were wondering. I was truly great at something, once.

No one in my group could out-eat me, including – and apologies, for this was the poor blighter's genuine nickname – Fat Cunt Barry (FCB if we were in a shop or around prudish parents). I would sometimes eat two full dinners. No problem. My most infamous Tardis guts incident was the Blackout and the Ambulance. Back when I was seventeen and a half, I cracked my head open from overeating at an Indian buffet lunch. I nutted a whole building. Headbutted the fuck out of a curry house.

That morning Jessica and I had had an argument and she had gone off crying with one of the girls from our group. The rest of us had decided to go to Albany Tandoori. It's still there today. I remember the name of the eatery clearly as it was the last thing I saw before the blackness came, the blood, the chaos.

Albany Tandoori had a very special Sunday deal. Not just a buffet. They're as common as a cardamom pod in a dansak. No, Albany Tandoori had All You Could Order. You paid a cover charge, and as long as you had cleared your previous plate, they brought another dish. On this particular day I had not smoked anything, and I'd had maybe half a lager courtesy of my fake ID. Shaun, Little Mike and two other friends all wimped out early, managing two main courses and a side at most. The closest to catching me was Shaun, who did a biryani and a half plus three breads. I went on to eat three full chicken tikka masalas, three rices, and three complete peshwari naans (we are taking the pre-meal pop-padoms, onion salad and chutneys as read). This was way beyond previous quantities. As a cocky flourish, I finished by eating a flower from the vase, plus the contents of the ashtray. Disgusting, but man points as far as my mates were concerned. Remember, Dave Kane had set unrealistic testosterone targets, which forced desperate measures. I stood up and roared – legend status secured. The smile faded quickly as I felt some awful rumblings. Waves of nausea I had never experienced before came over me. Had I, finally, overdone it? Was I a mere mortal after all? Might this be the time I threw up and disgraced myself? Showed myself up as the true beta-gamma male that I am? I tossed down my cash and went out on to the street to gulp down fresh air. In Enfield and Essex we call this chucking a whitey.

'You all right?' Shaun asked. This was just before the era of camera phones or I'm sure he would have started filming and laughing.

'Yeah. I think so.'

Everyone was now stood outside. Little Mike later described to me what happened next.

Have you ever watched someone pass out? There are two ways of going. The straightforward drop, where you, hopefully, gently crumple to the ground – or the walk and drop, which I did. The walk and drop normally happens to the type of person who refuses to give in to unconsciousness. In illness, in sleep, in everyday life. You know who you are. The ever-active. Passing out is the purest test. Even with the brain fully switched off, the body goes for a little walk. A sort of chicken walk, with knees low and bum absurdly sticking out. An idiot body refusing to give in, even without a pilot. That's what my body did. My mates just thought I was doing a silly walk. I was known for them. It was just pure luck I did not chicken walk into the road and die, a dead cock. Instead I walked away from them, then back, then pitched forward, headbutting the glass door with the Albany Tandoori logo on the way down.

When I came to, I thought I was blind, but it was blood, pooling in my eye sockets. Claret going up in a fountain. I had cracked my head open. My friends were gathered around me in a circle. It was as though I were in my own grave and could observe my own mourners. I had no idea what was happening – an aneurysm, a stroke? I could not speak, or move.

When the ambulance arrived I had to be lifted into a wheelchair. Every stitch of cloth on my body was red, right down to my pants and socks. I could only speak slowly and slurringly. I knew where I was, but my body was not working. Turned out I had smashed my head so hard I had given myself concussion. I have no memory of the ambulance ride. I was wheeled into casualty in a neck brace. It looked much, much worse than the pitiful six stitches with no follow-up appointment that the injury would eventually turn out to be. I'd begged Shaun not to answer my mobile should it ring, but it did, and he did, and before the Indian nurse could even get a needle into my head or dispatch me to a concerned colleague where my brain would be scanned for anomalies, my dad was there and in my face. Mum, the lieutenant of worry, flanked him.

'Fucking hell. My boy. I knew it.'

'Dad . . .'

'A junkie! Do you owe someone money? I'll kill the cunt!'

'Stop swearing, Dave!' My mum looked tiny behind him.

'I wasn't beaten up, Dad.'

'I knew it! Then it's some shit you've taken. What crap have you put in your body? Tell me so we can get you off the junk. Tell me what you're on!'

All I could manage in a whisper was, 'Masala, Dad. Masala.'

He never believed me; he went to his grave believing it was a drug-related incident.

Food. I loved it. But without a job I couldn't keep getting takeaways and Jessica would probably dump me. Wanking and hungry. No thanks.

At this point, aged eighteen and just about to discover

watches, the scar on my forehead, a Harry Potter-style mark I still bear today, was fresh, the stitches not long out.

I needed some money. I'd seen a job advertised – selling watches. A position on Bond Street flogging exclusive time-pieces to the world's rich. Yes please. I might be a dropout, an idiot with no exams – a rockstar at the weekend who intended to peg it before the humiliation of middle age (forty). But I could sell. Oh, I could sell.

13.

You Pay, You Say

At eighteen, I'd already had many jobs pushing various merch (all legal, unlike many of my contemporaries).

One summer holiday I had actually gone door-to-door selling the Vorwerk vacuum cleaner (don't worry, no one had heard of it then either). My pitch was simple: 'Madam, do you mind if I vacuum your house while you watch?' But ultimately no one wants to buy a machine they've never heard of from a sixteen-year-old boy they don't trust. I did manage to flog some to friends and neighbours, which meant that for years there were embarrassing reminders in airing cupboards around town of the machine I'd once forced upon them. My area manager was a sweaty man called Brian. He had the type of moustache a sex offender would long for. He informed me with a solemn face that I'd missed my targets and they needed their demonstration machine back, and that was that.

Another selling job involved myself and Steven Epsom pounding the streets selling frozen food. We went door to door selling the Eismann delivery service. We secured the subscription-based orders, and a van delivered the nosh a week or two after. The idea was to get people to sign up for a monthly delivery. It was pretty dispiriting trying to sell to mostly scared, confused old ladies who weren't ready to move from tinned into the heady world of frozen. It also didn't help that one of the biggest sellers was some creamy meatballs called Bobby's Balls. At seventeen it was impossible to take that order without laughing, then losing the order when an offended old dear slammed the door in your face. My 'granddad' Ken (Nan's fourth or fifth husband) was our boss, and always angry at how unprofessional we were. He drove us to various Enfield and Essex streets in his Metro. He had crippled sideways arthritic hands by then and, towards the end, a diabetic stent in the base of his skull. He never whined about it, but he would often cry out 'Fuck me gently!' when shocked or surprised – like when another car approached with its full beam undipped.

'Fuck me gently! Audi bastard!'

And the Metro would continue along the Crooked Mile which borders Enfield and Essex.

Steven and I still say 'Fuck me gently' to this day. To my shame, we used to 'do the hands' as well. Ken was an awesome man. A well-spoken ducker and diver, who I'm sure had spent some time with Her Majesty, although I've never confirmed this. He was cultured but street at the same time. The poor bastard had just about everything that can go wrong with his body go wrong. But even with a stent in his neck, a walking frame, glasses, failing ears – he still sold door to door. Grafter! And he smoked a pipe too. No wonder my nan loved him. It was like some part of him was immortal, even though his body was dying. Nan was heartbroken when he fell out of bed and died one night. I like to think he let out one last 'Fuck me gently!' and then popped his clogs. Gone to the big VAT inspector in the sky. Man, he hated VAT.

*

Mum and Dad were relieved that I had got a job. Mum's relief was more that Dad's anger would simmer down.

'But it's shop work, boy. Should get a trade. A real profession. A man's job.'

'It's something, Dave. It's a start.'

'It's not a shop, Dad. It's a showroom. Closer to selling cars. The cheapest watch is £1,400. We're actually supposed to say "the least expensive watch".' I smiled suavely.

'A showroom, Dave!' my mum put in like a backing singer.

'Grand and a half for a fucking watch. What kind of twat spends that?'

'Kyle Phipps has got one,' Mum put in.

'Exactly, the twat,' said Dad, clearly thinking of the Ferrari, the double brandies ordered at dinner. 'Liberty-taking cunts,' he added, confirming the thought pattern.

'I can make money on commission too.'

'How much?'

'One per cent.'

Dad laughed.

'Yeah, but the average sale is six grand – and at least once a week we sell a £20,000 watch.'

I watched him do the maths. Two hundred sheets for twenty minutes selling. 'I suppose it's a start, boy.'

I hoped so. 'At least I'm not going to uni or anything like that, eh?' I put in, accidentally edging it with a shade of a sarcasm. It surprised me. What exactly did I resent?

Dad shot me a look.

'You pay, you say, boy. Once you hit eleven you're a man in some cultures.'

Eleven??

Had I been making a dig? Maybe I had, but the expression on his face reflected his truth back to me: I'd made my situation. And once you get past the grey age of sixteen years old there is no one else who can make your situation. Great-granddad Wolff's golden rules, now our house rules, were frequently restated if anyone showed signs of weakness. Two of them were at play here.

Never rely on anyone. They *will* let you down.

Take care of number one, and fuck everyone else.

'You're the one that fucked about at that Essex college,' Dad said.

'Dave, let's enjoy our shepherd's pie without swearing, please.'

'Fuck's sake!'

So that's how I ended up selling watches. Becoming a horologist was so unlikely that it was once suggested that I had invented it. But it's as true as a Rolex Chronometer's timekeeping. I put on a cheap suit and started work in a shop selling timepieces.

There are many good things to be gleaned from pulling yourself up. You quickly learn to make a target and kick for it. You learn financial independence, and it makes your skin thicker than a lizard dipped in concrete. If you get trained early enough in life that you must cover your own back, you get a strong spine. But my plans for a higher education got left behind, an unopened book on a shelf I could not reach.

I smashed the interview, and within a week received my

written offer from the Swiss Watch Company. I would start on the first of the next month as a sales assistant in the Bond Street 'showroom' (not 'shop', mind you). A whopping 9K a year plus 1 per cent commission on any timepieces (not 'watches') sold.

A short meeting followed with Mum and Dad, and we agreed I would pay monthly 'keep' from my wages. This is a very upper-working-class concept. Regardless of how flush the Mum or Dad is, no matter if you're busting your balls to save up for an education or to better your life – 'keep' must be paid. A portion of your wages taken each month and put into the family pot. It trains you for real-life rent paying. Everything is about preparing for the hardships that will definitely come your way. *Life is shit and hard.* (Rule no. 1.) Start learning that as soon as possible, boy. There is a self-worth in paying your way. Many sheltered 21-year-olds learn the hard way via credit cards, loans and poor decisions.

Dad always said, 'Wipe someone's arse for long enough, eventually they shit on your hands.' Or maybe that was Keats.

Plus, once you're paying, well then maybe you could be *saying*. Now and again, I might get some influence in what went down at home. I was eighteen after all, a man, another thing my dad had been telling me since I was twelve.

'You're a man now, boy.'

Turns out man x boy = jester.

But I was wrong. Paying keep did not automatically give me any power at home, and it was my *paying*, but not having my *say*, which led to an explosive disagreement and me moving in with my nan just one year later.

*

My watch-selling career, three years long, was pretty unremarkable apart from a surprising fact: I loved it. I would be misrepresenting my past if I didn't admit that not going to uni at eighteen and instead being forced into the banality of a shop-floor workplace to taste the grind of the nine to five was the best thing for me. Much better than:

'Poncing around Vietnam . . .'

Three years of tedious full-time work aged eighteen was an inoculation for the rest of life. There were two, opposing effects – one was to show me I did not wish to work in a shop for ever, and the other was that I thrived when talking to people about shiny things with complicated moving parts. I adored selling, and what I was selling. Beautiful machines made from precious metals. Eighteen months' craftsmanship from start to finish. Exquisite chronometers with more mechanical complexity than a Ferrari, and many with the same price tag. I held watches worth £150,000. I sold one for £48,000 and the client paid in cash. The thrill of bringing the sale from buyer to closure was an electric rush I still get today. In 2019, words are now my shiny things, packed into the white van of my mind, and I cannot wait to lift them out and show them to audiences. Swiss watches taught me how to sell, an essential skill in the two careers I went on to have, and it also gave me, in the best motivational way possible, a massive class-based chip on my shoulder, a chip that pushed down on me till I pushed back, looked in the mirror and made that change – *shamone!* (If you're under twenty-one, that was a reference to Michael Jackson, who was this really big pop star when I was growing up, and by the time this is published may well have been disgraced.) Envy. What a complex, fierce, brilliant fuel. Green, yet harsh on its environment.

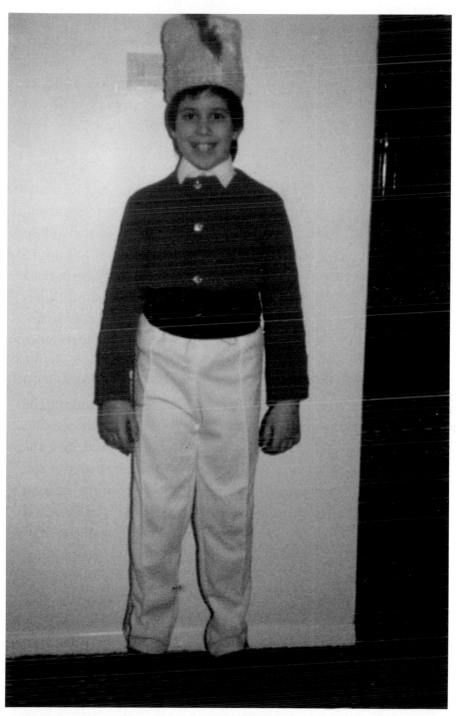

I've never enjoyed being the centre of attention.

Above: My two nannas - they couldn't have been more different. On the left is party animal Joyce (also known as Maria), who took me in when I walked out of mum and dad's, and on the right is Eva (who's surprisingly smiling here).

Below: Dad with my alcoholic auntie Brenda. She moved to America, but would violently cameo in my childhood several times.

Two places where Dad was happy the Warren Wood pub (**above left**) and on holiday in Menorca.

Always trying to find common interests with Dad – and usually failing. The wind blew up my T-shirt (**above right**) and for a second it looked like I had bodybuilder pecs.

Moving in with nutty Nanna Joyce (**above**) changed my life – the Kane Curse was finally challenged. So much so that it took me five months from enrolling on a distance learning course to a grade A in A-level Sociology – the quickest by many months. I even won an award, presented to me by Betty Boothroyd (**below**).

Graduation day! Marred only by Dad fretting about the traffic on both the North and South Circular roads.

Left: My dad, suddenly old-looking, stood in front of his hated Mercedes Elegance.

Below: Dad, aged fifty, flexing his guns in Florida, on the holiday where there was nothing for us kids to do apart from 'roast on the white-sand beach'.

It was while on this holiday to Cyprus that Dad's heart finally gave up. Eerily, this was taken the day before he dropped down dead.

Only once did someone who sounded and seemed like me come into the shop – I mean showroom – and he found himself humiliated by my manager, Herman.

'I'd like a Rolex Submariner, please,' said the twenty-something Essex lad. I smiled at him and he nodded back.

'Are you sure?' cut in Herman, with acidic snootiness. Our store manager had no modes between slimy friend and angry butler. Herman had known straight away something was wrong – people never purchased like that. They liked to be seated, spoken to, pampered. They are prickly about price, and want at least 10 per cent off.

'Yeah. Submariner. The one in the window—' and he started getting his wallet out. 'The grey one.'

'That's stainless steel, sir,' said Herman, but the 'sir' was spat out like 'peasant'.

'That's handy. Don't want it stained,' he said laughing and laying two notes on the table: a ten and a twenty.

'Excuse me, sir, what's this?' said Herman, like a monarch inspecting a filthy glove. We were not quite yet in the era where someone who appeared and sounded common could surprise you in a *Pretty Woman* way and turn out to be minted. This was still the time of 'looks poor, sounds poor, probably is poor'.

'Thirty quid,' he replied. 'Keep the change . . . it's been a bit of a good week. Cash work!'

I saw now he was younger than I first thought, maybe even seventeen or eighteen – my age. Poor fucker. He wasn't joking or trying it on. He was just sheltered and poor and naive. I felt a stab in my chest.

'Keep the change?' screeched Herman – two years later I would hear my first Lady Bracknell declare 'a haaaandbag' and it made me think of Herman – 'keep the change? It's *two thousand seven hundred and seventy pounds.*'

Silence, then: 'I thought it said twenty-seven, seventy.'

I tried making eye contact as he left the shop, but he never looked up.

Most of my punters (sorry, clientele, Rodders), were either rich and Middle Eastern, or posh English splashing out for their lucky brats. Three years of watching kids my age being shown around a shop by doting parents buying them 'graduation' gifts began to take its shoulder-chip toll.

'This is my son, Oliver,' said a white-haired dad one day as he sat opposite me in the showroom. 'Tell him, Ollie.'

'Well,' said Ollie, thin, posh, happy, 'I just got a first.'

Aged nineteen at this point, I did not have a clue what 'a first' meant. Not one person in my social circle or family would have used it. The first time I heard the phrase 'a two-one' was when I applied to university two years later. It was a world completely unknown to me, but little scenes like this kept piling on the pressure to travel there, to have a look.

'He's being modest,' put in the father. 'A first from Gonville and Caius . . .'

'Cambridge,' added the son when he saw my blank look.

I would humiliate myself over a decade later by mispronouncing 'Caius' while being interviewed. It's pronounced 'keys', not 'kye-usss'.

'Anyway,' the posh dad said, 'I'd like to buy my Ollie an Air King.'

A beautiful, steel, date-less Rolex for his adored son; a simple, elegant choice. I felt an irrational belch of fire . . . Angry envy – let's call it energy. Why should I be this side of the desk? Random accidents of birth began not to suffice as explanation. Things were shifting and stirring, but the break would not come while I lived under my dad's roof. The silverback's hold was too much. For me to move out Dad would need to do something so shocking that I would become a plastic leftic and move in with my nan. It was about a girl. I foolishly tried invoking 'I'm paying, I'm saying' – and it backfired horribly.

14.

The Cockney Klansman

I'd been at the Swiss Watch showroom for a few months when things with first love Jessica came to an end. My relationship with her, courtesy of Abigail, was the deepest, most intense and unhealthy breed of first love – a common ordeal for most of us. We met at a Lady Margaret's school ball in Surrey, me and my mates invited there as guests of Abigail. There had been lots of innuendo talk that this shy, blonde girl one year younger than me found me attractive.

'Bloody hell, Kane's gonna get laid,' Warren shouted.

'Indeed,' Steven Epsom agreed, pointing forward the Chin of Ecstasy in approval.

This was only the second time in my life a girl had chosen me. The first was Shagger Gina. That first evening of knowing Jessica started in the exact same dire pattern. Me avoiding her, not mustering the courage to even walk over to this stunning girl. I spent the first part of the night gazing at her through the window of an adjacent room. In the end Wayne had enough. He took me round a corner and produced an illicit bottle.

'Mate, take a slug of this.'

I swallowed a massive mouthful of bitter liquid – whisky. I was sixteen, I had only been drunk once, so the effect was instant. Wayne slapped me around the face. I adjusted my curtain hair and bowled straight over to Jessica.

'Do you want to go for a walk?' I said, invoking the standard teenage euphemism for come around the corner and snog me, please.

'Yes,' she said. 'Certainly.' So she was well-spoken . . . I felt a proletariat twitching in my pants.

Moments later I had my first proper kiss with an actual human girl. It was passionate, clumsy and earnest. We pulled away from each other, regarding each other's face like two botanists with special orchids; and we both knew that something had been started that could not be stopped. It wasn't pleasant, or fuzzy, or exciting. It was terrible, and hot, and uncontrollable.

At the end of the night, I kissed her and said goodbye. Six of us illegally crammed into Steven Epsom's Ford Escort and we drove back to Enfield. In the darkness, I silently cried. I'd fallen in love instantly and so deeply that I wept. I made sure no one saw, though. I didn't want to look like a wanker.

'Kane's crying!' someone said.

'Gay!' said someone else.

My three-year relationship with Jessica was almost standard teenage stuff, save for the sprinkling of bleak, intense behaviour spells, and stuffed full of exploratory shagging. The loss of my virginity was neither dramatic nor comically clumsy (annoyingly – would have made a good chapter). We both rather enjoyed it. In fact, we felt a bit let down that there wasn't bloody spraying, tears and operatic confusion.

Thank God for porn. Thanks to mucky films I knew where everything was, and what all the bits did. Back then, late-night comedy on the telly – old men and snarky women complaining 'No one knows where the clitoris is' – used to make me cringe. It's right there. How thick are you? My porn usage was in the sweet spot. Not too much of it, as broadband Internet had not yet arrived, plus everything I did see was simply men and women giving head and fucking. Nothing unusual, so my teenage brain hadn't warped into extreme shaving, misogynistic shagging, nor anything demeaning or cruel. I was a virgin, but I knew the manual back to front. I approached a woman's body the way I've approached everything else that I've had to work hard at: with diligent study and a passionate practice which gives the illusion of ability. The girls of my generation were (I hope) the last batch of girls who had not masturbated much (or at all) by the time they got into their first relationship. This is a disaster – like an Essex mum trying to speak French on day one of her holiday after zero study. Impossible. Of all the girls me and my friends dated, none were orgasmic by sixteen, even eighteen. None. We were the first generation of lads who could be mocked if we didn't sort that out. We were responsible for her pleasure. Poor Jessica thought she'd been electrocuted the first time we managed to 'blow her biscuits' – but once we did that, we were off. Shag Shag Shag.

So sex was easy. Managing our dads was a little trickier. My dad, meaning well, made crass jokes here and there that made us feel awkward.

'No porking in the conservatory, please!'

And when Jessica was out of earshot: 'Nice girl, boy – but no tits.' Wow, there's a joke that hasn't aged well.

When it came to staying over, I have to say Mum and Dad were cool. I'd never really had many friends allowed to sleep at the house, but they let Jessica sleep on the Z-bed in the lounge almost every weekend. I think my mum sensed I might actually die if we didn't see each other, and about this even Dad seemed relaxed. I guess when I was 'getting my end away' some sort of male pride trumped his passion for no one staying over, ever.

Jessica Sutherland's dad Leonard was a different creature. A cold throwback from almost Edwardian times. A softly spoken, vicious little hamster of man, to whom I did everything possible to try and endear myself but he would not have it. It wasn't me, it was the fact his daughter was sixteen, and in his head it was the year 1905. I only stayed at their house once, Christmas, and I was given a stubby can of Heineken while we all sat in clock-ticking silence waiting for the Queen's speech. It was a house frozen in time, the furnishings all lime green and plasticky, exactly as they had been when the Sutherlands had moved in in 1972. As buttoned as he was, a few times Leonard boiled over. I'd been at their house and it was late. I was just about to get in my Vauxhall Nova and leave. Jessica was already in her dressing gown, with a nightie underneath – hardly crotchless panties, but from the way Leonard exploded, it was like he'd walked in on us shagging in a chapel.

'Jessica! Good God!'

Neither of us knew what we'd done wrong. We were just saying goodbye. Not snogging, nothing.

'What are you wearing' – he marched her into the bathroom – 'with *him* here!'

Jessica, nearly seventeen now, couldn't help laughing – it was so ridiculous. She was in a tatty blue dressing gown and an old maid's nightie. But the laugh was followed by a hollow slap.

'Your reputation, Jessica!' And he slapped her again. 'Your

reputation!' It's the only time in my life I've ever seen a woman being hit.

Her reputation? It was the type of phrase my great-grandma would have used.

'You need to go,' said Jessica, her cheek glowing red, eyes flushed with embarrassed tears.

We had two good years after that – attending jungle raves, being sickeningly in love. I was no way stable enough to make a girl happy; by now I was insecure about everything. I had zero confidence about my skin (covered in spots) and my place in the world. I had no focus. I was shit. Everything I do will be shit, etc., etc. I was smoking too much weed, plus everything else. I must have been very difficult to date. I had a rotten temper too. Not against people – I've managed to go my whole life without ever hitting anyone. My anger was against things. Computers that didn't work. Cars that didn't start. Poor Jessica witnessed some seriously mad shit. I ripped off wing mirrors, punched through doors, destroyed computers.

When Jessica turned eighteen she decided to train to be a nurse. We picked a hospital near me so that we could be close to each other, but by the time she started training, she was done with my childish outbursts – and I can't blame her. Unfortunately, my love for her was just as deep, now tinged with jealousy and possessiveness as I sensed her moving away from me emotionally. It was one month into her training before she shagged a doctor. She told me straight away, one night when we were eating pizza. I fell to the floor sobbing and beat up the pizza boxes we'd just had delivered. A low moment.

I went round to her nursing accommodation a few days

later. They would not let me in, so I actually cried and begged on the intercom.

'What do you want?' said Jessica, when I eventually made it into her room.

'I love you. I love you – I'll die without you.' I believed it as I pathetically repeated it.

'No, Russell. I'm sorry, no . . .' she kept saying over and over, like an exorcism.

I will never forget the sight of my snot and tears on her black shoes.

Her dad had been due to collect her at that moment. It was the first time he was nice to me. He escorted me from the building humanely, arm around my shoulder, and I've never seen Jessica Sutherland since that day.

'Me and Jessica are finished,' I told my dad the next morning.

'Fuck it, boy. She had no tits,' and as vile as the sentence was, it made me smile.

In those weeks after the split, I began partying way too hard, and I found myself in an emotional state that not many other lads seemed to suffer from. I fell in love with anyone who looked at me. A kiss was honestly enough to have me writing poetry. And sex? At this confused stage, I called myself a love grenade: fine so long as the pin was still in, but once the pin was removed, 'I love you!'

There was this one girl called Becky. She worked in the Breitling showroom a few doors down from where I worked. She was coming out of a relationship too and everything about my decision to pursue a new one with her was flawed and dangerous. Yet one thing led to another and in very little time we were groping each other behind a Sainsbury's in Liverpool Street, fondling away the wait till our trains went out to Enfield and Essex respectively. I'd come so close to true despair during my break-up with Jessica that I couldn't believe I was even touching another woman. It felt wrong and right at the same time; a form of cheating. The relationship with Becky had as yet gone no further than snogging, but in my mind we were married, kids, the works. You do get clingy men too – we just hide it better. Some of us pretend to be bastards simply to be appealing to women. It's all so bloody confused. Thank God I'm hitched now.

Becky and I were on our third or fourth date at All Bar One (when it still felt like an upmarket wine bar and not a place where you got wanked off in the toilets by Karen from accounts) when Becky dropped a bombshell, I mean, a wombshell.

'Don't panic. But I've got to do a pregnancy test.'

'But I only kissed you.'

'Shut up and listen. Me and my ex, we had unprotected sex just before we broke up and . . .' She was crying at this point and I regretted my preggers-by-kissing gag. 'I'm three days late. I shouldn't even be telling you. I'm sorry.'

Pause.

'The bill, please!'

Not exactly Viagra (which hadn't been invented yet), and anyway, why can't they invent a de-agra? One that takes away sex drive. I think many men secretly long for that drug. Maybe they could bottle the feeling you get upon hearing the word *Brexit*? Yeah. That would work.

Also, I didn't say 'The bill, please'. That's what a *normal* lad-man might do. No, I was hit by a wave of crushing protectiveness, plus, and I've never admitted this before, but I hoped a bit that she *was* pregnant. Now that is messed up, but the idea of loving her and her little baby was instantly appealing to my heartbroken, chemically ruined self.

I think I'm going to leave a gap rather than analyse what it means – but seeing how I dote on my daughter now, I imagine part of me has always longed to have a stab at sacrifice and see what it felt like, to flout Take Care of Number One in the most meaningful way possible. Bringing up another man's baby. It's the ultimate Take Care of Number Two and Three. Take that, Great-granddad Wolff. I wanted to be saintly, gentle, different to the silverback. How can you rebel when inwardness is required? Surely a rebel needed to be outward-facing, loud and destructive – I was none of those things.

'Wow,' I said, feigning blankness.

'Do you . . . not want to see me again?'

'I . . . I . . . want to see you more.'

I wish I had the discretion gene, the gene that's good at keeping secrets, which lets a stoic man bear an illness without even telling his family, but alas I have the opposite gene: I tell everyone everything. I'm currently making a living out of it. I'll tell a taxi driver about a prostate examination if he asks.

Later that evening, oversharing was my downfall. It led to the biggest break me and my dad ever had. I decided to tell my mother. Why? My mum did not need to know these details. It was not even a confirmed pregnancy, and the girl was not my girlfriend, yet I could not help myself. Talk, talk, talk.

That night, I slipped out of my Topman suit, and after

Dad had farted his way upstairs to bed swearing about how tired and unlucky he was, I confided in my mum over steaming mugs of tea.

'So, this Becky.'

'What's going on? Something's up – I can tell.' She was tender, but suspicious.

'Well – she thinks she might be up the duff by her previous boyfriend.'

Pause. Then: 'Shit. Swerve it.'

'I actually like her, Mum.'

'But what about the ex-boyfriend?'

I hadn't considered that. 'I don't know much about Dayo.'

'Dayo?'

'Adedayo – that's his name. He's a DJ.'

'*Adee Dewoo*. That's his name?'

'Yes.'

She dropped to a whisper, as though the KGB were listening. 'Black?'

'Afro-Caribbean,' I said, gently correcting.

You could have driven a UKIP van through the gap in the silence.

'Swerve it,' she said again. And then again, 'Swerve it. I'm off to bed.'

And that was that.

Only it wasn't.

At all.

My mum carries the same gene as me: talk about stuff for hours and hours to anyone. And it wasn't even twenty-four of them before she herself thought it would be a good idea to confide in the Cockney Klansman himself. Dad.

'Dave – Russell's white girlfriend has a black ex, who

might be on the scene.' I bet it was that blunt. And it sent my dad full Liam Neeson.

Now, looking back, and being generous to my old man (what choice do I have?) – his main worry was just that some 21-year-old man would be hanging around our house having a problem with me muscling in on his baby. It was just that Dad chose to lay racist paranoia over the top of it.

The situation would not have ignited like it did if I held similar views to him. But the scenes I was partying in, the philosophies I danced to, had taken hold strongly of my jungle-music heart. By this time, I was nineteen, and deep in the Peace and Loveism clubbing scene of North London. Racism, to me and my white and black friends, was the prejudice equivalent of flares. Not even offensive, just ridiculous and something from yesterday. To us, for a few glorious years, racism wasn't evil, it was just silly and old-fashioned, like rickets or scurvy. Painful, yeah, but being eradicated; something to be smiled about while the MDMA took its rebel army through your body and into your brain.

Apart from a few pill-stealing idiot policemen, we were winning – the younger generation had seen the light. Every Sunday, we found ourselves hugging each other on the dance floor at 6 a.m. as DJ Ratty dropped 'One Family' by Some Justice, a tune that still gives me goosebumps to this day. So when our little bubble popped inward and bleak reality was revealed, many of our reactions were much stronger than they might have been. I knew my dad and his generation (remember the age gap between my mum and dad; he was almost two generations above me) divided the world along colour lines. Different-coloured people probably want to take your shit and make it their own. The philosophy, the fear, was that simple. I'd met some old pensioner Rastas who felt the same. I hadn't realized it could ever affect a random skinny white boy like me. But it did.

It was 7 a.m., everyone rushing around the breakfast bar in the kitchen. I'd just served myself a bowl of Golden Grahams, sponsored by Diabetes. Mum looked sheepish, then she dashed out of the room like a terrorist who knows the explosives are ready. And it was just me and my dad, and the bomb.

'That bird, boy . . .'

'Huh?'

'The bird . . . the one you're seeing at work.'

'Becky?'

'Yeeeeahhh, mon!' he said with an aggressive, parodic Jamaican accent; the sort Chubby Brown would do, then call everyone a snowflake if they got offended.

'What about her?'

Dad took a mouthful of tea. Burning hot tea. I've only met a few people in my life who can swallow tea when it's magma-hot like that. He also liked to take food hot out of the microwave with no oven glove. I once saw him peel an egg straight from the pan.

'I don't want her in my house.'

'What?'

'I don't want *that* in my house.'

'I never said I was bringing *that* over.'

'Well, you won't be, will you?'

The 'my' of my house . . . Not 'our' house. Not even the neutral 'this' house. But 'my'. The jet of piss was marking the wall. The silver fur was displayed, fists pounding the ground. Time to test my strength, for the first time ever.

'I don't understand,' I lied. 'I don't follow.'

'Yes you do, boy. I don't want her in my house.'

I heard a creak from around the corner. Mum, earwigging.

'Right.' I was confused about how to respond. After all, I hadn't planned to bring Becky to *our* house, but now, on principle, I thought – well, I might want to. And why shouldn't I? 'Go on then,' I said, in a tone which nudged dangerously close to standing up for myself, 'tell me why.' I naively thought calling his bluff would shame him into silence. It had the opposite effect. There was no pause, no thought. Just:

'She's been banging a coon.'

'Dave!' My mum from the next room, listening in like Polonius.

'Are you serious?' I asked.

'*Fucking* serious. You bring that in my house – up the duff – you got any idea what will happen? There'll be his mates climbing up the walls – breaking in. Your muvva'll be attacked. They'll stab the fucking cats . . .'

He went on. And on. And I'm surprised as I sit here typing that I've found the need to sanitize and cut what he *really* said. I've left out the more repulsive parts, I think to protect him, but also because I'm still embarrassed. To this day.

'Dad. Calm down.'

'Fuck off! My house! She ain't coming in,' and then he actually dropped an 'I'm paying, I'm saying'.

For the first time since I'd been born, at aged nineteen, I answered back in a slow, steady voice: 'But you aren't, are you?'

'You what, boy?'

'You're not paying. For my room, I mean. You take £150 off me a month. I should be allowed to have a visitor over for a cup of tea if I want. It's my room – I'm basically renting it off you.'

There was a short pause while he weighed up his response: 'You ain't got nothing. It's my house.'

I still can't believe I had the balls to say (and follow through) with what I threatened next.

'If I can't bring Becky over, I'll move out.'

'She ain't coming in. I don't even want her in the front garden.'

'Right. I'm moving out. Tonight.'

'Go on then!' said Dad, laughing like I was a little boy trying to lift a car into the air. But Dad was about to learn what everyone else who knows me quickly learns. I stick to what I say and follow it through with annoying willpower. I packed a bag, took it to work with me and that night went 'home' to my nan's.

15.

Nutter of all Nuts

This book may be about the X-Man that is my father, but I feel I should tell you more from my mum's origin story. If you're hoping for an interval of normality or conventionality, I am about to disappoint on a *Shameless/Eastenders Christmas Special* scale.

You may wonder why Mum was living with my great-grandma, her nan, when she met my dad. Where was my nan, her mum? Was she dead? Did she have a disability and was unable to raise my mum? Was she a go-getting career woman who chose the life of a feminist pioneer in the city rather than the drudgery of child rearing?

No.

She was an alcoholic, weed-smoking, wild party animal mental bastard who went through six children. And four husbands, one of whom died on the toilet, another on the floor. The rest ran, as fast as they could, or she did. The tales of her are wild and conflicting. Yet, as you may have guessed already, I absolutely adored her.

Nan was only just sixteen when she fell preggers with my mum. A slim girl, her gestational bump was like someone had taped a basketball to a broom handle. As soon as my mum was born, Nan handed the baby straight to my great-grandma

Connie (who lived till I was eighteen, by the way – and who I also had an amazing relationship with).

Great-grandma Connie was more like you expect a grandma to be. Silver curly perm, book-reading, park-walking – affected gentility had completely removed her working-class accent. I guess *she* was my grandma in the grandma sense. Her daughter, my nan, was my grandma in the Jimi Hendrix/Amy Winehouse sense. Inspiring, dangerous, clever and untamed. But as a mother to my mum, bloody useless.

I think of my mum's birth scene as a baseball tableau: Mum firing out of Nan, and my great-grandma catching her in a cushioned glove. And that's where Mum stayed. My nan (she was called Joyce, btw, although she hated the name and liked to be called Maria – how *do* we solve a problem like . . .) soon fled the family home and was off with her next fella. Five more children soon popped out. Some stayed with Nan, some ended up elsewhere, but only my mum stayed with my great-grandma Connie. Yet against all odds, my mum and her siblings, half or full, have always been tight. My mum's dad Peter, Granddad Peter, is still alive today and I visit him when I can. He's a manly man, still playing bowls and talking about hunting. Ledge. He went on to marry and have four more children – and my mum is reasonably close to them too. That makes her one of ten – and we're not even Catholic.

Mum's first few years were lived in that snugly overprotective cocoon of smiling, gentle Connie – plus, living in the spare room, with her husband Ivan, Connie's older daughter, my great-auntie Eileen.

Great-auntie Eileen is a carbon copy of Connie. And Great-uncle Ivan is the dad figure you would design on a computer. Thoughtful, interested, funny and kind. At the time of writing, Eileen and Ivan are still alive and well and a massive part of mine and my mum's life – Minna, my daughter, adores them. Really, they acted as parents to my mum. Those two and Connie.

Amazingly, when my mum was three years old, my then eighteen-year-old Granddad Peter went for sole custody of my mum, and won. That's how shit my party nan's conduct had been. But when the day came for my mum to go and live with her father Peter and his new partner Pat it became clear that she had become too attached to Connie, Eileen and Ivan – and it was agreed that she should stay there instead.

This amazing, kindly threesome raised my mum, and I'm lucky to have known them all. But, to my shame, as seems always the way with books, films and telly – the most interesting of that whole lot was not the hard-working, decent people, it was the H Bomb Joyce, my absent nan. That whirling dervish of damage. The crazy, swearing, quaffing, smoking, self-annihilating anomaly in that quiet, urbane household. Great-auntie Eileen, like her dad (Connie's husband Great-granddad Frank – a darkly quiet man whose arteries clogged up like the M25 and dispatched him into the slip road of deadness early doors), was a draughts person. Great-grandma Connie spoke nicely; she had managed various upmarket kiosks in her youth. What. The. Hell. Happened. To. My. Nan? Two girls, Eileen and Joyce. Raised in the same house, in the same way. One grows into a sort of cuddly vicar's wife, the other into bad girl rockstar – an angry, oozing stick of booze and profanity.

Nan's first enemy was an overdose of good looks. Like the girl in Disney's *Frozen* who accidentally freezes everything she touches, Nan heated up any man she went near. Maybe true love's kiss could have cured her too – but sadly that kiss often led to a baby and more chaos. She was a knockout stunner. Grade A, jaws on the floor, lads, Elizabeth Taylor stunner. Many of the girls in my family are beautiful (before I get angry phone calls), but Nan was too much. Bit Natalie Portman, much more Sophia Loren. And if you're cursed with beauty plus an inability to process male attention, then the result is usually: foetus. Second problem. She was totally batshit loony. Not in the clinical sense, but in the Ibiza summer season sense. As in 'Darren went fucking mental in Ibiza and had to come home again and now he's on pills'. But Nan never 'went home' from her holiday. She stayed at the party. Exactly when she made the transition from party abandon to chronic addictive illness, no one seems to know, but the girl, and then the woman, drank. But not like the semi-alcoholics you might know. She really drank. She drank as we breathe. She smoked as we blink. She would wake at 6 a.m., pour a triple vodka, add orange juice, light an Embassy Filter, and that's how she powered through her day. She managed to work at various intervals, but once she got into her fifties she was usually in bed by 7 p.m.

One time I accidentally tasted that first drink of the day. We were up and getting ready for a wedding. I had been awake about twenty minutes and entered the kitchen in a pre-caffeine daze for my morning shot. Back then I had a 'people's espresso' as my morning drink: a heaped teaspoon of Maxwell House instant coffee and two tablespoons of hot water. I clicked on the kettle.

'Morning, love,' Nan said, there, as always, in her dressing gown made of a fabric I'm going to call Immortal Turquoise.

This deathless dressing gown, an almost holy item, belonged in one of *The Lord of the Rings* movies as a magical object which ten Frodos could not have hacked through. If she was indoors, she was in the turquoise garment. Sometimes a short trip to the shops would be completed in the same spectral cloak. That morning, as usual, she was drawing on her trademark Embassy Filter fag, like an aboriginal Australian sucking snake venom from a bite, while stirring a saucepan of Goldilocks-perfect porridge. The fag and the cooking. If only there had been an Olympic sport for maintainers of ash-length, my nan could have found fame in Los Angeles or Rio. She always had a single grey finger of filth tantalizingly hovering over the pan. More than once I saw the ash drop in. She found it hilarious.

'Adds to the flavour, love.' I honestly believed it did.

If ash fell on to the living-room floor she would tread it in. 'Strengthens the carpet.'

I believed that one till I was twenty-one.

I said, 'Morning, Nan,' sipping my people's espresso.

'Sleep all right?'

I poured myself an orange juice. A moment later I picked it up for a swig, only, at 7 a.m., to discover it was not my morning juice, but hers. I should have noticed – the colour wasn't right. A thin yellow rather than orange. There were ice cubes in there too, with polar swirls of boozy mist. The taste – mixed with my coffee – was foul enough to put me off vodka for nearly a decade; the flavour equivalent of sticking your finger in a pencil sharpener and turning it. Vodka for breakfast: that's how my nan started her day.

Nan stood in as a father figure at my most critical time. She was an aggressive supporter and encourager of the craziest leap anyone in my huge, disparate family has ever done: an A-level. An actual fucking A-level that got an actual fucking A grade.

I was nineteen when I moved in with my nan. I lodged in a box room in her housing association flat on a council estate in Enfield. The room just took a single bed, no room for a wardrobe. I made do with glued-on coat-pegs on the walls. My shirts loomed over me as I slept like shit ghosts in a Gothic novel.

These were the three years during which I transformed myself, worked out who this chavvy nobody was supposed to be, and Nan, my Joyce, my Maria (or whatever the mad drunk was calling herself that week), my absolute nutter of all nuts, the kernel of the nut itself, Nutella McCashew – she lit the fuse that ignited a fuel cell, the energy of which fires these key-strokes today, and which, if you're ever kind enough to see me live, propels the thermal charge which rips across the room, regardless of how big or small the room I'm playing. Something cracked in me, but luckily, it cracked at the right angle. Three weird, brilliant years, living with the wildest nan ever to walk (and zigzag and kick) the earth.

It's hard to explain how living in the box room of a housing association flat with no furniture, carrying a self-defence knife in my work bag* and smoking yet more weed, became the period of my life wherein I made the most positive, active changes.

Most would *not* describe my nan as a successful human.

---

* It was a cheese knife, and it was my own big mouth that caused the problem to arise in the first place. Thank God I never tried to use it. I thought the cheese-stabbing prong on the end was threatening but really the only thing it was good for was Brie.

Six children, all of them imperfectly parented, and my poor mum, abandoned altogether – although, given how amazing Great-grandma Connie and her older daughter my great-auntie Eileen turned out to be as substitutes, perhaps the best thing that ever happened to her.

Even back when I was nineteen and righteously angry, it felt treacherous giving my nan any recognition or love, seeing how she had abnegated so much of her basic responsibility towards my mum. Today it feels like full treason; now that I'm older I can appreciate how she made my mum feel. After all, it was my mum and dad who *made* me. My old man who worked his pecs off. My mum who cleaned and dinner-ladied; who fought to get me into a school that was a bit less shit than all the others (but turned out to be stuffed with Godders and a pacdophile); who walked me to the local panto-mime society and to the church hall to take acting lessons when I was nine. The trouble was, when I got to nineteen I needed a shove in a new direction. My old man's approach was to push you under, to teach you how to hold your breath in the mucky tub of life. Things were gonna rain in your face, you'll need strong lungs, start practising how you sink; after all, you're going down anyway. My nan's approach was to walk around that bath of water, laugh and let the plug out. This was her whole life philosophy; many times I heard her say this:

'Laugh and the world laughs with you. Cry and you're a cunt.'

Here it is in Latin.

Non irrideas et mundi subsannavit te. Clamo ad te et cunnus.

I don't know if that's correct, but it's the type of linguistic mischievousness my nan would have adored. And, besides, to cry about it being wrong would make me a . . . You get the idea.

In the three years Nan and I lived together, it was our mantra. Sometimes we were laughing when we recited it, sometimes we were crying. She picked me up off the floor when I was broken; she skipped when I skipped; she told me to rebel, to take the gamble – even to embrace debt and the wildness of going to uni. Sod my steady job.

Here's another of her phrases:

'Fuck her dirty knickers!'

Puer eam knickers sórdida.

We used this for girls, men, things – house keys, anything. And for jobs. Yeah – employment, the filthy undercrackers of the slave class. Working was for squares. To become a loafing, reading student was so far from anything I recognized as the correct way to live that only a failure and a rebel could have lit the way for me. It's something my old man would never have understood. Work wasn't always salvation; sometimes it broke you.

'Laugh and you'll get laughed at. Cry, and then it's done.' That maybe would have been his version.

My nan lived on patch of dog-shit-coloured suburbia sublimely called Freezywater. Essex was two minutes' walk from the front door, and London was three minutes the other way. Freezywater itself was nowhere, not even in Hertfordshire. It was *Shameless* meets *Game of Thrones*, a mysterious thing that somehow *is*. The estate Nan lived on was more violent than a ginger's sunburn, but it was close to Turkey Street Station with its direct line into Central London, and that'd do me.

I hadn't realized how funny it was to live on a road called Turkey Street till one Sunday morning at 7 a.m. when a group of us travelled back from a Strawberry Sundaes hard house rave. We'd picked up this random American girl, and as we stood there in the bright reality of a post-clubbing sunrise, she howled the laugh of an experienced pill-user, repeating the word 'Thanksgiving' over and over.

'My God – Turkey Street – that's just so fucking funny. Thanksgiving. Thanksgiving.'

We went over to the local park and sat on the climbing frames, all cuddling in a human heap of warmth and imagining that life didn't get any better than sharing a dog-muck patch of local green space with pilled-up nutters we'd met on the Tube.

The all-white racist feud with Dad had simmered down within a couple of weeks. I remember feeling disappointed with myself. I had been sure it was the beginning of the tear that would estrange me from my immediate family for life. The drama and the finality of it all appealed to my boiling teenage mind, but within a few months a tacit peace treaty was in operation.

Oddly, for a man with a tendency to verbal tsunamis, no big sit-down speech was ever given by Dad, no discussion ever happened. Maybe he knew he was in the wrong, but he was also exerting his rights to be utterly bad and still be authoritarian – that's a fascist – and he knew it.

The easiest thing initially was for Sunday lunches quietly to resume. Maybe I was just too forgiving, or high, or much more likely couldn't be arsed to maintain a stance. I would never have moved back, but a weekly roast I could manage, and so a few weeks after I moved in with my nan, I returned for my first Sunday lunch. Dad was on top form, soaked in Stella Artois and venting over a Costco leg of lamb about:

'That old cunt down the road. Helen Markham.'

Mum: 'Dave! Would you mind not using the C-word at Sunday dinner!'

'Difficult, when you're describing a cunt.'

Helen Markham was second in command to the aforementioned Hilda Black. My dad's beef with her had started the year before – a poisonous argument about parking and front gardens. We had (treacherously in their council eyes) paid to have a slope put in, and the neighbours saw it as more evidence of unforgivable pretension and 'ways'. White-haired pensioner Helen Markham was an original troll, before Twitter – and actually looked like a troll. A defrosted mound of pork mince with a pubey white perm. She moved from house to house gathering hate and falsehoods for her and Hilda to disseminate. She was a miserable old bint with four dogs and a thin pipe of a husband who lived in the pub. She was Hilda Black's lieutenant, her Himmler, and the two of them used to hang off the gate together gossiping and planning the next character assassination.

'Just ignore them, Dave.'

'Fuck 'em. They need to be told. I made something of myself. That's why they hate us.'

This flash of my dad's self-pride was something new. So part of him *did* believe he'd achieved something. Things were stirring up inside me. Maybe it was something to do with the different perspective that moving out gave me. Most Sundays there was something I could laugh at or be astounded by; some of it too offensive even to describe onstage later on:

'India, Pakistan . . . same fucking thing . . . they should nuke the lot.'

But my God, I would love him to have lived through Brexit. I could have just held a Dictaphone to his mouth and the stand-up would write itself. You selfish bastard, Dad. I needed you for jokes.

Life at Nan's was dysfunctional, but it was exactly what I needed. Working in a watch shop by day, smoking weed in a council flat by night. At weekends, I partied hard and risked my health and mental well-being. With all the rules removed I could have gone down; instead, with Nan's help, I started to see the nonsense of it.

'You will fail. Life is shit.'

And Nan corrected: 'Life is chaos, love. Run at it.'

I could give up my job now. I could take MDMA now. No one is actually stopping me.

'Do you know what rules are?' Nan said, sloshing a Smirnoff.

'What?'

'Bollocks. That's what they are. Swinging fucking bollocks.'

I began to feel more daring. More invincible. Even though my skin was grey, and I felt tired and dangerously on a come-down all the time, at work I was the top seller. Watches flew out the door on the wrists of smug bastards I would one day catch up. My brain was speeding up; something was happening that had nothing to do with the toxins I was putting into my body. I lay in bed each night at my nan's and I could feel that there was something I was supposed to do next – I just could not figure out what it was. But one random Saturday

I met the guide who would show me. She was the one thing I never thought I would experience: a properly posh girl-friend, much more so than Jessica, who was more genteel than posh. She showed me, quite accidentally, what I had to do next.

Some of us find when we look back that we can't pinpoint the exact moment we changed. It happened gradually. We made small adjustments. We stopped getting high, slowly knuckled down, and eventually things came together. That's not me! My waste-man days ended suddenly in a flash of comedown and revelation. In one hour, in one specific minute. I have the diary entry, the exact moment. I was twenty years old. Two things converged – the class-based chip on my shoulder finally shifted, and this awakening coincided with my meeting a well-spoken goddess called Emily, who showed me how the other half might live.

Turned out that although most of us are born into the level of wealth and success that we will enjoy for our entire lives, there is a hack, a cheat, that no one talks about, and that many cannot get the strength to execute. It's called: working your tits off in solitude.

16.

Breaking the Kane Curse

Emily was my second great love. Everything in between her and Jessica was just playing. Becky from work, it turned out, wasn't pregnant, and neither was she destined to be my lover. It was Emily who over a year later appeared through a haze on a dance floor at 5 a.m. and, out of nowhere, handed me her phone number.

It was a disgusting dance floor. Covered in Red Bull and body fluids. A few zombies crashed around in the dry ice, chewing their faces, eyes rolling, in an Ecstasy apocalypse. The hard house was winding down and the battle to get back to Enfield via public transport was almost upon me and my fellow fuck-ups. That's when she approached. No words. A tall girl just handed me her number, an actual landline, on a slip of paper, then vanished. Why the hell would a five-foot-nine-inch model-looking fittie do that to a pigeon-chested mess like me? But she did. I called her the next day when we were both still tripping and witty. The connection was instant, and things moved quickly. I could never quite believe I was shagging her.

A book about my dad is not the place to dish the intimates on my wild and bumpy chemical romance with Emily. But she is a catalyst of my story because of what she showed me. A glimpse of *the other side*. My old man had always believed, and in good faith, that uni was 'a waste of fucking time'. You could earn a proper wage with a proper trade. Agreed, there was a brief period when I was eleven when my mum thought I might be a 'barrister or something', but I think we all just liked the sound of the word, not the cost and the parental sacrifice that it would take to make that real. Poncing about with books was expensive, expensive with Dad's wedge – and might lead nowhere. People rarely make it to the other side of the tracks. Only a lot of 'cash in hand' through a trade, or stockbroking, or winning the Lottery could guarantee you rural Essex: the mansions Dave dreamed of in Nazeing, Chigwell or Epping. Books won't get you there, *you silly bastard*. Only punishing graft and luck.

'And trust me, boy, we don't have any luck. The Kane Curse.'

Dad would invoke the Curse even for something minor like a drink spillage or traffic jam.

'Waheey. Lovely. Fucking delayed. We'll probably miss the flight – the Kane Curse.'

When I met Emily, I still totally believed in the Curse, in fate; the insurmountable mountain of graft, the impossibility of change. But living at Nan's was stirring things up. Order was to be sworn at: 'Fuck the system.' Bad luck was to be run at face-on, debt to be welcomed, uncertainty embraced with a maniac's twisted smile.

'The electricity's run out, love,' Nan said once.

'Shall I run to the shop?'

'Why?' she said. And we sat in the dark laughing till we cried.

Nan and I had a telly from Radio Rentals. You had to put a pound coin in the back of it for a few days' viewing. When it ran out in the middle of a programme we were enjoying, we would laugh – get off on the bad luck of it.

'*Coronation Cunts* more like!' she once hollered.

This devil-may-give-a-shit wildness started mixing in with my toxic envy at all the rich kids coming in the watch shop to buy Submariners and Datejusts.

'Go on, Anthony. You got two As and a B. You're off to Durham. Choose your timepiece.'

'Thanks, Daddy.'

Fuck you, Anthony! Silver spoon, bell-end. All the books and leisure and cosy learning. Yet these Anthonys, Ollies and Lukes were average boys. When I was talking to them in the shop, yeah, they had acquired more knowledge than me, a lot more, but I was just as nimble. Bugger me. It was dawning like a sunrise over Turkey Street . . . I'd wasted a love of knowledge and an innate ability to play around with it. There had been no grammar-school skimming off for me in my comprehensive borough; no bookish but indulgent parent who knew what to do. My school was just a wasted six years, and now I'm a shop-boy stoner slipping watches on to the limp wrists of posh twats. Dad might be wrong about uni. What if the mighty Dave was wrong, just this once.

I do not think I'd have taken my class-treachery further had it not been for goddess Emily. I was so into this girl that I overlooked my greatest insecurity: dating a girl who, once in heels, is taller than me. The love was instant, deep and dangerous. By the September of that year she herself started university, coincidentally at Middlesex, just a bus ride from my nan's. This meant that now, when we spent the night together, I was waking up on a campus; commuting to my shop job from student halls. It'd been jealousy-making enough staying in her leafy mansion with her wealthy parents, but that felt far enough from my life that the bitterness was kept at mild. But waking up at Middlesex University – an institution seven miles down the road from where I was living in the box room of my nan's housing association flat (carrying a knife for safety) – was the slap in the brain I needed.

I can recall the exact morning. I was due in at the watch shop for a half-day, at 2 p.m. It was this accident of timetabling that put me face to face with the glorious sight. I kissed Emily on the forehead and walked out of her digs on to the central green of the campus. It was a warm September day, and students who looked and moved like me were just sat there enjoying life, no shits given. Reading. Talking. Laughing.

Why the hell is it them sat there, absorbing literature in a leisurely fashion, and not me?

It was a simple but devastating question. Now and again, heads were tossed as banter was batted back and forth. Were they laughing at me? No. But maybe they should be. A few scruffy, happy bodies dashed across lawns to lectures; some nerds queued at the bookshop then left gripping fat books on subjects that immediately seemed fascinating: criminology, psychology, structuralism. Intellectual porn was revealing its slutty leg to me. My God, the biggest stress these bastards would face that day was which interesting thing to learn next, and which bar to spend the evening in, enjoying a pint for a pound with newfound friends. Social connection everywhere. Knowledge everywhere. No bullies, no idiots, and any wasters were doing it with a book in their hand.

'No cunts,' Nan had said later that night. The one thing she turned out to be wrong about. Cunts are everywhere.

My breathing became shallow and I had to sit down on the

grass for a full five minutes, so violent were the flashes of revelation in my head. I missed not one train, but two. I felt like Jim Carrey in *The Truman Show*. I had just seen the cameras and lights of working-classness, and it was all fake. All a set-up. The show started filming at my birth. My dad, a manual labourer, was cast. So I got the part of Shop-work Son. Well, fuck that! I didn't accept it. I demanded my place on the grass, reading books like a ponce. I am a ponce! I want to throw my head back and say something clever while calm, pretty people look on. I want to dance till 1 a.m. in a student bar surrounded by people with spectacles, not tattoos. I want my cheese knife to be only for cheese – any sword will be a pen.

I walked through those uni gates a different person. If you like Marvel comics, it was my radioactive spider moment: sudden, dramatic and transformative. I was bitten, and suddenly found a power that had been absent my whole life. For GCSEs I could barely absorb the names of Henry VIII's wives, or the chemical symbol for lead. But something had just switched me on; the bite had put something in me. Fuck lead (chemical symbol Pb, btw), I wanted to burn like a magnesium strip – and this time it wouldn't explode in my face.

At work, during afternoon tea break, I frenziedly made a note in my diary. I needed a record of the moment. I was sucking on a fag in the smoking room, and I knew that this was a profound moment – not a promise, but a plan.

'Today is the day I change my life. I will redo my A-levels, and I will go to university, and I will get a first.' It was as simple as planning a trip to the shops.

That evening as I told my nan my plans, I showed her an advert I had found.

'I can do an A-level, Nan. Right here – in the flat.'

'You might wanna smoke less of that then,' she said, pointing to my spliff.

'Yeah.'

'Or more, love. Fuck it! Whatever works, darling. And you will . . .' And she staggered to bed.

The National Extension College. You learned A-levels at home on your own: quite literally out of a box. Once a week you mail an essay to a tutor you never meet. You are totally and utterly on your own, with just your own vim and self-motivation. Perfect for me. Middle-class teachers so far had not inspired me; no one believed I was anything special. But I would prove it. Now, I was the most white-hot, determined soul I knew, and I poured that energy, my nan lashing at my back with swearing and wit, into the most appropriate A-level I could have chosen. Sociology: the study of inequality and social anger.

The next day I got some good news from an education counsellor: as I would be twenty-one by the time I went to university, I needed only one good grade at A-level. I phoned the National Extension College, and the moment that beautiful box of sociological words arrived, I became a crazed and obsessed council-estate professor. I made a full time-table for every day, weeks in advance. By the time I got in from work and had eaten one of Nan's legendary toad-in-the-holes, it was at least 7 p.m. I carved my night into study chunks. I studied before work, I studied during work. I made mountains of index cards and I studied on the toilet, in the bath. (Bathing at my nan's was something of an art. I had to lower myself in around her bath lift and old sponges. Hardly a Champney's spa treatment.)

'You're gonna nail this, you mental bastard,' said Nan

through a crack in the bathroom door one night, ice clinking in her vodka glass.

After a few weeks, when I knew it wasn't just a manic impulse, I told my mum and dad, who instantly asked:

'How you gonna pay for that – with your kidneys?'

'I'm saving, Dad. I need £80 a week to live on for three years. That's a year of selling watches from now – if I live like a monk.'

'Good luck, boy,' said Dad neutrally. Neutrality was progress.

But I didn't believe in luck, or curses. Graft, plus geography – being in the right place, but working your nads off.

I still partied on Saturday nights. I continued being truly, madly, deeply involved with Emily – but my focus was the studying; and I had become impatient, jittery. I wanted to sit the exam almost as soon as I started studying. The recommended timescale for a part-time A-level was two years. I was going to have a stab at six months from box arrival to passing.

I had to sit my A-level exams as an 'external student' – on my own little table, slightly apart from the normal kids at Enfield College. Three three-hour bastards. My pen went through the paper a few times, scratching the desk. I was writing up until I was told to stop. I cannot recall once struggling to bring information to the front of my mind. I answered the questions set, but I did so with the fury of a builder taking out a connecting wall with a sledgehammer.

I knew I would get a good grade.

It took me five months from enrolling to A grade. One of the highest A grades in the country that year, and the quickest by many months. I won an award, presented to me by Speaker of the House Betty Boothroyd. My mum came with me to the ceremony. It was a surreal day: the penny had dropped that the secret to most things in life was an insane work ethic. How prosaic – no one wants to find out that there is no magic shortcut, only graft. Fuck. Dad was right in his own weird way. Take care of number one.

I felt now that I was unstoppable. Knowledge could be attacked the way Anthony Joshua has attacked boxing from the age of fourteen. Just go down the gym, use what nature gave you and out-train everyone else. My three-year journey to a first-class honours degree, and the Ede & Ravenscroft award for academic excellence, would be a blast. 'I'm gonna enjoy this,' I said to myself, like someone who has discovered a hack no one else knows.

17.

Squiggles on a Page

The day I arrived at Middlesex University, Dave Kane was on vintage form. He had surprised me by offering to help move me in. I think once Dad saw my bank account loaded with the twelve grand self-saved funds needed, and the exam result in my hand, he conceded:

'This learning bollocks was worth a shot.'

We loaded the Transit with my stuff and backed the van into a space on campus marked *No Parking*. I was three years older than everyone else, which straightaway drew attention (as did the fact that I appeared to have a bouncer moving me in), but for once it was good attention. Twenty-one really was the sweet-spot age for uni for me. Still young enough to hang with the eighteen-year-olds, but old enough to know what they don't: that if you fuck this up, you might end up selling watches to people who *did* finish their degrees.

'Wait till they see this, boy,' said Dad, beaming with pride as he carried a roll of carpet down the corridor in my halls. Neighbours gawped as my old man proceeded to carpet my room, paint it and install a mini fridge. He fixed my door, and sorted the seals around my windows. It was the proudest I ever felt of him. A posh chair from a junk shop was placed into my room as well as trippy ceiling mobiles. The room announced me as someone who was sure of their identity, strong and a bit weird. Here was a halls room of character; someone people might want to know. The mash-up of working-class ethic with angry cleverness was an instant hit with my new posh-kid connections. I had made several friends, from all backgrounds, before my dad left paint-spattered that evening.

'Good luck, boy,' he said – and the first of my two hugs I would ever receive from him were administered. Fuck me. Maybe *he* was proud of *me*, too?

The only bad thing he did that day was when he was try-ing to be funny. It took a good ten trips to the Transit and back to get my stuff, and Dad thought he would help me by assessing 'the female talent, boy'.

Women of every background, shape and size streamed past us. Young feminists, artists, nerdy science types. Gay girls, straight girls. Posh girls, common girls. We were all equal at last. I'd never seen so many clever, driven women in the same place before. These women would be my future friends, debat-ing partners. Being deeply in love with Emily, I was under no mating pressures. I was a neuter like my mum's Burmese cat Theo. Yet Dad thought it would be hilarious to grade the women out of ten as we passed each one.

'Phwoar! Eight out of ten!'

'Dad – no.'

'The tits on it, boy, fucking hell!' Then: 'Six out of ten – big hooter.'

'Dad, please.'

'Four out of ten. Shame. Pretty face.'

'Oh God.'

And then said: 'Rhaw!' He was using an acronym he'd invented. It stood for 'rather have a wank'. Part of me died

as he said it, but part of me laughed too. This was my conflicted path.

It's still my conflicted path. I have a bawdy sense of
humour, I laugh at things I shouldn't – yet I'm so angry at
injustice and political incorrectness. That's the intellectual
cross-breed my dad and university created. A mongrel who
bites the hand that teaches it.

It would be way too boring to detail my caterpillar-to-
butterfly journey at university. All the other memoirs I've read
do it. Normally at Cambridge or Oxford. And they always
bump into people with whom they will end up collaborating
before jetting into media-land to be lauded. As much as I
loved my degree, this was not my experience. I found my
voice, yes. I absorbed poetry, literature, drama. I wrote my
own plays, short stories and verse, eventually getting trans-
ferred on to a specialist wing of my degree for creative
people – all of that was amazing, and I benefit from those
three years every day of my life. The problem was, I had so far
to catch up that in the end it left me socially retarded. I made
wonderful friends over those three years, but the sheer scale
of my academic climb meant I couldn't deepen those friendships at that moment. I could make a connection but not
lavish time on it. My new friendships were like fireworks that
promise long and lasting explosions but in the end were just
exciting launches. I really am profoundly sorry for that. I have
maintained not one friendship from university, yet this was
the group of people who lifted me higher than I could ever
have dreamed. It's a problem that's carried on into my current
career. I find myself torn at the end of a day's work. Everyone
is in the green room, wine flowing, but that voice, that sociology A-level voice, is still chattering away in my head.

'Yes, you could stay for a wine. Or you could get an amazing nine-hour sleep and outperform your goals for tomorrow.'

Striving: it's a boring addiction. But it's mine.

To catch up at university and conceal the moon-crater gaps in my knowledge space, I had to do a few weird and extreme things. Applying myself to the work of my degree was the easy bit now that I was in an environment where I would be left alone to sculpt and chip at my coursework projects; after all, I could solve anything with Dad's 'graft' approach. But the foundations of my learning needed retro-fitting or else it would just be a matter of time until I was exposed. Think about it, I was twenty-one years old and I had hardly read any important books. My sociology was on point, but my litera-ture stopped at *The Lion, the Witch and the Wardrobe*, and my vocabulary was pure council estate mixed with some social science jargon. I needed an artificial intervention. So I started with authors whose names began with A – and I simply began reading. I gleaned this scheme from a book called *Nausea*, whose author's name I pronounced 'Sar-tra' until someone posher gave me the French execution of *Saaaatr*. There is a character in it at whom we are supposed to laugh: a working-class intellectual nerd who starts at A in the library and reads through to Z as his way of catching up with the privileged kids. Well, fuck it, it seemed like a good idea to me.

Every morning, no matter how drunk or crazy the night before had been, I rose a full two hours before everyone else. Sometimes Emily was unconscious on the bed next to me as I moved around to my reading position. I read as many pages as I could of any author who was *not* on my English Lit. course. I started with Austen, then Brontë, and so on all the way through to Zola in translation. (A French author – an exotic fruit in an adjacent orchard. From him I got hooked on Balzac, George Sand and eventually my great love Flaubert.) I tried to read fifty–fifty men–women so the girls would think I was cool. (I ended up getting obsessed with Iris Murdoch. I read everything she wrote, novels and philosophy; even joined the Iris Murdoch Society, travelling to Oxford for extra courses and lectures.) Each time I reached Z (or Y, not many decent Zs), I started again from A. My wall was covered in literary maps. It seems inconceivable to me now, with my encyclopaedic love of literature, that at twenty-one I was yet to read a word of Dickens or Trollope (I ended up much preferring the latter; we have a lot in common work-ethic wise). I had not yet seen Shakespeare performed. I started attending theatre alone – crap, fringe performances for a fiver – just to absorb the text. If I was walking, cleaning, travelling, then I had an audiobook running. It was an unrelenting stream of words. I bathed in books. This was how I caught up my reading to everyone else's.

'How the fuck you retaining it?' asked Dad one Sunday lunch.

'You could retain the Haynes manual for the Transit?'

'I suppose. That's survival, though.'

'Same.'

Dad smiled, sort of. 'He's a fucking nutter, Julie.'

A few of my mates said this too: that there was no way I could be properly absorbing literature if I was reading that quickly and intensely.

But I think absorption is more about how interested you are, how deeply you are into something, than how long you do it for. To me, the literary world was like someone pulling you aside and telling you the most delicious gossipy secret, dripping in details that tattoo your consciousness. You don't need to be intelligent to soak it up, you just need to be *profoundly interested*. Your nosiness will gobble up every syllable; your vicious curiosity will pull in every phrase. That was me in the company of 'posh' books. Books that were not intended for a peasant, for a nobody. I felt I had broken into a forbidden library, and I planned to steal everything. That is still me with books; I read at least two to three books a month. As crazy as my life is now, I'm still doing it – though not going A through to Z. I stopped that when I held my degree certificate and it said 'First'. Time to read organically now.

There was one practical problem with this literary foie gras method, however. My vocabulary. I had the normal vocabulary of someone from the Essex/London borders – but the books I was mainlining did not. They were full of words I could not pronounce or understand. So I came up with another pragmatic solution. It's only recently I've felt comfortable enough to reveal how I cheated the vocabulary system.

Every time I encountered a word I did not know, I would look it up in my beloved Chambers dictionary and create an index card for it. I would revise these cards every day. As the pile grew, I divided them into daily batches. I came across the first word within a few pages of my very first book that September: Austen's *Pride and Prejudice*. The first 'elite' word I ever 'carded up' was 'impudent' – appropriately. But then I had another problem, didn't I, my working-class readers. I've never heard this word – so how the fuck do I pronounce it? The Internet wasn't quite in people's rooms yet, so I had to actually learn the phonetic symbols at the front of the dictionary. It was the only way I could be sure I wouldn't make an ignoramus of myself. (*Ignoramus* was word 247. And you can have *raa* or *ray* as the middle sound.) *Im*pudent. Emphasis on the *Im. Pyooo. Dent.* Then I would add to the card its noun and adverb forms (its *cognates* – word 1891). Impudence and impudently. The meaning I scrawled at the bottom ('bold and cheeky') and that was one card done. By the time two years had elapsed, I had thousands of these things, and I was deeply secretive about their existence. The thought of someone learning I was manually expanding my vocabulary rather than organically having done so filled me with shame and dread – but the reality was that once I had passed fourteen or fifteen years old I was never going to magically acquire the spiky words I needed to hold on to the mountain of academia and climb.

I was careful with the usage of my new word-darlings. I didn't run into the student bar with my broad Essex vowels and shout:

'Hey, Ollie, fancy an impudent night out?'

I'd have been busted in a second.

The uncomfortable reality is this. If you are from a certain background – whether it's racial, religious or class – you can't use certain words, use certain types of language, without people around you smirking. If you're a Boris, an Ollie or a Benedict and you walk into a pub with people you don't know and open with: 'How exquisite to be here. Obstreperous patrons, but a wonderful ambience . . .' you could smile warmly, and your syntax and words would mark you out as a member of the educated world. You are posh, so it sounds nice when you say *obstreperous* (emphasis second syllable *strep*, meaning rowdy and noisy). Now re-run the scene with an Estuary accent; or give the sentence to a boxer – and we

smile patronizingly, or laugh at the absurdity of the polysyl-
lable coming from a stereotypically unusual mouth. The
instinctive prejudice. Humans are at it everywhere.

So I waited, always learning my cards: during *ablutions* ('on
the toilet', card 579), while *ambulating* ('walking', card 349).
And I only stopped learning the card when I found the word
naturally on the tip of my tongue, *osmosis* complete ('absorbed
into the system', card 629). Even then I would only dare drop
it into my writing, not my speech. It would take years for the
words to find their way naturally into my sentences, for me
to use them without remembering the dirty shame of their
provenance: after all, they weren't my biological word
children – they were adopted, illegitimate, stolen.

University was easily the happiest three years of my life. I
walked away with the only first awarded in my year; and the
money I had saved lasted perfectly – down to the final week of
my final term. Over the three years, I did not work a single
Saturday in any shop. This is part of the reason I did so well.
While others worked in the summer holidays and saved their
money, or travelled with their rich parents, I stayed in, greedily
hoovering up the coming texts. I stayed in my halls during the
holidays, savouring the cosy solitude. Only one summer did
Emily and I do something different. We bought Interrail cards
and went around Europe.

Dad drove us to Dover and left us at the ferry port.

'Be careful, yeah, boy?' And the second hug he ever gave
me was awkwardly administered.

That month railing around Europe was amazing. We lived
in a tent and cooked on a tin pot stove. I was free of all planning, tidiness and organization. Heaven. I realized on that trip
I had a wasted aptitude for languages. If only I had discovered

it earlier, I wouldn't have to make do with just English for the rest of my life. Still now though, when I'm on holiday, within a few days, my wife Lindsey starts getting annoyed as I babble away in Hindi, German, Greek, French . . . whatever. I only ever get to polite exchanges, and I forget it as soon as I get home, but I love it. My love of speaking in other lingos has nothing to do with intelligence, by the way, but everything to do with showing off, being accepted. I've always had a need to be understood, liked – on the Europe trip with Emily, it pushed my brain into French, Italian, German. Shallowness can be very powerful when leveraged (see current career).

Love though . . . Emily and I were feeling the strain in our relationship. Founded as it was on warehouse raves and getting seriously mashed, when the haze cleared there wasn't much there. We didn't shag that much any more and I was bored with raving. Books turned me on more. The intoxication of our travel experience, plus shared uni friends, trundled us on another year, but we split up during my final semester. I should have enjoyed my first period of being confident and single but, alas, as a sufferer from serial monogamy, I had only seven days of 'being a lad'. The first party I went to the following Saturday, tears from the Emily break-up still fresh on my cheek, I met a feisty Glaswegian called Joanne and jumped feet first into my new, toxic, doomed, long-term relationship. It would be four years before we split up and her mum hassled me about property.

I'd done it. I had my first-class degree. Yeah, OK, I'd jumped sideways from my hardcore literature and society studies into the BA Writing arm of the degree; but, it turned out, that was exactly where I needed to be – not that Dave Kane understood it.

'BA in Writing?'

'Yeah.'

'As in fucking squiggles on a page?'

'No, Dad.'

He was joking. Sort of.

'Writing! Fuck's sake. Can you earn wedge from it?'

But it turned out you could. Good news was coming my way within a few months.

A lot of people exaggerate when they say they 'put themselves through uni', but I really did. I'm proud of it. I wouldn't change it, and I don't feel hard done by, or that it's something negative for me to bitch about. It was something strengthening. I wanted it, I did it. I payed, I sayed.

In the whole three years, Dad only gave me money once. I was back one evening for a home-cooked meal in my second year, and Dad had had a few Stellas. His eyes were glazed, and I could tell he wanted to say something nice to me but just didn't have the words or the tools to do it properly.

'You're doing well, boy, ain't you?'

'Yeah.'

'Just do something. Something. Know what I mean? Fucking . . . anything . . .'

'I better go. The bus.'

'How much is a cab?'

'Seven quid.'

My jaw fell fully open as he went into his pockets and pulled out everything in it. Eight pounds sixty-three pence. I have never forgotten this hallowed sum.

'There you go, boy. Get a cab tonight.' And then his face returned to normal, like a spell had worn off.

£8.63. Plus what I had saved. That's how I funded my degree.

My graduation ceremony, and Dad was on excellent, day-ruining, miserable form. Looking back, I should have just taken my mum. She would have got off on me being 'star of the show' – the only one to get a first on my course; the miracle poor boy with a silly board-hat on his head, scroll in pasty hand – an actor pretending to be middle class in a fringe-theatre production of an Alan Bennett.

I just watched a brilliant advert for Netflix where a woman of colour powerfully speaks about always feeling like you're walking into rooms where you sense you don't belong, where no one looks like or sounds like you, where you feel you should keep your mouth shut and not speak. There is a shot of the phenomenal Hannah Gadsby (gay stand-up, please check out her paradigm-shifting special *Nanette* on Netflix). The narrator implores us: 'Let's make more voices, let's create more space.' Well, I would never pretend to understand what living in the poisonous fog of prejudice must feel like, but the words of that narrator struck me deeply. I spent the first twenty-five years of my life experiencing those feelings. Every room I wanted to walk into had people there because they were born in the right place, to the right people; and if I tried to speak, only a whisper came out. None of my friends, and not one of my cousins, would ever get the chance even to turn the door handles of those rooms. That's how big my chip was, a McCain's Fries factory of insecurity on my shoulder about being common, thinking common – sounding common – being a fake chav who'd learned his words via index cards. A pretend version of clever. My graduation day was the first time I realized that where and to whom you are born, something you cannot control, should never dictate what you can do . . . and anyone who tries to control people because of the accident of their birth needs to be called out and corrected.

'This is Wembley, boy,' said Dad joylessly as we parked his new, bigger, blacker Mercedes Elegance in the Wembley Conference Centre car park. It was a car he both loved and resented. He'd always wanted a Mercedes Elegance – but the monthly payments made him hate it a bit at the same time. 'Fucking Wembley!'

'I know, Dad – it's amazing, isn't it?'

'Tenner for parking! Cunts!'

'It's an amazing venue though, Dad.'

'The South Circular Road is amazing, boy. Amazingly shit. Finishes at 5 p.m., right?'

'Yeah.'

'Fucking hell. Traffic – we're shagged – is there no way we can get away at four thirty?' he said as we marched to the pay-and-display machine.

'Dave!'

'It's all right, Mum, I'll check.'

And that was the tone for the day. Not: *how amazing I'd self-started, self-funded and gained a first* – but *let's hope the traffic won't be 'murder'* and therefore wind up Dad.

Dad pushed open the doors of Wembley Conference Centre and there were all my friends, my new peer group – *the educated*. I was on edge, in a nervous, silly mood, and for some reason I introduced my mum and dad to the novelist Sue Gee with these words:

'These are my parents, they are both transexuals.'

It was completely out of context, apropos of no running joke, a totally weird and offensive thing to say. But there, I said it. Sue Gee smiled politely – I was the course's eccentric, energetic and, most of all, unlikely success story. In fact, in my second year when I sat the test to transfer over from the Literature wing of my degree to the more creative Writing arm – I failed the paper. The short story I had submitted about a broken heart was maudlin, amateurish and full of desperate flowery language which strained to show off my posh new vocabulary. I was devastated to be told I had not made the cut, and I begged for a face-to-face interview with course leaders Sue Gee, the poet Maggie Butt and creative writing guru Susanna Gladwin. I used charm and desperation to convince them I might just do well on that creative course.

'Give me one semester – and I promise to progress from appalling to bad.'

Humour sealed the deal, and I began working even harder than before. As with everything I've ever done, I had no natural ability or talent, just a thousand times more energy than anyone else was willing to put in. And that's enough. It's better than ability. Don't let anyone with natural gifts tell you otherwise. I'm not even sure there is such a thing as natural gifts – maybe we can exempt the height of a basketball player, or the size of a jockey, but even then I'm not convinced. Here's my formula:

Accident of Birth x Energy = 'Talent'

And that's it. That prosaic formula will make tough reading for many small business owners and artists. But remember: if the 'accident' of your birth is loaded with too much prejudice, shackled with too much damage of whatever kind, then no amount of energy will save you. I grew up with boys and girls like that. When I read about what happened to them, I experience a type of grief. Maybe I've been a bit cold by not adding 'luck' to the equation.

My graduation day was unpleasant for Kane senior. The self-employed master of his own timetable did not appreciate being chaotically shoved from room to room by smiley, frizzy-haired academics with thick-rimmed specs, sloshing plastic cups of cheap wine around as they used the foreign language of the educated. It is the only time I can remember my dad looking, incongruously, small. Plonked there among all the posh, verbal parents – all confidently comparing notes – he seemed to shrink into almost nothing. They all spoke the same language – they all knew the rules. But he stood apart, awkward – culturally different, a tiny non-native.

There was a big stage in the main room and students went up one by one to receive their degree certificates from the chancellor of the university. It is still the most important and transformative moment of my life: full butterfly, the chrysalis shed. When it was my turn I looked out into the audience for my parents. Mum was beaming, Dad looked confused, like he was thinking, *What is the point of all this; why do they make it so we get stuck in traffic at the end?*

I turned and faced the chancellor, and thought it would be hilarious to offer a comedy fist-bump instead of a handshake. He looked put-out, no one laughed. It was just awkward, desperate showing off by me – *I must try and turn that into a job one day.* I exited ascending stairs on the other side of that stage like a Christian rising up out of baptismal waters. I was middle-class now. I still sounded like a twat when I spoke, people will still think I'm thick, but now I had confidence: and that, mixed with determination, is a killer weapon.

I found my mum and dad and showed them my certificate.

'I'm so proud,' said Mum and we hugged. 'You came first.'

'Well done, boy,' said Dad, but I knew he was thinking about the time, and the veins of London's roads clogging towards traffic thrombosis.

It was 3.30 p.m. Parents now mingled with tutors, all drinking red wine from foam cups, throwing back their heads and remembering their own uni days. I wanted to drink wine from a foam cup too. I wanted to say witty things in a circle of mothers, fathers and academics. But Dad was our designated, booze-less driver; and now he was pacing.

'To be fair . . . it is mostly just standing around now, love,' said Mum, trying to find a compromise, as always.

'M25. Fucking murder, boy. Hours we could sit there. The table is booked at Papillon's for eight p.m.'

Yes, my table, for my day, I screamed, but internally. *My afternoon.* Why can't we just once be like the others? Join the crowd, drink the shit wine, get the packed, chaotic train, be the last to leave – get caught in the rush – be one of the idiots, the mugs, the people muddled in with everyone else. Why not? This is my most significant moment, and I was one of the highest achievers here, a good grade – I'd done this. No one had ever admired me before this educational mission began.

'It's building now, I reckon. One accident and the whole motorway is fucked, boy. That's the problem.'

'It's not worth the stress,' said Mum.

And so we left.

After four years (if we include the initial months of my impossible A-level), twelve grand of my own money; after defeating every demographic prediction a sociologist might make after looking at where I'm from, we walked out. Bye, Sue Gee. Bye, Maggie Butt.

'I knew it,' said Dad as we merged on to the South Circular Road, 'chock-a-block with cunts!'

I didn't reply.

'Rush hour starts at 3 p.m. really.'

'Well done today, Russ,' said Mum.

'I'm fucking starving,' said Dad. 'I'm gonna ruin a steak. Ruin it.'

Food was how we celebrated in my family.

'Big portions, boy. Massive fucking portions – and top quality.'

The showy meal out was my dad's favourite way of being generous. He had a catchphrase for restaurants. Any birthday or for the firm's Christmas do (which was just my dad, as he was self-employed), we would go to the Akash or Papillon's, and he'd announce:

'It's Christmas/Easter/birthday/graduation – you can order whatever you like.'

Mine and my brother James's eyes would widen. Could he mean king pr— but then Dad would jump in with . . .

'Anything you like . . . except king prawns . . . don't take the piss, boys.'

Every time.

For me and my brother, the king prawn was the holy grail of food. We'd tried it now and again, maybe off someone else's plate – but at twelve quid for six prawns, it was a dish we could never get signed off by the alpha. The monarch of meats was rarely ordered in my childhood. My dad was a meat auditor too, always checking that all pieces of chicken or prawn were present and correct before he started eating:

'Five fucking prawns, Abdul! You having a laugh?'

And it would go back to the kitchen to be topped up with more ocean kings.

Another of my dad's staple commands: 'Order a shashlik!'

And often we did. The shashlik was my dad's go-to display meal. A Bangladeshi speciality that came from the kitchen sizzling like a magician hitting a Vegas stage. It's a smoky up-yours to all the other diners who have ordered merely a *normal* chicken tikka main course – unsizzling, unspecial idiots.

'Mugs,' Dad would say as he watched amateur curry eaters not even squeezing their lemon slices over the boring, non-frizzling tikka.

We would hear our shashliks even before the kitchen door opened on to the restaurant's dining room.

'They're all looking,' Dad would say proudly. 'None of them have ordered sizzlers. None of 'em.' Then, inhaling the steam, 'This is the bollocks – not literally of course.'

But on my graduation day we didn't go for a curry, we went the next one up – the French bistro Mum and Dad sometimes went to: Papillon's in Barnet Village. I know Dad, in his own way, wished to reward this proud moment; show me the maximum respect with a full-blown Papillon's meal. It was to celebrate both my graduation and my coming birthday – a double. It would be exactly three years from this point, in the same restaurant, that I would see my dad for the last time.

We settled into our red leather seats and ordered lots of fantastic things, yet I felt a creeping numbness as we waited for our food.

'You all right, love?' said Mum.

'Just tired from it all,' I said.

'Black pepper skate wing, boy. How about that? Fucking hell . . . wait till you see it! It's like a tent flap . . . ain't that right, Barney?'

And the head waiter came across, enthusing about black butter, seasoning and fish.

I had only had a couple of glasses of wine, but I felt wobbly, like reality was fading out. I excused myself and went to the toilet, where unusual things happened.

I looked at myself in the mirror and realized, fuck, that's that. You have just achieved your goal, and you don't have another. More numbing was the thought that I had dreamt up a scheme and it had *actually worked*. That's not what I had been raised to believe. My internal script said 'you can think something up, but it will fail'. But it hadn't failed. Every step had worked. I smiled at my new middle-class reflection, a wonky, fake smile, and then a profound, disturbing thing happened. I'll preface this by saying that although I'm highly strung, I'm not a self-harmer, I don't have loads of dark, juicy revelations to spill, but on this occasion some sort of goth gasket blew. The mixture of finishing my degree, with Dad's doom behaviour, sent a power bolt through me and *BANG!*: I headbutted the mirror. It wasn't planned, I didn't feel it coming on. I just did it. Boom. Hard too. Thankfully, it cracked only at the corner, and it was a discoloured piece of glass – no one would notice it in the dingy toilet lighting. More problematic was my head with its jet of blood at the parting. I must have been in that loo a good five minutes, building up little layers of bog roll, then repositioning my hair to cover the tiny gash.

'You sure you're OK, love?' said Mum as I rejoined the table.

'My tummy . . . all the nerves from today . . .'

'You're not gonna waste this fucking skate, are you?' said Dad, pointing at Barney who was carrying the Moby Dick of fish to our table.

'No, Dad,' I said blankly. 'I'm gonna eat all of that.'

And I did. I drank all the wine too. It was a night of cele-bration, yet I went to bed empty, dead and a little bit mental.

18.

Bank of No One

Before August arrived I had decided what I wanted to do: teach and write. I would teach all year, and write all summer. Novels, non-fiction, kids' books – anything. Maggie and Sue helped me on to a last-minute PGCE which started that September.

'Teaching, Russell? Are you sure? They'll be lucky to have you,' said Maggie, kindly.

'They need more male teachers in primary school, and I love telling little people things.'

I do. I genuinely do (more so now). I was excited to start my PGCE. There was one problem. I had nowhere to live and no funds. I took a job in credit checking – which most people would hate, but I absolutely loved. Nosing in on other people's debts and discontents fed both my voyeurism and schadenfreude self-esteem. Dog shit on my shoe? Not to worry, there's someone covered in shit over there . . . I've never understood debt. To me, Dad made it as terrifying as a paedo snatching you off the street. I'm not exaggerating. Dad was genuinely *less* scared of sex offenders than he was of credit cards and loans. *At least you're the victim when you get assaulted . . . you create debt, you're the arsehole . . .*

'See that, boy,' he said once, pointing to a watch, face filled with a bitter pride, 'I can't afford that. So I'll never fucking buy it. Know what I mean?'

'OK.'

Another time, when I was younger:

'See, if we were hungry, do you know what I would borrow to feed us?'

'A tenner?' I think I was about eleven, so this seemed loads.

'No. We'd simply not eat. Never, ever borrow anything from anyone. *Go without!* Going without is what a man does. A credit card is just a form of poncing. Weak prats. Like a toddler that wants a rattle, can't help itself.'

And that's how I grew up: terrified of those little bits of plastic my mates flashed around. Access, American Express . . . None of the adverts worked on me. I laughed at the credit-card forms people filled out at uni. Sure, when I was living with my 'fuck-the-world' nan, I'd briefly considered 'rinsing' the banks so I could fast-track it to uni. Nan would have backed such a scheme.

'We come into the world naked and with nothing, love,' she said once, lighting one Embassy Filter with another. 'It's a sin to go out with more.'

'What about leaving stuff for my kids one day?'

'And what does that teach them?'

'I see your point.'

'Have a laugh, love. You're a long time dead. If you need to borrow, take it – do what you gotta do.'

But that was a step too far for me. At the last minute, I chose graft and saving as my weapons to prise open the door of university. Nan and Dad did agree on one thing, though: give your kids nothing; or at least don't give them too much. Getting fuck-all for free when you're younger puts you on the steroids of self-reliance in adulthood. Yeah, I've had to do everything myself, but the world is full of feet-draggers who want something for nothing from their parents. Would it really have done me any good to know my dad was going to bail me out or fund whatever I did? I've never believed in sitting back and waiting for Mummy and Daddy to rescue me with their hard-earned cash. Life was never explained to me that way. Save and strive, or go down. My dad went too far – but he enabled my lifting of big weight. My ability to save is the Schwarzenegger's bicep of my mind. All I've needed was 'my clothes, my shoes and my mountain bicycle'. (If that *Terminator* reference is lost on you, please never speak to me again.) All this programming for carefulness is why I found that silly credit-checking job so fascinating. To die of hunger was more honourable than to borrow, in the World According to Dave.

Still, here I was: no real money. How could I fund a teaching qualification when I would not be able to work, even part-time?

'Can I move back into my old bedroom, Mum?' I asked, a sinking feeling in my stomach that always came when I actually needed something from someone. It's a feeling I've never grown out of, or mastered. Although I'd lived with my nan before, I'd been working then – and she had no income at all. As I wouldn't be working, I assumed my parents would support my move back in.

'The door is always open, love.'

So, aged twenty-five, back to living with Mum and Dad and yet to start a career. I laughed when I heard people saying 'bank of Mum and Dad'. You lucky, cotton-woolled bell-ends. This would need an actual bank.

'Welcome to the real world, kid.' Another of my dad's

favourite maxims. 'Life's tough, and even the bits that aren't are fucking expensive.'

A PGCE needed dosh. I was starting from zero, so I went into my local Barclays and managed to persuade them to *invest in me*.

'It's not a loan then . . .' I said, turning pale.

'Well – you do have to pay it back, but it's more an advance against new business – you becoming a teacher,' said the bank manager, sensing my allergy to debt. I placed this bit of borrowing in the *mortgage* section of my fiscal brain – not proper debt; sensible costs to build something bigger.

I wonder if that bank manager was supposed to authorize that investment – normally only for self-employed business starters. Maybe he bent the rules for my benefit? If you've watched that recent Fyre festival documentary on Netflix, well, I was by this point in my life like that guy who was so desperate for bottled water he would have done anything. And if the bank manager had asked me, yes, I would def-initely have sucked him off for the loan. This was the ticket off my island. With £5K I could live while I trained to be a primary-school teacher. After I bought my books, paid my costs, I'd still be left with £400 a month. It could be done, just.

'So that's the plan,' I said, sat opposite my mum in the kitchen, chatting over steaming mugs of tea.

'Right,' she said, looking at the serious papers I had fanned out, 'so you've got the loan, I mean investment.'

'Yeah. I start September. I'll be out of your hair by the fol-lowing June.'

'Don't be silly. You'll always have a home here.'

It was all too easy – and I was right to be suspicious.

Twenty-four hours later we were back in the kitchen, more tea brewed, totally different atmosphere. I knew by Mum's face that whatever came out of her mouth next was via Commandant Dave – and she wasn't comfortable delivering the ruling.

'You had a busy morning, love?'

I'd had a day off credit checking, so I'd been to Enfield Town to pick up my glossy teacher-training textbooks. (Shit! Remember shops? The idea of going on a bus to shop now seems so old fashioned. Like using a well, or having syphilis.) I'd spent the rest of the day holed up reading about the psychology of eight-year-olds. I was genuinely pumped for my future.

'Right,' Mum said, 'the thing is – obviously – stay here as long as you like but the costs . . .'

'Costs?'

'The costs of you being here.'

Wow. Maybe I was about to be billed for my own conception too? I imagined my dad explaining the invoice.

'I did spunk off and create you, boy, and that is a cost to *me*. It's a hundred pounds, compounded into today's money – shall we call it a grand?'

'There won't be any costs, Mum,' I protested. 'I'll just eat a bit of whatever you guys are having – or I can use my uni fridge in my room and make my own stuff . . .'

'I meant the *keep* costs, love.'

'Keep? Keep is when you're working. But I'm not earning, remember – I'm in training. It's still education to become a primary-school teacher.'

'Exactly. But you've got that loan . . .'

'That's for everything, though.'

'So how is £50 a month? Fair?'

And that was that. The borrowed amount which I had carved into twelve modest chunks in my head was now minus a crisp £50 note for every month while I trained and stayed at Mum and Dad's. This was the purest 'take care of number one' and 'I'm paying, I'm saying' I had ever witnessed. All hail the alpha. But, again, at the time I didn't whinge – I just thought: well, fuck it, it's cheaper than renting a shithole in Cheshunt.

Living at home, however, meant battle with the silverback began again, exactly where it had left off. Nothing had changed. There was no adjustment for me being twenty-five and fully a man. No concessions were given me for having educated myself and made excellent prospects. I was under the dominant male's roof, and therefore I was the same as any blackback male. Age meant nothing, particularly as I was not yet 'earning', merely 'studying', and only paying a reduced rate of *keep*. The arguments were the same as ever, me liberal and bookish, Dad Tory, angry and into metal things that go smash. I was the rogue, challenger male back from university – from that other gorilla nest across our Rwandan jungle. My back fur, although still black, had threatening silver flecks, the patina of education and silly middle-class ways. It was during this tetchy summer, before I'd drawn down that loan (in the end, with a fantastic twist, I would never draw it) when I decided to become a vegetarian.

These days, it's yawningly common to be a vegan – more passé than growing a Shoreditch beard or liking French bulldogs. I wonder – is a bandwagon *itself* made of meat? (If it were, vegans would never jump on it.) When I was twenty-five, vegetarianism was the diet-conformist equivalent. It was totally banal to go veggie; it had the equivalent shock value of staying out till 7 a.m. *Ouuh, so daring and hippy* . . . But my dad didn't live in our century, or even the previous one. I'm gonna plump for the Bronze Age. My radicalization into vegetable eating had happened one morning on the way back from clubbing. A few of us had wondered into a farm in rural Essex – all off our tits – and coming face-to-face with a cow I experienced a weird, spiritual connection. It lasted only a few minutes before the word 'cunt' was being shouted at me by a startled farmer. I ran away from police sirens into some bushes. I fell asleep in something prickly. I can still remember the cow: *287*. That was her name, stapled into her ear. 'I'll never eat meat again.' I lied, as it turned out.

I managed three or four days of covert broccoli consumption before Mum became suspicious. Maybe you're thinking, why didn't I just cook my own meals? No deal! The kitchen was not for a lowly tenant's use. Toast and tea-making, perhaps, but full meal authorization, *no way*. Paying keep = all-inclusive. And no other meal plan was available. I would have to come clean to Mum.

'Oh fucking hell,' she said. 'Dad's gonna go nuts.'

I resisted telling her that, come to mention it, we were going to need a lot more nuts in the cupboard.

Had I been telling her I was gay or converting to Islam, it would have been easier. Meat was one of my dad's measures of a man. The true silverback rends flesh from bone and eats it with closed fists while swigging ale.

'Steaks, boy. Massive steaks . . . Protein, boy . . .' etc.

Dad was happiest when he was unloading the Transit after a meat run to Makro.

'Try and lift that, boy!'

I couldn't. I was eight.

'Whole leg. Whole bloody leg of lamb. Freeze it, Julie – we'll have it at Easter with pints of mint sauce. Fuuuuck! Handsome!'

Meat was one of the last things holding me and Dad together. We had no sport, films, books . . . nothing of common interest, but when he watched me demolish a whole rotisserie chicken from Tesco, the wonky smirk of pride on his face was unmistakable.

'That'll go straight to your guns, boy.'

'Three sets of ten bicep curls?' I had replied, my chin glazed with dead bird fat.

'Exactly. But make sure you do the triceps, too, or it'll look like a wasting disease in your arms.'

'Right.'

'Like muscular dystrophy my cousin Brian got.'

'Yep. Got it.

Don't get me wrong, my dad loved veg too. Cauliflower cheese, dripping-soaked spuds, sprouts – the backing singers to the Luther Vandross of his meat solo. He was no veg denier – it's just that to him, meat deniers were thin, weak and probably paedophiles. Dad cited two men he knew that were veggies: both thin, quiet men.

'It's hard to get big, not without protein. Can't be done. I used to eat thirty eggs a day when I was training.' The thirty-eggs claim again.

'Vegetarians can eat eggs,' I had put in.

'Don't take the piss, boy. Anyway – it's not just the muscle. Look at the pair of 'em! Both nonces.'

'Dave!' Mum objected.

'They fucking look like 'em, Julie. Kiddy-fiddlers. Mark my words. Fucking vegetarians.'

Vegetarians represented everything my old man hated and feared. All the lefty, self-satisfied things he felt he could never be. It was straight out of the manifestos of Effeminacy and Decay. To turn veggie was to start wiping your arse on the Union Jack, a kick in Thatcher's vag – intolerable. But I had made the move, and I would have to tell him. It would be the last great battle me and the alpha would have before he popped his meaty clogs just a couple of years later.

I waited till Saturday.

'So, Dad, I—'

'I already know. Your Mum told me.'

'I can just have more of the vegetables at Sunday lunch?' I said, drawing a blank on suitable things to say.

'But, love,' Mum said, 'they'll be cooked in the same oven as the meat.'

'That's OK, Mum.'

'It's fucking rib-eye this weekend as well. You fucking nugget.'

'Not a chicken nugget, though,' I joked bleakly.

He was weirdly calm, more upset than angry.

'I just feel better for it, Dad.'

'You do whatever you feel, boy.'

Seeing him broken, downcast, was worse than seeing him angry.

'I've just got one question,' he said ominously. 'Who did it to you?'

It was such a strange way of phrasing it. Not why or when or what made you, but *who* did it. He was still just that big protective ape and I was his tiny boy. It was the tone of a

Muslim dad asking his son in 2019 how he got radicalized. That's how seriously Dad took my departure from meat eating: a challenge to the Western world. Of all the things I could have done to break away and start out as an alpha on my own, denying the Sunday roast, it turned out, was the most powerful.

'Just a lad from university,' I lied.

'I knew it. I fucking knew it,' he said, imagining a lefty villain grooming me into lentil-hood.

I'd lied because I wanted to give him the peace of his world view remaining intact. The poor old (but not that old) knackered angry bastard. But come September it all changed again, and by the October I was moved out, this time for ever.

Now and again, in real life, ludicrous plot devices happen that instantly move the story on. It's amazing, and hard for people to believe, yet while I was on lunch break from my credit-checking job, doing some preparatory browsing of a teacher-training book in a crummy, cramped staff room, I got the phone call that changed everything; the news that built the bridge from Dave's nest, and led me towards my own silverback domain.

'Hello, Russell?'

'Oh my God, Sue?' It was the novelist Sue Gee.

'Are you sitting down?'

'In a staff room.'

'An adverting agency has approached the writing department to ask if we had a suitable graduate for a copywriter placement. I immediately suggested you.'

Long pause. 'What?' I had no idea what a copywriter was, I thought it was something to do with law and copyright. 'As in solicitors?'

She laughed. 'No! Like Fay Weldon and Salman Rushdie used to do . . .'

'Thinking up headlines?'

'And much more. It really is a very brilliant thing.'

'Fuck.'

'Precisely, Russell. Shall I tell them you'll call?'

And that was that. Fourteen days later I was walking into one of the top 'through-the-line' agencies in London. Through-the-line meant they did all types of copywriting: adverts, in-store, on-pack, even terms & conditions; and I did not care a solitary shite which genre they threw me into. This was working with words. This was playing with words. A sea of language to be harvested and shaped, and I was getting paid for doing it.

I breezed through my three weeks' trial, and in September that year I sold my teacher-training books in stunned glee. I was hired, but couldn't shake the feeling the whole thing was a horrible joke being played on me by the middle classes. Would I turn up on the first day at the office only to have a bucket of pig's blood tipped over my head, while tall people laughed and pointed?

My starting wage turned out to be modest, but it doubled every six months for the first eighteen months of my sparkly new career. I was officially the first person in my family, in my street – fuck it, as far as I know, in my postcode – to get a proper professional job, not grafting with my hands but sat around on ironic pink cubes of furniture trying to think up puns, headlines, whole campaigns. It was as though someone had pressed the on-switch at the base of my skull. I went to things called 'brainstorms' – glass rooms with clever people shouting out witty ideas and being accepted and supported in their suggestions by the other smiling people in the room.

It was like being on drugs but I was sober. This was the real rave, this was my true party.

A few months went by, and Dad finally passed comment. He was in full Stella-Artois mode: 'Fucking hell, boy. One of us made it. A decent job.'

'I can't believe it.'

'They're paying you mug wages, though.'

Ah – there it was – the fleck of negativity. But this time I went along with it. It was easier than contradicting him, or forcing him to realize that if I made creative director, at the rate I'm going I could easily be on 100K within seven years. Dad never lived to see me earning more than twenty-five grand a year. I always wonder what he would have made of it. I'm sure he would have felt pride tinged with his own sense of thwarted ambition. One of us had made it, but it wasn't him, 'the wanker builder' as he called himself. Me earning more than him would be the equivalent of chucking ape-shit at him. He would never have conceded silverback status.

19.

Silly English Boy

That first year of making my own way provoked me into one of my most un-Dave experiments yet: travelling without a plan. It was to be my most extreme camping trip. Agency life was exciting, but full on. I was on a break from Joanne, and I needed mess, so I decided to do something I'd never done before. Get on a plane, on my own, and go somewhere random. Properly random. I selected the destination by pouring myself a large drink and spinning an Argos globe.

'Whenever it stops, that's where I go,' I said, half to Dad, half to myself.

'What you gonna do if it lands on Iran, boy? You gonna go to Baghdad? Silly sod.'

I left his error uncorrected.

OK, so I had one rule. Wherever my finger landed, I would go there or to the nearest country described as safe on our government's website. I would go for three weeks, no matter what. I booked the days off work even before I had selected the destination.

I spun the globe and *boom*.

'Ha ha. That's Africa, you twat,' laughed Dad craning in, sloshing a Stella.

'Excellent,' I said, peering at the tiny typeface. 'Botswana.'

I don't know if I'd ever heard of Botswana at that point.

Most 25-year-old graduates had done a bit of travelling. I'd seen Europe, but not Africa. I researched – Botswana was tricky to get to, but safe and friendly.

'The Okavango Delta swamp, Mum. That's where I'm going.'

'Just go down Brixton when it's raining, boy. Save yourself some wedge,' Dad chimed in, racist, but chipper. He seemed tickled by the idea of me doing something so adventurous and independent – like when a toddler pretends they're going to work and you smile benignly at their silly child fantasy.

It would take three flights, and the next day, I booked them. I used the first travel agent I phoned – no price comparisons made, no shits given, and apart from travel jabs, that was all the prep I made.

'The cost of the fucking malaria pills, that'll be a jab to the face, fuuuuucking hell,' Dad had counselled as I popped my first pricey dose of Malarone.

All I knew was that I would be getting off a light aircraft in Maun on 21 September after sixteen hours travelling. The first flight from London to Johannesburg was hell. An old couple had blocked me into my window seat with a sentence that still haunts me to this day:

'Have you made your *final* visit to the toilet?'

And then the selfish old bastards stretched out for the full twelve hours. I needed a wee so badly that I pissed a blood diamond by the time we landed in Africa. I still have window-seat panic attacks to this day. I'm an aisle person, free and independent.

I was supposed to call my mum when I reached minuscule Maun airport in northern Botswana but I was too busy being in shock. There was one little passport man, who waved me through, and a smiling cleaner lady. In the arrivals 'hall' a few useless shops that were not open in the 3 p.m. heat looked grey and dead. The fifteen other people on my flight were all waved on to a rickety minibus which swept out of the tiny car park in front of the airport in a cloud of orange dust before I could ask anyone for any tips. The only other human I could find was a ten-year-old girl out front, who found me and my massive rucksack hilarious. She did a full point and laugh, then returned to playing with a bit of carrier bag and a stick. I was stranded – no contacts, no options. My plan had been to go 'into town' but it turned out there wasn't really a town, and no way of getting into it.

I sat on my rucksack drinking water and about thirty minutes later a pickup truck with *Backwater Campsite* painted on went past. It had some cool-looking, twenty-somethings in the back – and a blonde girl who waved at me with her fingers as she whooshed past. I'd read a mention of Backwater in my Lonely Planet. I scribbled down the phone number from the van's side and begged the cleaner lady to let me use a phone. That's how I blagged it to my first campsite in Africa. From that inauspicious start I had the most amazing seventeen-night adventure. Within half a day I was friends with a group of Dutch and American people, some of whom I recognized from the pickup. We clubbed together and rented a guide and some *mokoros* – a sort of canoe – and cruised over the Okavango Delta camping, stopping to make settlements on mud islands with tree shelters. Our guide dug us toilets and served us weird tinned semolina with bits of dried meat in it (my vegetarianism long dead by now). I purified swamp water with some chlorine pills I had bought from Millets and never thought I would actually use. The taste of mud and chlorine is vile until you're thirsty, then it is nectar. It was the most free and grown-up I had ever felt in my whole life. The most opposite of a neat house, a small mortgage, and a holiday with an all-inclusive wristband.

After that first swamp trip, I hitchhiked around Botswana with no fear or questions, sitting in the back of pickup trucks driven by African dads who seemed more chilled and serene than my own. My co-passengers were goats or children or both. The word seatbelt never occurred to me. But the best bit of the trip? That's easy: Leonie Brandstatter, the finger-waving goddess from the truck. I had found someone more daring, more reckless than me.

She was twenty-one years old and had been hitchhiking across southern Africa totally alone. When I encountered her at Backwater, she had just crossed Namibia with nothing but a hitchhiking thumb, a backpack and a tent. She was funny, confident, kind, Austrian and very pretty.

'No chance,' I said to myself as I masturbated dolefully in Backwater's open-air shower. 'None.' She was the popular girl of our informal group. 'But my God, just imagine . . . Stop it!'

None the less, I found myself talking with her at the end of each night. We liked the same shitty wine and the same good writers. I was going through my European literature phase so it accidentally looked like I knew much more about Arthur Schnitzler, Thomas Mann and Hermann Hesse than I actually did – it was recent knowledge rather than deep. It was one of the sweetest coincidences that I had a copy of Schnitzler's *Dream Story* on that trip. Not only is he Austrian, but the story is erotic too – we naturally had some pervy chats safely draped in an outer coat of art.

We took another swamp trip, six of us plus guides, and as we arrived on our mud island the bombshell was dropped that I would have to share my two-man tent with Leonie. This was something I had never done – a boy/girl platonic tent with just two people. Very awkward for me, but she was not fazed at all, brazenly getting changed next to me, shimmying out of one set of knickers and into another like we were both sexless five-year-olds, or jovial female friends. It was the most friend-zone feeling I have ever experienced. Every time she got changed, I faced the tent wall like *Rain Man*.

'You are very funny, English boy,' she said, laughing at my crushing embarrassment. 'It is only our bodies.'

'That's the problem,' I joked weakly.

We went two nights with her as the camp's lead fire-stoker, water-purifier and drop-toilet administrator. We walked around the delta with guides during the day, and played Yahtzee dice games around the fire in the evening, the six of us comfortable with the prevailing Enid Blyton vibe. The other four were couples; Dutch – who politely spoke English even when I wasn't part of the chat.

In the cosy (and very hot) darkness of our two-man tent, Leonie kept asking me about the authors I loved; she seemed genuinely interested in my answers. She in turn was happy to tell me about her work with disabled children back in Austria. Was this girl for real? Confident, kind, selfless, bright – and with eyes that went through me from the tips of my hair to the depths of my pelvis. My heart thudded in my chest, and my pants, but I gave her no sign I fancied her. She even checked at one point, as most girls have whenever I've been single, whether I was gay.

'You sure you don't like the boys, English boy?' she said, eyes sparkling.

'I'm not André Gide!' I said, dropping another literary European author, like Michael Jordan smashing a ball through a hoop.

'*Sehr witzig*,' she said. It had become a little catchphrase.

On the third night of swamp camping something amazing happened – right in the middle of her teaching me a song. We were side by side in our weird 'girl mates' tent. It was too hot and sticky for sleeping bags, and the front of the tent gaped open so that we were both bathed in the orange glow from the dying fire. She was in knickers and bra; I was in a modest T-shirt plus baggy boxer shorts – I just couldn't bring myself to go top-off.

'My hat has three corners . . . tell me just one more time,' I said. 'I've nearly got it . . .'

'OK,' she said. '*Mein Hut, der hat drei Ecken. Drei Ecken hat mein Hut. Und hätt' er nicht drei Ecken, dann wär' er nicht mein Hut.*'

'I love it when you sing that,' I said.

'*Ja?*' she said. 'And do you love this?'

And the kiss came as totally unexpected. Not exploratory and romantic but deep and passionate, like one of the Channel 4 European films where you could sometimes see a boob after midnight. My dick was instantly harder than a maths test.

'Yes,' I said, 'that was very much liked.'

There was a moment's silence and then she said something I could never have imagined an English girl saying.

'Russell?'

'*Ja?*'

'Do you find me attractive?' she said, almost in the comedy accent we would do for a German soldier in a film.

I laughed. Our platonic two-man tent, in chaos from a kiss, suddenly felt much smaller. 'Er. You are, of course, a pretty girl . . .' My God, I was Hugh Granting it. Stuttering. *Just kiss her.* But I could not kiss her back. I could not find the courage. She smiled at me for a full two minutes, then lay down. I thought I'd blown it, but she smiled and said:

'Shall we have full sex?'

And there it was. The Germanic version of a pass. She actually used the word 'full'.

'I'm sorry?'

'I haven't had full sex yet on my African trip, and it would be very enjoyable to do so.' She was speaking like she had been programmed by a fifteen year-old boy who was on some sort of behavioural spectrum.

I laughed. 'Well, rather that than partial sex.'

The joke was lost in translation: 'We can have partial sex if you like. This I did in Namibia with an Italian boy. I thought you might enjoy intersex more.'

'Yep. Yes, I would.' What else could I say? I was now throbbing like an Essex girl's face after fillers.

There were three other tents with us on the trip – and guides too – so it was the quietest shagging I'd ever had, and the most unexpected. The next morning, she was exactly the same. I wasn't. I made sure we were together for the rest of my trip. After a few days, she began doing cute things, like tracing my face with her finger, talking about Austria – about me visiting the country one day. I fell in love. Horribly, juvenilely, deeply – like stepping into a lift shaft and falling down into the motors. On our last night together we treated ourselves to a hotel room. It was the first bed she'd slept in in months, but she didn't seem to enjoy it – like it broke the studenty continuity of her trip. Still, we had an amazing dinner with actual cutlery.

Right in the middle of the meal, unprompted and totally without context, she said: 'If you come and see me in Salzburg, I will shave my vagina for you.'

My fork hovered in mid-air, my hand stopped working.

'Silly English boy. Still so shy. You wouldn't like that?'

'I . . . er . . . would love to see Salzburg.'

She laughed till she cried, and the final thin resistance around my ruined heart gave way.

'I love you,' I said.

'No,' she replied, 'that is too dangerous.'

'So is shaving your badger.'

She laughed again. 'What is badger . . . *mein Gott! Dachs!*'

When I boarded my tiny plane the next morning, I cried into the biltong I had bought for the flight. I had a beard. I was heartbroken. I was lost for love.

'When I get back from my trip, we shall see, *ja?*' she had said, speaking like an inscrutable man character in *Sex and the City*.

Leonie still had another seven months left to travel – and I knew that our one fortnight of love, both of us living in different countries, both of us being young . . . it seemed inconceivable it could go any further. I bandaged up my heart and started to forget her. Even though the Internet could have kept us connected, Leonie refused to use it while she was travelling – she didn't use any more hotels either.

When I got back to the UK, me and my ex, Scottish Joanne, decided to try one last time to make it work, but all

I ended up doing was moving my Austrian emotions into a Scottish house. Joanne and I limped along in recriminations for another year, throwing gravel and swearwords at our resurrected romance. We split up after a massive argument about a Chinese takeaway. Joanne was a really nice girl, I was trying to be a really nice boy – we were just totally incompatible and way too young. To make it worse, we'd bought a house together.

'Do not buy a gaff with Joanne,' Dad had warned.

'It gets him on the housing ladder,' Mum put in.

'Housing prison. She'll rinse him like a fucking dishwasher, Julie,' Dad had said.

After the break-up, Joanne and I had to live together for a further six weeks. We had one bedroom and one sofa, and we decided it was fair that we should take it in turns having the bedroom as we were equal, and both working. This was a massive mistake on my part. I soon found myself cast as the patriarchal bully who made a woman sleep on the floor. Joanne's family naturally had it in for me, so I decided that rather than fight back, rather than try to hang on to the house, I would use the tactic that had got me through the playground at Church School: enjoy being punched. It's the one tactic that your opponent never expects – come at them, and enjoy it when they hit you. Nine times out of ten, they will hit you less. People mostly hit you to see you scared. Wear a metaphorical gimp mask, encourage the punching and they lose their venom. Joanne moved out, and it was left to me to sell our house in Essex. I knew what was coming. They wanted me to do all the admin of finding a buyer, and then they would fight me for what they felt was theirs. But I was ready.

One day at work, her mum called me, ready for the show-down. It was very satisfying to disarm her.

'Zat Russell?' said the formerly friendly Glaswegian accent.

'Yeah.'

'It's Joanne's mum.'

'I know.'

'Just so you know, now you got a seller for the hoos, Joanne will be taking any profit, or we will never sign the documents!'

She was so sure I would fight. Instead I said, not even sarcastically, but with love: 'Yeah . . . OK.'

'What?'

'I think that's fair. All the distress she's been through.'

'You'll give her the house, just like that?'

'Whatever she wants, Maureen.'

There was a pause. Plenty of breathing, the receiver covered, muffles.

'And we'll be wanting £3,000 cash too.'

'Right.'

'That's the deposit she put in!'

This was true, but over the year I had paid the bills and the mortgage, that had been our deal, but still, I couldn't resist saying, 'Her deposit?'

'Yep!'

'I think it was £3,500. Let's do the full amount. I wouldn't feel right short-changing her.'

Silence.

'You're going to be a very lonely man, Russell,' she said.

'As long as I'm as kind as I can be, that's all I can do, Maureen.'

She hung up, defeated. I had an email shortly after the call confirming they would sign for £3,500. I borrowed the cash from Halifax that afternoon, and smiled as I sent the money across. It took me five years to pay it off, and every time an instalment left my account, it felt great – like a shoulder massage. Sometimes the best purchase isn't a thing, a holiday, or even an experience . . . it's freedom. I hope Joanne found happiness. I was never lonely from that day on.

By the time all that mess was concluded, Leonie – who did indeed contact me as promised a year later – got bored and offended when I failed to respond. I just couldn't get into anything complicated and heavy at that moment. The initial feelings had long cooled to a sort of Pompeii Eros statue. I could only remember how hot it once was. I received one more, old-fashioned, hand-written letter.

'I have given up on my English boy. It was our Dream Story. Goodbye.'

I left her missive unanswered.

'German birds, boy. They're the ones.'

'She's Austrian.'

'Whatever. Cracking in the sack. Hairy though,' Dad had said.

And I burst out laughing.

I found out years later that Leonie soon fell in love with a man who looked exactly like me and she still lives in Toronto to this day with pretty babies, and always has a smile. My God. Tent sex. Must stalk her again later.

20.

A Mug's Game

I made Head Copywriter the same year my dad stubbornly ignored the throbbing breathlessness in his chest. It's more manly to die than give in, remember. That was also the year I did something else no one in my family dreamed of doing at my age: I bought my own house – but with Glaswegian Joanne: a cursed place. Our relationship was crumbling before we even completed on the sale. Our romantic connection was dead, yet my advertising agency life was soaring. Dad, at the time, had had a bit of a dry patch with his insulation business and was about to do some private chauffeuring to top up his income.

'Let's see if you can show us these "copywriting" skills then, boy,' he said, saying 'copywriting' the way Ray Winstone might say 'hummus'. It was a genuine challenge but thrown at me in a 'let's see if you can catch this' way, like when someone chucks you an expensive vase. They want you to smash the fucker really.

'What do you need?' I was back at the Castle for Sunday lunch – and as always, although I had now without doubt made my own manly stamp on the world, I remained a boy in his presence.

'I need a business card for my chauffeuring. Gonna use the Mercedes Elegance to earn some wedge.'

I paused and, as had been happening to me at the agency, the solution for the headline leapt straight into my head. It was weird. I was scared to say what I had thought up, not because I thought Dad would be negative about it, but because it was a form of showing off, a form of cockiness in solving his problem so quickly. That was 'flash' behaviour, and as I well knew, all 'flash' people are cunts. Still, I blurted it out: 'How Would You Like to be Driven in Elegance?'

'That's brilliant, love,' said Mum.

Dad nodded and smiled. One of those side smiles in a martial arts movie when the novice gets in one punch and the master allows it. 'Not fucking bad, boy.' It's still one of the proudest moments of my life (up there with one day in 2019 when I converted a kick at Twickenham in front of 82,000 people for charity – that would have blown my dad's heart, even had it been healthy).

Glaswegian Joanne and I limped through that summer. She seemed to get more Scottish the more wrong our relationship went. I worried she might actually turn into a caber and smash my head in. Her even feistier mum had now begun her campaign of getting into my mind about property and consequences, and how I'd be lonely my whole life if I dare split up with 'wee Joanne'. Around this stressful time, there was also a change in my attitude to the copywriting path. Not the craft itself – I love it to this day and would happily go back to it – but the lifestyle that came with it. As brilliant as agency existence is, it's way too intense for anyone trying to maintain a normal life. Weekends, evenings, birthdays – if there's a pitch on, you stay at work. No exceptions. People slept at work – they definitely shagged at work. Copywriting is the junior-doctoring of creativity – you do it out of passion and love, and 100-hour weeks are the norm. No overtime. No extra pay. When you're new, the cleaners earn per hour at least double what you do. You love it, but it fucks your life. Every aspect. It killed the last remaining bits of me and Joanne. One evening as I was working on some copy at 10 p.m. and eating cold pizza, I decided on a strategy to get something back just for me: I would try something unrelated to marketing, let off steam, get a hobby. I considered starting an MA in literature – but turning up to an evening course with any regularity would be impossible (I did eventually manage a post-grad certificate in Modernism). Art, pottery, climbing. I considered many things. But the creative planner at work, Steve Dorfman, kept nagging at me to try one particular thing.

'Try stand-up, you'd be good at it. You always make people piss themselves in the office.'

So what, I thought. Yes, I'd done that my whole life. It was my August-baby, son-of-an-alpha male survival trait: make bullies/girls laugh and hope to stay unpunched/touch boobies at some point. To me, totally normal. Being funny was like having brown hair. Plus, I hated stand-up. I found it boring. I'd never been to watch it live, it was something that held no interest for me at all. I liked books, sex (group sex by the toilets it turned out), and going to Ibiza. Also Ibiza. And Ibiza too. Plus, standing up onstage and pathetically begging pissed strangers to like you? No thanks. What tragic needy twats stand-ups must be.

'Try it once, you pussy. Think of it like a bungee jump. For the ego.'

Steve Dorfman, if you're reading this: thank you. Thanks

for the weird peer pressuring. I literally only did it to shut you up. Completely disinterestedly, with no passion, goal or motive, I thought – fuck it. I'd give it a go. I could never have known what all my emotional tension and paternal-driven self-doubt, plus energy and adrenaline would create: Lee Evans on crack, basically.

I googled stand-up, clicked the first link, phoned the first person, and planned for my first and only comedy set for the end of September. By bizarre – actually, I'm gonna go with *macabre* – coincidence, it turned out to be just one week after my dad's funeral.

I saw my dad one last time. That August was stupidly busy, four pitches and my first television marketing campaign, but somehow I made time for my birthday meal out with Mum and Dad. Joanne was there. We had argued before we went out; we were in the final month of our relationship. It was a sombre night at Papillon's. Dad, however, was in good spirits. Food. His thing.

'Fucking skate wings, boy!' Dad started on a big meat speech. 'Does a nut roast have wings? Fuuuucking hell. Nut roast.'

The atmosphere quickly turned tense when I idiotically started talking about something from the news. I had learned years before never to discuss any current affairs with my dad as he was guaranteed to have the opposite viewpoint. This was the time when there was still a debate about whether the UK might adopt the euro.

'It could be for the best, Dad,' I said, tearing a baguette and dipping it in balsamic. 'No more exchange rates etc . . .'

'Are you fucking kidding me?' And then he laid his philosophy out and ended the debate. 'Listen, boy. Why would I want *one euro* when I can have *one pound*? You see? A pound . . . it's fucking better . . .'

Thank goodness all that European debate has died down in the years since then.

We hobbled through an awkward meal trying to find other things to talk about. Eventually I gambled. Might as well see what the oracle thinks.

'I'm, er, I'm gonna try stand-up comedy next month.' I knew my dad had tried it once when he was about my age. He had been a Red Coat in one of the holiday parks, done a whole season telling jokes. Whenever I had tried to push him for more details, he closed down. I think he may have got further than he let on – actually done a few gigs in London and Essex. Over the years tantalizing details would leak out. *He knew Mike Reid – they gigged together.* He got a non-speaking part in *Doctor Who.* He did some modelling. But none of it knitted together as a story – and he would always fall back on being 'a lowly tradesman' – to be pitied and dismissed. Still, the fact he had some contact with this craft meant a naive part of my mind was hoping for some positive comment.

'You what?'

'Yeah. In September.'

'Pah!' He laughed. 'Tried all that shit. Mug's game, boy.' And that was the total of my old man's commentary on what I've ended up funnelling my whole life into.

We drove back to mine and Joanne's in the Mercedes Elegance. I felt like a little boy in a car seat sat in the back, uneasy silence filling the car like a fart. Mum and Dad were supposed to pop in for a coffee, but Joanne and I lived on a road that was awful for parking. Dad reversed and moved forward a few times trying to fit into a space, the tension building in the car as gaskets flew out of his head.

'What a cunt of a road!'

'Do you want me to get out and guide you in, Dad?' I said.

He thundered back at me: 'I've got a lot of fucking car here, boy!'

And that was that. Mum politely said goodnight. Joanne and I got out of the car and Dad sped away. Away . . . Those were the last words my old man ever said to me. *I've got a lot of fucking car here, boy!* They summed up everything about our relationship. Me wanting to help, to assist, for him to see my efforts and accept me, acknowledge me – and him, full of fury and disappointment, a big lump of metal that could not be steered, his life, the *elegance* that never got there.

A couple of weeks later, Mum and Dad went to Cyprus, and one night, with absolutely no build-up or warning during that evening, he dropped down on the floor with a massive heart attack. He lived for another thirty minutes after that, defiantly and stubbornly spitting at the world.

'Give Russell my watch . . .' Those were some of his last words, Mum told me.

I held it together when I found out; and at my dad's funeral. I had to, for my younger brother, who by then had abseiled deep into the cave of mental illness and cut the ropes. I did the whole funeral day in 'fake me' mode – like one of those housewives from the 1950s who cheerfully wore Marigold gloves but secretly wanted to hang themselves. It was a good send-off. He wasn't a happy man, but he was respected. That was my dad, and now he was gone. Did that make me a silverback? I wasn't sure.

Exactly seven days later I found myself at the Comedy

Barn in East London. I told no one I was going through with the stupid idea of doing a stand-up comedy gig. The venue was packed with laugh-hungry strangers, and I was at the side of the stage with a bunch of attention-seeking misfits. I felt totally unlike them. I was still grieving, confused, and very nervous. Joanne and I had broken up the day after my dad's funeral, and her mum had been taunting me about how they would take me to court about the house. No mercy was given for my bereavement. My head was messier than a toddler's colouring book. I had no jokes, I didn't really like stand-up, and the audience comprised pissed-up city wankers.

'Just try it once, mate. Something to tell the grandkids,' said the MC for the night just before the show began.

'Yeah, cool, whatever,' I replied, eating my third Imodium. I had been shitting liquid nerves since 4 p.m. that afternoon. I didn't even know how to get a microphone out of a stand. Yank it? Toggle it free? I hadn't bothered to check. I didn't really care anyway. I heard the MC call my name, which didn't sound like my name, but like a silly made-up word someone shouts when they're drunk. I wobbled up the stairs and on to the blinding stage with the body language of a sex-cult victim. I pulled the microphone out of the stand and stared out into a blanket of blinking, silent faces. I knew I needed to start talking, but all I could hear was my dad's voice:

Pah! Tried all that shit. Mug's game, boy.

You're probably right, Dad, I thought as I began speaking into the microphone, you're probably right, you miserable old bastard.

ABOUT THE AUTHOR

Multi-award-winning comedian, presenter, actor, author and scriptwriter **Russell Kane** is best known for the BBC Radio 4 podcast *Evil Genius*, which has become a flagship show and was the best performing original podcast on the BBC Sounds platform. Russell's other podcast, *Boys Don't Cry*, also features regularly on the iTunes podcast chart.

Recent TV appearances include *The Apprentice: You're Fired*, *Stupid Man, Smart Phone* and the host of three series of *Live at the Electric*. Other TV appearances include *Live at the Apollo*, *Michael McIntyre's Big Show*, *Love Island Aftersun*, *Comedians Giving Lectures*, *8 Out of 10 Cats*, *The Crystal Maze* and *Celebrity Juice*.

Winner of Best Show in 2010 at the Edinburgh Comedy Awards, Russell went on to make history as the first comedian to win both the Edinburgh Award and Melbourne Comedy Festival's Barry Award in one year.

Russell is currently touring his sell-out show *The Fast and the Curious* throughout the UK, Ireland and Scandinavia as well as continuing his ever-popular topical online rants, 'Kaneings'.